The Valiant Woman

ELIZABETH HAYES ALVAREZ

The Valiant Woman

The Virgin Mary in Nineteenth-Century
American Culture

The University of North Carolina Press *Chapel Hill*

This volume was published with the assistance of the Greensboro Women's Fund of the University of North Carolina Press.

Founding Contributors: Linda Arnold Carlisle, Sally Schindel Cone, Anne Faircloth, Bonnie McElveen Hunter, Linda Bullard Jennings, Janice J. Kerley (in honor of Margaret Supplee Smith), Nancy Rouzer May, and Betty Hughes Nichols.

Cover photograph: Julia Margaret Cameron, *Blessing and Blessed*, 1865. Digital image courtesy of the Getty's Open Content Program. Cameron posed housemaid Mary Hillier as the Madonna in dozens of photographs.

Library of Congress Cataloging-in-Publication Data
Alvarez, Elizabeth Hayes, author.
The valiant woman : the Virgin Mary in nineteenth-century American culture / Elizabeth Hayes Alvarez.
pages cm
Includes bibliographical references and index.
ISBN 978-1-4696-2741-0 (pbk : alk. paper) — ISBN 978-1-4696-2742-7 (ebook)
1. Mary, Blessed Virgin, Saint—Symbolism. 2. Mary, Blessed Virgin, Saint—Influence. 3. Mary, Blessed Virgin, Saint, and Christian union. 4. Christianity and art—United States. 5. Christianity and literature—United States. I. Title.
BT603.A48 2016
232.910973'09034—dc23
2015026762

For Isabella Cusano Hayes

and

Elizabeth Theresa Alvarez

Mary was not only a holy dove hiding in the clefts of a rock—a pure virgin called to feed with her milk, and cradle in her arms, a heavenly guest; she was a valiant woman, whom the Lord delighted to place in turn in every situation of life, in order to leave to the daughters of Eve an example to follow, and a model to imitate.

—Abbé Orsini, *The Life of the Blessed Virgin Mary*

What does the Holy Ghost especially admire in her? Not her sweet and amiable temper or her gentle disposition, though of course she possessed these qualities, for no woman is perfect without them. No; He admires her valor, courage, fortitude, and the sturdy virtue of self-reliance. He does not say, "Who shall find a gentle woman?" but rather, "Who shall find a valiant woman?"

—Cardinal Gibbons, *Harper's Bazar*

Contents

Illustrations

Acknowledgments

I am grateful to the faculty of the University of Chicago Divinity School, who guided this project in its earliest stages. Martin E. Marty and the late Jerald Brauer sparked my early interest in American religious history. I am deeply thankful for their warmth, generosity, and wisdom. Bernard McGinn, Margaret Mitchell, and the late Martin Riesebrodt spurred my thinking about gender and religious identity in various places, times, and contexts. Richard Rosengarten taught me how to approach novels and other literary sources, and stepped in when I truly needed him. Catherine Brekus and W. Clark Gilpin gave me untold hours of support, stretched my thinking, read early drafts, and encouraged me throughout. Catherine has been and remains a mentor in every way, offering encouragement, strategies, feedback, and practical advice, and I am grateful for her friendship.

I am also indebted to Edith Blumhoffer, the staff at the Public Religion Project, and the faculty and staff at the Martin Marty Center for the Advanced Study of Religion for the lessons they gave me in research and public scholarship.

I owe much to my wonderful colleagues in the American Religious History and History of Christianity working groups at Chicago, especially Amy Artman, Jonathan Ebel, and Paula Gallito Shakelton, without whom I would not have discovered the questions that continue to preoccupy me.

I wish to thank the librarians at the University of Chicago for all their assistance. I am also indebted to the various libraries that allowed me access to their collections, particularly the Turro Seminary Library at Seton Hall University, the United Methodist Archives and History Center at Drew University, Jennings Library at Caldwell College, the Marian Library/International Marian Research Institute at the University of Dayton, Hesburgh Library at Notre Dame, Paley Library at Temple University, and the New York Public Library. Laura Ruttum Senturia at the Colorado Historical Society; Michael N. Cook at Cornell Library's Home Economics Archive: Research, Tradition, and History (HEARTH); and staff at the Library of Congress graciously offered time and assistance to help me find needed illustrations.

My colleagues at Temple University have also been tremendously supportive of my work, ready with leads, advice, and diverting stories. I thank them all for their friendship, especially Rebecca Alpert, Douglas Greenfield, Laura Levitt, Richard Libowitz, Elliot Ratzman, and Terry Rey. I am also grateful to Linda Jenkins and Emily Mears for their generosity and administrative support.

I would like to thank my editor at University of North Carolina Press, Elaine Maisner, whose persistence, encouragement, and advice made this book possible. I am also grateful for Assistant Editor Alison Shay's and Project Editor Jay Mazzocchi's frequent help.

I have been blessed with a tremendously supportive and wonderful family. My parents—Ann Hayes, Ted Richuitti, and Jeffrey and Karen Marra—contributed meals, child care, and gentle nudging to "keep working." Laura Barrett supported me with friendship and research advice. James, Caleb, and Phoebe Alvarez have grown up with this work and have made me a happier and more thoughtful person. Most important, I am grateful to my husband, Marcus Alvarez, who has supported me in every way through this process. He has traveled to locate resources, read drafts, manned the fort so I could work, reconnected me to the world, and helped me hold on to my vision when it got murky. I thank him for making my goals his own and for bringing joy to the journey.

The Valiant Woman

Introduction

Francis Lieber, the celebrated German American political theorist and author of the "Lieber Code" of military ethics, described encountering Raphael's *Sistine Madonna* as one of the seminal moments of his life— comparable to watching Napoleon's forces enter Berlin when he was six. As a young man, Lieber journeyed a hundred miles on foot from Jena to Dresden, where he immediately sought out its famous art museum. There he found himself standing in awe before Raphael's vision of the Virgin Mary, cradling the infant Christ while standing on billowing clouds surrounded by countless, nearly imperceptible angel faces. Lieber recalled being so "overcome" by emotion in the gallery that he attracted the attention of a stranger, Dorothea Tieck, daughter of the Romantic poet Johann Ludwig Tieck. Tieck spoke with him at length and, approving of his profound response to the painting, "encouraged his sentiment."[1] Biographies of Lieber cite this anecdote as evidence of his particularly "generous and sensitive nature," but accounts like this were not uncommon. Nineteenth-century memoirs and travelogues frequently depicted Protestants (Lieber was Lutheran) finding themselves moved, overwhelmed, and transformed by encounters with Marian art.[2]

A few decades later, Louisa Parsons (Stone) Hopkins, a well-known poet and kindergarten movement advocate, lyrically described her ideal kindergarten, highlighting the Marian reproduction presiding over the imagined scene. "In the morning hour," she wrote, "as they fold their little hands and sing the prayer and happy song with such a reverent and believing spirit, the scene is holy and blessed. The picture of the Madonna, which hangs upon the wall, seems almost lit up with glory at such a bringing in of the glad tidings of joy to childhood. Multiply the kindergartens and train up motherly teachers . . . to have each generation better trained for life than the last."[3] In her vision, kindergartens were nearly sacred spaces with Mary's prominently displayed image signifying both the female, motherly spirit of the movement and its sanctifying, nonsectarian Christian environment. To the Congregationalist Hopkins, kindergarten teachers were surrogate mothers, professional mothers, and Mary was the symbol par excellence of motherhood devoid of Old World European or Roman Catholic associations. Kindergarten movement journals were filled with similar accounts, by authors who suggested that Marian art played an important, even crucial role in successful kindergarten environments. The journals themselves were illustrated with sketches of Madonna and Child groups and copies of famous Marian paintings.

As these two glimpses suggest, Marian imagery was vividly present in nineteenth-century America despite widespread Protestant discomfort with Catholic Marian theology and veneration. An upsurge of interest in Marian themes among Protestant elites in these decades has been well documented. Nathaniel Hawthorne included Marian characters in many of his books and was fond of Raphael's *Madonna del Pesce*.[4] Harriet Beecher Stowe displayed a reproduction of Raphael's *Madonna of the Goldfinch* in her parlor in Hartford, Connecticut; owned several other reproductions of Marian paintings; and included Madonna figures and motifs in many of her books, especially *The Minister's Wooing, Uncle Tom's Cabin,* and *Woman and Sacred History*.[5] Henry Adams, Margaret Fuller, and George Elliot explored Marian themes in their works.[6] And famous art critics like Anna Jameson and John Ruskin, along with artists like Samuel Morse, recommended renowned Marian artwork for its moving content as well as its technical achievement.[7] This interest in Mary has been explained, primarily by literary historians, as a limited, elite aesthetic trend. But as I began to research visual and literary depictions of the Virgin Mary in nineteenth-century America, I quickly discovered that it was not only Protestant elites who embraced Marian art; her imagery proliferated in popular culture as well. While Mary was generally absent from American Protestant churches (except for her yearly starring role in Christmas nativity plays), she was increasingly present in mid- to late-century visual and print culture. When lithography and other printmaking technologies were developed, reproductions of Marian paintings were consistent best sellers. Raphael's *Sistine Madonna* was widely held to be the "best" painting ever made, and public school teachers throughout the country hung prints of it on classroom walls. Popular magazines such as *The Ladies' Repository* and *Harper's* routinely ran spreads of renowned Marian artwork. Poetic allusions to Mary were myriad, and overtly Marian characters populated domestic fiction, not just Catholic fiction. A wide range of novelists, ministers, artists, and ordinary Catholics and Protestants were fascinated by the Virgin Mary, and together they elevated her as a symbol of idealized womanhood.

Raphael, *The Sistine Madonna*. From the Gemäldegalerie Alte Meister, Dresden
(Art Archive at Art Resource, New York).

This book is a study of popular images of Mary in nineteenth-century America. It explores the ways Americans imagined her and the meanings her figure transmitted—both religious meanings and gendered meanings. For nineteenth-century Americans, Mary was, among other things, a culturally constructed symbol of motherhood and womanhood whose content was contributed by both Catholics and Protestants. While contemporary readers may have difficulty seeing the Madonna as something other than a Catholic religious figure and her imagery as something other than an indicator of Catholic presence, it is important to recognize that Mary only gradually came to represent Catholic identity in America. Protestants were also interested in her as Jesus's mother and as the most prominent woman in the New Testament. From colonial Puritan naming practices, which made "Mary" a perpetual favorite, to the advent of early twentieth-century fundamentalism, which made Mary's virginity at Christ's birth one of the "Fundamentals" that defined the movement, Mary has been a meaningful figure to American Protestants.[8] However, beyond her role in Catholic or Protestant theological systems, she existed as a cultural icon with distinctive characteristics and narrative content recognized by nineteenth-century Americans. Christian themes and images formed a rich lexicon of meaning that Americans drew on to address a range of social questions. Religious figures, especially those that appear in the Bible, were employed as metaphors and cultural touchstones for various ideas. For example, Onan, the Sodomites, Deborah, Solomon, and Mary Magdalene were invoked in discussions of (in order) contraception, homosexuality, female political leadership, wisdom, and prostitution. Mary was an integral signifier in this web of meaning—an important symbol of female holiness and maternity for both Catholics and Protestants. Of course, she also existed simultaneously within various Christian communities as an important (and contested) religious figure. Because of these different roles, a range of theological premises and prescriptive gender content were implicit in the era's many representations of her.

There has been wonderful scholarship on Mary's role in American Catholic devotional contexts and several excellent treatments of Marian themes in American literature. This book, instead, focuses on her representations in nondevotional contexts and explores the impact of popular understandings of Mary on normative constructions of womanhood. Religious historians have often assumed that only Catholics were devoted to Mary, and when they have found evidence of Protestants' interest in her, they have interpreted it as exceptional in some way: for example, as a compensatory indulgence of the Protestant intellectual elite, a foible in the character of a particular historical figure, or an aesthetic trend. Likewise, women's historians have discussed the cult of domesticity and the figure of the Angel in the House, but they have rarely examined how Marian imagery in particular affected ideals of womanhood. This book makes the unique argument that Mary was an important figure for both Catholics and Protestants in the mid- to late nineteenth century, especially as Americans were grappling with anxieties caused by shifting gender expectations and economic change. I demonstrate that because of her role as exemplar of Christian womanhood, Mary was a shared, culturally constructed figure that linked together various Christian groups and helped shape the period's gender ideology.

My claims about Mary's cultural functions are not meant to suggest secularization: at the same time Mary was gaining prominence as a cultural figure, her theological and devotional role within Roman (and Anglo) Catholicism was also expanding and evolving. In time, Mary's identification with Catholic devotionalism in America would eclipse her other religious and cultural functions; however, in these decades, Mary played a prominent role in popular formulations of idealized womanhood. Significantly, I find that despite Protestants' rejection of Catholic theological claims and their vocal worry about Catholic Mary-worship, the Marian images Protestants created and reproduced had characteristics surprisingly similar to Catholic types. Rather than a diminished or theologically bounded "Protestant Mary," American popular culture abounded with images of Mary that conveyed purity and power, compassion and transcendence, maternity and queenship. This was due, in part, to a vogue for reproductions of great artwork from the Western canon. These paintings and sculptures predated the Reformation and were generally seen as part of a shared cultural heritage. The most popular dated from late Medieval and Renaissance Europe, when Marian theology and veneration were cresting. The Marian piety and enthusiastic veneration (more correctly, *hyperdulia*, which Thomas Aquinas described as the "highest species" of *dulia*, or "piety and observance ... whereby reverence is shown towards a man," which was "due to her ... inasmuch as she is the Mother of God") of that period was manifest in these works of art.[9] Since most Protestants rejected religious devotion to Mary, did not understand or accept Catholic veneration of the saints as intrinsically different than worship of God (*latria*), and did not embrace the Marian doctrines associated with these artworks, they were, surprisingly, producing and promoting images that they explicitly rejected as theological formulations.

In fact, they sometimes rejected images for these reasons. Especially because Marian art was a site of Catholic religious veneration, it could provoke iconoclastic responses. Iconoclasm was a significant element of the anti-Catholic violence of the 1850s, and the "violent destruction of images" in those episodes "constructed and enforced the category of idolatry as *the* mark of [Catholic] difference."[10] As a symbol of Catholic identity, Mary was discussed not just as a religious figure but also as a *category* of visual image. Thus while Marian art was sometimes classified as a subset of the Western art tradition, other times it was classified as a site of idolatrous devotion. As I examined nineteenth-century images of Mary, I carefully attended to context and intention—both of the presenter and of the viewer—which could dramatically shift the reception of Marian art. Protestant Americans sometimes embraced Marian artwork as "Christian," "religious," "spiritually uplifting," and part of their own valued cultural heritage, while other times they derided the same artwork as "Catholic" and thus idolatrous or dangerous. Despite this tension, Marian art was widely reproduced, displayed, and taught as basic cultural literacy.

Because underlying theological premises were always tacitly present in Marian images, Protestant use and embrace of these works is a fascinating point of departure, which I examine in detail in chapter 2. However, instead of focusing exclusively on either Catholics or Protestants, I highlight exchanges between them and the religious meanings that they created together.[11] Thus, the book does not dwell on Mary's role in the theological systems of Catholics or Protestants, nor on how she was understood by any particular group of historical actors. Rather, it traces how a wide range of Americans constructed and used her figure as a site to transmit, contest, and negotiate gender ideologies. Ideologies are deep social structures that create meaning, prescribe behavior, and define the range of options available to individuals. In the text, I treat Mary as a shared cultural figure whose content was one source (among many) for the maintenance and transformation of American gender ideology. An ideology "requires constant social interaction to preserve its structure."[12] In the case of Mary, the social interactions that created and maintained her figure as an exemplar of womanhood were often acrimonious. Cultural exchange was often invisible and unacknowledged, as images and meanings were transmitted between distinct communities without conscious intent. For example, Mary's growing prominence in Catholic devotional contexts triggered broad popular interest in her imagery, even among those who rejected Marian devotionalism. Exchange can also be negative, as groups define themselves against each other, heightening their distinctiveness. For example, Catholics' increased theological claims for Mary, expressed in the Immaculate Conception declaration, triggered vocal Protestant renunciations of her soteriological role and agitation over the "feminine divine."

Prior to the nineteenth century, Mary had a more fixed and minor role in American culture, but as the century progressed, her figure was increasingly prominent and contested. One clear reason for this heightened interest was the dramatic growth of the U.S. Catholic community, which grew from tens of thousands at the start of the century to more than 2 million at midcentury to nearly 14 million at the close of the century. From the 1830s through the middle of the century, Germans and Irish dominated Catholic (and non-Catholic) immigration, while huge numbers of Italian, Polish, and Eastern European Catholics arrived at the end of the century. Mary had been a subject of Protestant and Catholic contention for centuries, so the arrival of so many Catholics brought increased attention to her figure as a point of difference. But Mary, as a religious figure and site of devotion, also became prominent as a unifying force within the rapidly expanding Catholic community.

Catholic devotionalism, which grew rapidly in these decades, consisted of private participation in Church-sponsored activities that included feast days to honor a particular saint or doctrine, specified prayers, novenas (structured periods of prayer and church attendance over the course of nine days), the wearing of saints medals and cards, and other religious acts such as the adoration of the Blessed Sacrament. These activities strengthened an affective relationship between the devotee and the object of devotion, generally Christ or a specific saint. Many devotions originated or increased in popularity in the early to mid-nineteenth century through the efforts of local bishops, the publication of prayer books, and the spread of parish missions, which drew large crowds and popularized particular devotions. Marian devotions in particular—especially the Sacred Heart of Mary, the Seven Dolors, and the Immaculate Conception—increased markedly midcentury.[13] Through these means, immigrant Catholics constructed an unexpectedly consistent system of religious meaning that bridged diverse cultures. While national and ethnic tensions and distinctive religious practices persisted, devotionalism created a lexicon of shared meanings, intentions, and practices that gave texture and meaning to the identification "American Catholic."[14] Because of Mary's prominence in Catholic devotionalism, Catholics (and non-Catholics) increasingly used her figure to represent and consolidate Catholic identity.

This growth led Americans increasingly to view devotion to Mary as a marker of Catholic religious identity. Yet, surprisingly, this identification did not come at the expense of popular use of Mary as a female archetype. Marian imagery continued to proliferate in both visual and literary forms throughout the latter half of the century and was used by both Catholics and Protestants to conceptualize traditional womanhood, especially purity and motherhood. I think that these contradictory uses of Mary occurred simultaneously because of how necessary it became to shore up an ideology of womanhood in response to structural change and how powerful and multivalent her imagery could be in transmitting quintessential Christian womanhood. Industrialization, immigration, urbanization, and the beginnings of the modern market economy dramatically changed business and economic culture. The Christian values of meekness, humility, generosity, and self-sacrifice had been understood to be essential to the functioning and progress of a democratic state, but they were hard to reconcile with a burgeoning capitalistic economy based on self-interest and a more cynical view of politics. Because of these shifts, women became responsible for carrying forward these formerly shared values, freeing up men to pursue success in the market. Despite increasing divergence on Mary's theological role, the similarities I find in Catholic and Protestant uses of Marian imagery reveal that both groups hoped women could mitigate the dislocations associated with the emergence of the market economy and its individualistic ethic.

A particular emphasis on motherhood and domesticity developed as a counterbalance to the harshness of the emerging capitalistic market.[15] By creating a carefully delineated domestic space—a tranquil and sanctified realm—women soothed the conscience of a society transformed by the faster pace and morally suspect actions required by business. In the popular imagination, the domestic sphere bounded women and defined their identities. At the same time this domestic ideology was gaining ground, lower-class and immigrant women were working outside of their homes in domestic and, increasingly, industrial settings. These women were omitted from both the experience and the ideology of middle-class domesticity. The necessity of leaving their homes and children to work made their existence challenging to cultural models of gender. They were marginalized as persons, in part, because they could not embody the role of "women." The prevailing midcentury domestic ideology thus had an economic role in justifying and sustaining the emerging business economy and a social role in defining the middle class. Middle-class women actively contributed to the development of the norms of female domesticity by joining maternal associations, reading domestic advice books and women's magazines, and creating interior spaces that signaled piety and class status through the consumption of domestic goods. In these ways, women functioned as both foil to and enabler of the market.

While this "cult of motherhood" was fully under way by midcentury, scholars have shown that Catholics did not adopt Protestant domestic norms until later in the century. A sense of the sacredness of the family began to coalesce among Protestants in the antebellum period and among Catholics in the 1870s.[16] This was partly due to the economic realities. Immigrant Catholic families did not have the resources to set up households that exemplified the American domestic ideal, especially in terms of consumer consumption and women's availability in the home. Also, recent immigrants brought with them a range of cultural traditions and gender expectations that shaped their home lives in America. However, while a sentimental domestic ideology was not pervasive among Catholics until late in the century, attention to popular culture reveals that Catholics did not merely emulate Protestant culture but directly contributed to the creation of an influential female ideal. I show in subsequent chapters that sentimental domestic femininity—represented by the popular figures the Angel in the House and the domestic queen—was in fact deeply indebted to Catholic portrayals of Mary. While theology and devotionalism continued to make Mary a symbol of difference, Mary's ability to play this cultural role for both communities linked Catholics and Protestants.

It may be helpful to clarify my usage of these terms. Throughout the text, I use the term "Protestant" to describe the non-Catholic cultural tastemakers who wrote the newspapers, magazines, art guides, advice literature, domestic books, and religious tracts that made the Madonna a popular nineteenth-century figure. Some historians have argued that there was a Protestant evangelical consensus that created unity and held sway in the period. In their view, a unified Protestant culture is identifiable despite denominational and regional differences. Others have suggested that the notion of a Protestant evangelical consensus is a myth that obscures the stark and often contentious theological and cultural differences among

Protestants, and that the notion of a Protestant consensus is more aspirational (then and now) than evident. Historians therefore should not uncritically adopt assumptions about the unity of the past.[17] It is, of course, problematic to write about American "Protestantism." There were abiding differences between Protestant groups in the nineteenth century that manifest in public conflicts, splits, and competitiveness, as well as in the repeated hopeful efforts toward Protestant unity and revitalization. These include the revivals of Charles Finney; the reform efforts of Josiah Strong, John R. Mott, and Walter Rauschenbusch; and the creation of pan-Protestant organizations such as the American Home Missionary Society, the American Evangelical Alliance, the American Bible Society, the YMCA, and the Student Volunteer Movement. Even efforts toward unification suffered from internal conflict and often splintered or failed. However, despite divisions and differences, the "Protestant mainstream" enjoyed significant cultural power.[18] Protestants perceived themselves to be culturally dominant and entitled to shape and define American culture. In reality, the national ethos was shaped by the interaction of assorted groups of Americans of varying religious affiliations. But part of the desire for, and assumption of, Protestant consensus in the nineteenth century was an attempt to shore up existing Protestant cultural authority.

The project of drawing Catholics as conceptual "others," which often involved prescribing and bounding the use and meaning of Mary, was an attempt to construct a unified, normative community. Over and over, authors of varying denominational backgrounds asserted that their critiques of Catholic Mariology and Marian veneration represented the "Protestant" perspective. This was a strategy for achieving consensus, not evidence of it, and in analyzing the "Protestant" voice, I am examining a public negotiation in which various individuals and groups defined themselves as an unified entity against an imagined Catholic community that they formulated to serve as foil, scapegoat, villain, or even victim (of an imagined criminal Catholic hierarchy). This hoped-for unity was not merely presumed but often explicitly asserted, as when the compiler of *Methodist Pamphlets for the People*, a series of anti-Catholic tracts, claimed them to be nonsectarian examples of a shared Protestant mission: "It is believed [the pamphlets] contain nothing to which Protestants of all the leading Orthodox communions will not subscribe ... They will prove a valuable *vade mecum* to anyone who may be called to defend the faith once delivered unto the saints against the novelties of the Man of Sin, ... the corruptions of Popery."[19] As writers like the

Methodist compiler of the pamphlets presumed to speak for and to the typical American, they contributed to a generic Protestant voice that a majority of Protestant Americans identified as inclusive of themselves. While denominational publications with specific theological commitments existed, the majority of newspapers, women's magazines, and popular literary and general interest magazines adopted this voice of presumed Protestant consensus. Standardized Sunday school curricula, public school Bible reading, and Christian moral teaching also contributed to a sense of broad Protestant consensus.[20] Additionally, anti-Catholic writers frequently quoted and reprinted each other's tracts, articles, and books; for example, Methodist publications ran theological articles by Presbyterian professors, Reformed theologians wrote introductions to Baptist-authored books, and general-interest magazines ran articles by Episcopalians and Baptists side by side. Finally, socioeconomic privilege and control of the media magnified the cultural impact of this "Protestant voice."

Still, while Protestant cultural power was real, the primacy of their experiences and perspectives was not. Religious groups in America constructed their identities and developed their values reciprocally. Cultural influence is a two-way exchange between majority and minority cultures. Religious communities took both active and reactive stances as they shaped each other. And all contributed to the creation of a shared American culture to which they looked for their national identity and against which they defined their particularity. Nineteenth-century Protestants used terms including "Catholic," "Romish," "Romanist," and "Papist" to refer to a cultural construction—the imagined Catholic community. But Catholics were just as invested as Protestants in constructing an imagined unitary Catholic community, both transnationally and in America. Thus, both Protestants and Catholics of varying classes, ethnicities, and religious affiliations imagined and reified the binary religious categories of "Protestant" and "Catholic," despite the wide range of cultural and religious differences concealed by those terms. In the text, I use the word "Catholic" when analyzing anti-Catholic rhetoric or referring to the broadly defined but recognizable "Catholic voice" that emerged in Catholic newspapers, books, advice literature, magazines, and fiction in the period. This term is not meant to minimize the diversity of lived Catholic belief and practice in the United States. Whenever I refer to specific Catholic individuals or groups of Catholics, I locate them religiously, ethnically, and socially. However, it is important to recognize that the culturally constructed figure "Mary" was related in complex and shifting ways to the equally constructed category "American Catholicism." I analyze these constructs by closely reading the discourses in which they were collectively built by Americans. In doing so, I remain aware of the imbalance of power between various groups.

One of the primary ways in which power inequity was manifest was in the rhetoric of Catholic "otherness." This discourse was pervasive in nineteenth-century America and led to real violence and discrimination. At the same time, attraction and longing existed alongside Protestant hostility toward Catholics.[21] This book argues, in part, that previous historians have overstated the "otherness" of Catholics. Protestants were extremely critical of Catholics, but as I demonstrate, part of the reason for their hostility was that they shared so much else with Catholics as Christians. In particular, they shared a cultural inheritance that marked a particular canon of religious music, painting, sculpture, and architecture as indicators of elevated taste, and they shared gender ideals that drew on various theological interpretations of the figure of Mary. Because of such similarities, differences were rhetorically magnified. More powerful groups could define their opponents as "others," but it is important to remember that "such politics are based not in an account of radical otherness, which is a matter of absolute difference, but rather on a notion of proximate otherness, which involves differentiation from one's near neighbors who share anthropological similitude with us. So . . . the other 'is most problematic when he is too-much-like-us or when he claims to be-us.'"[22] Historians can sometimes accept the vociferous insistence on Catholic and Protestant difference, from both communities, too much at face value. Despite centuries-old contention between Protestant groups and Catholics over the appropriate role of Mary in Christianity, Catholic interest in Mary was not alien to Protestants. As I demonstrate in the text, nineteenth-century Catholics and Protestants argued so vociferously about Mary because she was a shared potent symbol of womanhood and motherhood that remained crucial to them both.

THIS BOOK MOVES through the second half of the nineteenth century in a broadly chronological schema, beginning in chapters 1 and 2 with responses to the Immaculate Conception declaration and ending in chapter 5 with the rise of the New Woman and the domestic queenship motif of the 1880s and 1890s. Some sections of the book are organized more thematically. For example, in chapter 2, in addition to responses to the declaration, I also sketch the growing prevalence of Marian imagery that proliferated with technological advances in the print industry through the second half of the century. In chapters 3 and 4, I not only examine the content and impact of several books that were published in particular years but also trace their representation of broader trends and their continuing effects in subsequent decades.

The first chapter treats the 1854 declaration of the Immaculate Conception of the Virgin Mary as Catholic dogma. The process leading up to and culminating in the declaration received detailed (and often biased) coverage in the U.S. press. The proclamation intensified and publicized an intractable theological disagreement between Protestants and Catholics. Its culmination surprised many American Protestants: with its strong affirmation of Catholic theological distinctiveness, it was a step away from conciliation. The debate that followed the proclamation offers a unique window into popular understandings of Mary's role. In the chapter, I examine the broad outlines of Protestant attacks on and Catholic defense of the doctrine, the reception of the doctrine by both communities, and the role that Mary played in signifying religious identity.

The second chapter focuses on the gender rhetoric that emerged in the Immaculate Conception debate. In articles, editorials, and pamphlets, American Protestants publicly stated their beliefs and fears about the meaning of Mary's womanhood and objected to the dogma in explicitly gendered language. An analysis of this rhetoric reveals that the implications of the doctrine for Mary's public function as an exemplar of Christian womanhood was a factor in the sectarian debate over Immaculate Conception theology. I also explore popular visual depictions of Mary in sources including art books, art exhibitions, lithographs, magazine illustrations, and other reproductions, and examine the gender characteristics transmitted by these images. Taken together, chapters 1 and 2 highlight the intensity of Catholic and Protestant theological disagreement over Mary, which contrasts with the underlying convergence in the content of popular Marian imagery that I treat in subsequent chapters.

In chapter 3, I examine the cultural impact of the work of Anna Jameson, whose 1852 book *Legends of the Madonna* became the authoritative text on Marian art and remained influential throughout the century. I argue that Jameson's book helped to popularize Marian art, legitimate Protestant interest in it, and shape public taste toward stronger, more independent depictions of Mary. In chapter 4, I examine Marian imagery in American domestic fiction, focusing on one Catholic and one Baptist author. Catholic convert

Anna Hanson Dorsey influenced popular Catholic conceptions of Mary through her many domestic novels, which were characterized by their Marian spirituality and hyperpure Mary-derived heroines. I analyze her 1887 novel *Adrift*, alongside an 1888 novel by Baptist minister Alexander Stewart Walsh entitled *Mary: Queen of the House of David and Mother of Jesus*. I show that Dorsey and Walsh used parallel strategies for employing Marian themes to address the late-century "Woman Question." Employing maternalistic arguments, each writer suggested that an elevated and egalitarian understanding of womanhood, modeled on Mary, would lead to social reforms that would protect women from exploitation and give them an expanded sphere of action without overturning their domestic role.

Finally, in chapter 5, I explore the Marian-derived rhetoric and imagery of domestic queenship that evolved in response to and alongside the New Woman. While such rhetoric was used both to resist and promote the "cause of woman," queenship had the potential to establish a less sacrificial model of womanhood. Because Mary's queenship was a culturally available, traditional image of female transcendence, it provided a way to invoke female power without undermining, or appearing to undermine, traditional social norms. As the New Woman rose to prominence, some Catholic and Protestant authors drew on more powerful aspects of Marian theology, particularly her unmediated relationship with God, her centrality to the salvation narrative, and her authority over Christ as his *mother*, to create strong, Marian-inspired heroines who were more autonomous than traditional models. These motifs drew on Mary's theological power to create models of womanhood with more personal agency and self-determination. However, the theological content embedded in Marian imagery always included traditional, nonthreatening virtues—such as gentleness, humility, and maternity. A Marian model of womanhood, even the powerful Queen of Heaven, implicitly transmitted these more traditional female virtues alongside more autonomous ones. In some cases, domestic queenship helped justify women's entrance to the public sphere by cloaking increases in activity and power in reassuring, maternalistic rhetoric. However, these same elements also constrained the future usefulness of the Mary symbol to woman's empowerment once significant gains had been made.

A FEW FINAL COMMENTS about my sources and approach. I use both visual and literary sources to uncover and trace the development of Mary as an American cultural construction. While Mary was notably present in elite Protestant literature and Catholic devotional materials, I focus instead on popular cultural sources because they allow a broader and more nuanced view of her function in American culture. Due to male control of media and publishing houses, I necessarily find a predominance of male voices when examining public arguments about Mary. However, despite women's restricted access to many vehicles of public expression, women contributed to the construction of the American Madonna. While women were underrepresented as journalists, theologians, columnists, and editors, they were well represented as novelists, poets, and essayists. I treat a variety of woman-authored texts in my analysis, including the works of writers Eleanor Donnelly, Anna Dorsey, Elizabeth Eastlake, Estelle Hurll, and Anna Jameson. I also examine women's contribution to the Marian female ideal through their display of Marian visual imagery in domestic spaces and quasi-public spaces such as kindergartens, settlement houses, and public schools.

I include visual sources alongside textual sources in my analysis because they were an important site—possibly the most important site—for the transmission of Marian tropes in the period. Rapid advances in print reproduction created a visual culture that blurred and bridged the boundaries between elite and popular culture and transmitted meanings between religious communities. Because images were open to a range of interpretations and could be reprinted easily in various contexts, they open a window to sites where religious norms, assumptions, beliefs, and practices evolved in contact with other groups. When reading Marian visual and literary texts, it is also important to recognize that historical actors, like people today, were not always consistent. There were often tensions or even outright contradictions between their professed beliefs and their actual concerns, preoccupations, and assumptions about religion and culture. As one Victorian cultural scholar reminds us, "a cultural myth thrives in large part because it lives below the formulated surface of its age; rarely does it crystallize into explicit gospel or precept which the conscious mind can analyze and reject."[23] Persistent unsanctioned beliefs recurred and surfaced in both literary and visual culture. Thus, even though nineteenth-century American Protestants vociferously rejected Catholic Marian theology and devotionalism, they helped proliferate Marian images that transmitted characteristics derived from Catholic theology.

I also examine both visual and literary culture because these forms cannot be easily disentangled. Nineteenth-century Americans discussed, prescribed, and objected to Marian art, making a significant portion of the public conversation on Mary about visual representations of her. Marian images were a large subset of the Western art tradition, knowledge of which was fast being reclaimed as an indicator of refinement and class status. Likewise, many literary references to the Virgin Mary—in novels, short fiction essays, and poems—consisted of detailed descriptions of well-known Marian artworks. The fact that these passages were descriptions of paintings was often not acknowledged, but their evocation of famous art was unmistakable and would have been easily recognizable to most readers. Even when texts referred to biblical pericopes about Mary, or stories about Mary derived from Catholic tradition, they often described famous paintings in order to evoke an image in the reader's mind. Thus, the acts of reading and seeing merged as writers drew on a shared visual culture to communicate and contest religious and gendered meanings. In the text, then, I often analyze visual and textual images together. In doing so, I use the terms "visions," "imaginings," and "readings" of Mary to describe constructions of her figure. Because of this overlap, I use them interchangeably despite the fact that reading visual imagery and envisioning textual sources are figurative uses.

Also throughout the text, I generally use the word "icon" in its common, nontechnical sense of a figure being *iconic*: "a person or thing regarded as a representative symbol of a culture or movement."[24] Tracing the history of what exactly Mary symbolically represented—womanhood (what sort?), Catholicism, motherhood, domesticity, transcendence, power—is a main goal of this text. But the specialized definition of "icon" as holy image, the site of veneration and devotion (derived from the portrait icons of Byzantine Christianity) also applies in some cases. Nineteenth-century Americans used contextual clues to determine appropriate responses to Marian images: in this instance, is she an icon or merely iconic? Whichever function was determined, both uses were nevertheless religious. The power of Marian imagery as a source for theorizing womanhood depended on its ability to invoke the range of meanings generated by the Christian narrative and the underlying conviction that she was a religiously significant figure. For some American Protestants, Marian imagery was always iconic, in any context, and thus required iconoclastic rejection; but for most Americans, Marian imagery was a commodious symbol that contained and transmitted multiple conflicting but religiously and socially useful meanings. The tension in the definition of the word "icon" mirrors the tension in the reception of her imagery.

CHAPTER ONE

The Immaculate Conception of the Blessed Virgin Mary

Conflict and Conversation, 1854–1855

O Mother! I could weep for mirth, Joy fills my heart so fast;
My soul to-day is heaven on earth, O could the transport last!
I think of thee, and what thou art, Thy majesty, thy state;
And I keep singing in my heart—Immaculate! Immaculate!

—No. 82, "Immaculate! Immaculate!" *The Crown Hymn Book*, 1862

But brethren, it is not enough, in such a day as this, to abjure what is false; we
are taught by an apostle, that we ought also, to "contend earnestly for the faith
once delivered to the saints." . . . There are good men, among Romanists, . . .
Now then let us be prepared to show them "the good old paths."

—A. Cleveland Cox, *The Novelty and Nullity of the Papal Dogma of the
Immaculate Conception: A Sermon Preached in Grace Church Baltimore,
March 25th, 1855*

On December 8, 1854, Pope Pius IX declared the Immaculate Conception of
the Blessed Virgin Mary—her exemption, at the moment of her conception,
from the inheritance of original sin—to be the faith of the Catholic Church.
The newspaper *Univers of Paris* declared: "Two hundred Bishops were present. Never has such a multitude been seen. Rome is intoxicated with joy."[1]
American newspapers widely reprinted these pithy lines in the following
weeks and months alongside accounts of the ceremony and the celebra-
tions, explanations of the doctrine, and with equal frequency, Protestant
denunciations of it.

Witnesses described the ceremony as emotionally powerful: the pontiff
raised the question of Mary's conception, waited for confirmation by the
Holy Spirit, and then, with visible tears and a cracking voice, declared
the Immaculate Conception of the Blessed Virgin Mary to be dogma of
the Church. The proclamation received thunderous applause during which
attendants raised Pius IX, seated in his chair, onto their shoulders and carried him to the Chapel of the Virgin. There, he placed a jewel-encrusted

crown on a beautifully adorned statue of Mary. After the ceremony, the Basilica of St. Peter was lit with an estimated six thousand tallow and turpentine lamps to produce a "scene of splendor probably nowhere equaled ... indescribable."[2] As the building receded into the evening darkness, it became "perfectly invisible, while the immense mass seemed as if it were constructed of lights."[3] Processions and jubilation followed in the streets of Rome, and cities throughout the world celebrated into the night.

THE IMMACULATE CONCEPTION declaration—the proclamation of a doctrine already widely embraced by Catholics—was welcomed by American Catholics, but provoked vehement reactions from Protestants. The move of the doctrine to dogma amplified an intractable theological disagreement between Protestants and Catholics and was perceived by both groups as a bold and unapologetic assertion of Catholic Mariology. In countless articles and editorials, Protestant critics decried both the content of the doctrine and its mode of pronouncement. Some Protestant theologians, familiar with the historical arguments for and against the doctrine, engaged its complex theology; however, most objected to it on three main grounds: it grew out of Catholic tradition more than biblical witness; it was decided by papal fiat, not free religious debate; and most important, it seemed to place a female figure, Mary, on the same footing with the male Christ.

Catholic veneration of the saints, and of Mary in particular, had long been an area of theological discord and, more pointedly, a target for anti-Catholic propagandists who painted devotional practices as idolatry. But because the beleaguered pope made a grand gesture using a Marian doctrine to assert his spiritual authority, he moved Marian devotion even more to the fore. The declaration placed her figure at the center of the Church's identity in a changing world. Such a visible endorsement of Catholic Mariology reinforced the divergence between Catholic and Protestant attitudes toward Mary. However, Protestants did not simply give up using Marian imagery; instead, arguments over her were heated. The declaration reignited a contention for the right to use and define her role in Christianity that would continue into the early years of the twentieth century.

In response to the declaration, Protestants not only denounced Catholic Mariology but also publicly reflected on and clarified Mary's appropriate role in Christianity. Many more articles on Mary were published in these years than in previous decades. In these articles, Protestants articulated their beliefs about Mary and objected to her place in Catholicism, often focusing on her sex and her role as an exemplar of womanhood and mother-hood. I examine the challenges to American gender norms triggered by the declaration in chapter 2; here, I look closely at other pervasive themes that arose in these writings. The Immaculate Conception declaration accentu-ated the distinctive and, for many Protestants, unfamiliar aspects of Catholic Marian theology. The three most prevalent critiques of the declaration—that it was an authoritarian "binding" of Catholic minds, that it was "innovative," and that it contributed to an overshadowing of Jesus by Mary—were distinct expressions of already prevalent nativist tropes. Protestants feared the po-litical and social implications of escalating Catholic immigration, so debates with or about Catholics were often about the right to control and define American identity. The charge of authoritarianism, therefore, was driven by Protestant anxieties about papal control over Catholics, particularly about the opinions, behavior, and votes of foreign-born Catholics. The charge of innovation was also tied to fears of papal power. It was often expressed as an objection to the Catholic Church's claim to have the authority to teach ("de-cide") doctrine, which Protestants contrasted to the authority of a (supposedly unitary) "plain reading" of the Bible. Finally, the charge of Mary's overpromi-nence was tied to fears about Catholic transgression of (again, supposedly unitary) American gender, family, and sexual norms.[4] Protestants used these themes to portray Catholics as intrinsically outside "Christian" and "Ameri-can" categories.

Immaculate Conception: History, Context, and Reactions

A feast day honoring Mary's "conception" and later her "immaculate concep-tion" originated in the East by the seventh century and spread throughout Europe.[5] The objections of early twelfth-century abbot, Marian devotee, and theologian St. Bernard of Clairvaux that the feast lacked ancient precedent and was doctrinally misleading slowed its progress.[6] In response to his argu-ments, the feast was abolished or renamed the feast of the "conception" of Mary, rather than the "immaculate conception" in some areas. This seman-tic distinction accomplished little, however, because holding a feast to cele-brate Mary's conception (not merely her birth or her life) presupposed some set of miraculous circumstances surrounding it. The Church's en-dorsement or censure of the feast prompted theological reflection on the merit and status of the doctrine. In the thirteenth century, prominent theologians—including Dominicans St. Albert the Great and St. Thomas

Aquinas, and Franciscan St. Bonaventure—contended against it on theological grounds. The Dominican order, taking their cue from Aquinas's opposition, followed suit. However, among the doctrine's defenders was the great Franciscan scholar John Duns Scotus, whose writings formed a basis for the Franciscan order's committed support. Eventually, the European universities, beginning with the University of Paris in 1497, each decided in favor of the Immaculate Conception doctrine and required scholars to take oaths defending it. During the following centuries, theological subtleties were clarified and debates became timeworn as learned opinion coalesced in favor of the doctrine. This mounting support culminated in Pope Clement XI's 1708 decision to elevate the feast to one of obligation for the universal Church. However, papal support for the feast was not equivalent to propagation of the doctrine, and individual theologians, particularly Dominicans, exercised their freedom to oppose it. The dispute between Dominicans and Franciscans over the Immaculate Conception persisted. The long-standing divide was repeatedly (and gleefully) recounted in American periodicals in the decades before the declaration brought the issue to the fore, leaving American Protestants with an inaccurate sense of Catholic disunity on a subject that there was actually very little disagreement about.[7]

When Pius IX decided to officially resolve the question of Mary's conception, he took a unique and radical course of action. In 1849, while exiled in Gaeta during a period of extreme political unrest that many supposed would weaken his leadership, he issued the encyclical *Ubi Primum*, announcing his resolve to decide the Immaculate Conception question and requesting the prayers and advice of bishops worldwide.[8] It was widely recognized that the encyclical was not actually an open inquiry, but the first step in the formalization of the doctrine into dogma. A large majority of bishops replied with enthusiastic support for the doctrine. Their responses affirmed their endorsement of Mary's exemption from original sin, but it was clear they were also formal assertions of loyalty to the pontiff in exile. Only fifty of the six hundred or so bishops who responded to the encyclical expressed reservation, with some calling the doctrine undefinable or, more commonly, politically inopportune. Of these, only a handful actually withheld endorsement. All American bishops and prominent American theologians supported the doctrine. The bishop of Philadelphia, John Neumann, and the archbishop of New York, John Hughes, were particularly vocal promoters.[9]

When Pius IX called the convention in Rome to decide the question, it was largely understood to be a formality. The form of the convention was new; because it was not an ecumenical council and had no official avenue of representation, the assembled bishops formed an audience rather than a decision-making body. Two Jesuit theologians, Fathers Giovanni Perrone and Carlo Passaglia, wrote the main text of what would become the solemn proclamation, *Ineffabilis Deus*. Several attending bishops were asked to review and contribute to the prewritten proclamation, and minor changes were made, but no opportunity to debate the question was provided.

The most significant Catholic opponent of the doctrine was the French priest Abbé M. Laborde of Lectoure, who traveled to Rome to formally protest the proclamation and there was questioned and detained. His protest was not officially acknowledged. Laborde's account of his experience in Rome was widely publicized in the United States, and his book, *The Impossibility of the Immaculate Conception as an Article of Faith*, detailing his opposition to the doctrine, was published in the United States, France, and England and reissued in several editions during the next decade. Protestant critics of the declaration quoted it liberally and promoted it as evidence of Catholic disunity. The *Church Review*, for example, celebrated it as "one of the most remarkable books of the day" because it showed that even a "learned Papist who adheres religiously to the doctrine of Papal Supremacy" was willing to sacrifice his career to protest "the new popish infidel dogma" that was "ruinous to the case of faith." The review asserted that other Catholics would surely join with Laborde and that he "will not stand alone."[10] Laborde's book was placed on the *Index Librorum Prohibitorum*, the Vatican's List of Forbidden Books.[11]

While the convention clearly was not an ecumenical council, some bishops advised that an assembly of bishops should stand with the pope when he made the pronouncement, to signal their support and consent. However, the pope chose to stand alone. It was immediately apparent that the proceedings had implications beyond Mariology. The pope had declared doctrine solely on his own authority, he spoke alone, and his declaration was received without challenge by the bishops of the Church. The *Univers of Paris* epitomized the event in the widely reprinted line: "Peter arises, he speaks, he commands, he is victor."[12] The *New York Evangelist* quoted a Vatican propaganda office pamphlet conveying the significance of the mode of the pronouncement: "The Holy See is about to exercise its highest prerogative of infallibility, and the occurrence of so rare an event must necessarily engage the attention of the whole civilized world."[13] It certainly commanded the attention of Americans. While the aftermath of the Kansas-Nebraska

Act and the formation of the Republican Party dominated the news in a country less than a decade away from the eruption of civil war, U.S. press coverage of the Immaculate Conception proclamation was surprisingly extensive. Media stories expressed particular concern about increased papal power, at least over religious matters.

In an apostolic letter written after the convention, Pius IX clarified the implications of his action. He explained that, as pope, he had sufficient authority to define dogma without a general council and that the replies he received to *Ubi Primum* not only supported the Immaculate Conception but also the exercise of his papal prerogative to declare dogma. The bishops, he wrote, "entreated of Us with a common voice that the Immaculate Conception of the Virgin should be defined by Our supreme judgment and authority."[14] Emphasizing the legitimacy of such papal authority, Pius continued: "We resolved that We should no longer delay to sanction and define, by Our supreme authority, the Immaculate Conception of the Virgin."[15]

American Catholics were buoyed both by the means and the content of the declaration, while Protestants denounced it as an unreasonable assertion of papal power. The *New York Times* framed the issue for readers unfamiliar with Catholic institutional structures: "It is a cardinal doctrine of the Catholic . . . that infallibility necessarily resides . . . in the Church; but there is an old difference of opinion as to *where* precisely, in the Church, that quality of prerogative is lodged. Some maintain that it vested only in general councils; others that the See of Rome also may appropriate it."[16] Protestants did not agree that the Catholic Church was infallible in any part, but many Protestant denominations accepted the early ecumenical councils as authoritative and, despite rejecting the authority of later councils, sided with conciliar rather than papal control over dogma.[17] The *Times* article concluded with a quotation from a French bishop, who boldly announced: "Holy Father! Thou hast not only decided the Immaculate Conception—thou has decided thine own infallibility."[18] Sixteen years later, that implication was fully realized when the doctrine of papal infallibility, the pope's right to pronounce dogma apart from an ecumenical council, was affirmed at the First Vatican Council (1869–70).

American coverage of the doctrine and its proclamation was biased and often misleading. Journalists and editors especially mocked the exuberance of Catholics and their hopes for spiritual renewal. "You will hear by this mail that Europe in general, and Rome in particular, is 'intoxicated with joy,'" wrote a correspondent for the *New York Daily Times*: "Now, joy is certainly better than brandy to be intoxicated with; however, I don't like drunkards in any shape, and so I must protest against my being counted in the number comprised in the collective expression of 'Europe.' I am not at all intoxicated with anything, however the Pope may declare, for such is the telegraphed reason of such an uncommon inebriety—'the immaculate conception of the Virgin.' But, then, you will say, I am an heretic. Just so, and I accept my lot, come what will."[19] Jokingly appropriating the term "heretic," the correspondent used his minority status as a non-Catholic in France to reinforce his readers' privileged majority status as Protestants in the United States, while interpreting Catholic unity and celebration as collective delusional hedonism. While the tone of the report was entertaining and sardonic, the writer reinforced a "Protestant voice" of measured rationalism against an imagined Catholic emotionalism.

The French correspondent for the *Independent* likewise described the European reaction for American readers, writing:

> No one now is regarded as a good Roman Catholic who denies the future dogma; indeed it seems, from the most approved books and Episcopal charges on the subject, that the whole interest of religion in this world is to be concentrated upon the question of Mary's conception, with or without sin. All the troubles, wars, disputes, divisions in Christendom will end when Mary is declared sinless, so at least say the bishops. In a most astonishing charge, if any thing from that quarters could still astonish us, the Archbishop of Bordeaux ascribes all the calamities of this world to God, and all the blessings granted to it, to the virgin Mary. 'When was the queen of heaven's protection more necessary to us, than when the wrath of God threatens us on every side, . . . when the mysterious disease of the vine . . .' Think of the wine crops being restored by the Virgin Mary's intervention in spite of God's opposition to it![20]

His critique showed contempt for Catholic triumphalism and raised two of the three most common Protestant critiques of the declaration—the limitation of Catholic freedom of conscience and the question of Mary's authority, specifically the charge that the elevation of Mary comes at the expense of the authority God. The correspondent portrayed Protestants as reasonable observers who were "astonished" by religious absurdities. Protestant coverage of the declaration consistently struck this tone of wry amusement and patronizing rationalism. What was left unaddressed, however, was why non-Catholics were invested enough in Catholic Marian theology to report on, explain, and denounce it at all—never mind with such frequency. Articles about other religious "absurdities," be they Mormon or Hindu, were common and characterized by a similar mocking disdain, but they did not share the emotional, high-pitched, detailed engagement of Immaculate Conception coverage. While such derisive articles were outwardly distancing, this level of engagement revealed that Protestants had something at stake in Catholic belief and practice.[21]

The elaborate, triumphalist claims that Protestants objected to were, in fact, ubiquitous in the American Catholic response to the declaration. Catholics asserted that God would surely reward the Church's faithfulness to Mary by resolving the papacy's political fortunes, strengthening the position of the Church in America, delivering thousands of new converts, and ending wars worldwide.[22] John Hughes, the bishop of New York, expressed such hopes in his newspaper, the *Freeman's Journal*: "[The declaration] has given joy to the world, and is it too much if we expect from it the pacification of the nations, and a general prostration of heretical and persecuting forces! . . . The Saints and holy ones of past ages who have defended this doctrine . . . have predicted that this declaration would be followed by a time of great rest and advancement to the Holy Catholic Church."[23] The *New York Times* reprinted Hughes's triumphalist hopes, giving the Protestant public a glimpse of Catholic buoyancy. Hughes's remarks captured the mood of many American Catholics who received news of the declaration as a personal victory that renewed their hopes for their future in America. A papal pronouncement of a high honor for Mary affirmed their religious identity, which by midcentury had come to be characterized by devotionalism and by Marian devotionalism in particular.

No American Catholics publicly expressed reservations about the theology of the Immaculate Conception, leaving Protestant critics with only (schismatic Catholic) Jansenist opponents in the Netherlands or the Abbé Laborde in France to quote for evidence of Catholic disunity.[24] Some Catholics may have feared the increased scrutiny and Protestant censure that the declaration would trigger. Such fears were not expressed in print, but Catholic sermons and magazine articles occasionally admonished readers to support the declaration or to be more vocal in their support, indicating the possibility of Catholic reserve. Bishop Hughes drew on the pope's boldness in making the proclamation to encourage his audience toward a bolder public embrace of Catholic distinctiveness. He concluded his sermon on the declaration with the charge: "Let the Catholics of America acknowledge their past tepidity of faith, and hasten to shake it off. Let us betake ourselves to our great Patroness—Mary of Immaculate Conception."[25] Remarks like these indicate that years of intensifying nativism coupled with pervasive negative press coverage of the declaration may have caused some timidity and defensiveness around Catholic Marian theology. Still, most approved of its bold affirmation of Catholic faith.

As Bishop Hughes reminded his listeners, U.S. Catholics already had a special connection to Mary Immaculate: in 1846 the Sixth Provincial Council of Baltimore named the Feast of the Immaculate Conception the patronal feast of the United States, and in 1847 the "Blessed Mary, conceived without sin" was named patroness of America. U.S. Catholics had also fully incorporated the doctrine into their devotional life through observance of the feast, the growing popularity of the miraculous medal (printed with "O Mary, conceived without sin, pray for us who have recourse to thee"), and the inclusion of the "immaculate" descriptor in other Marian devotions. American Catholic embrace of the doctrine is also clear from the spur the declaration gave to Marian devotionalism. Already on the upswing, after the declaration, Marian devotions continued to grow in popularity, with the publication of devotionals focusing exclusively on Mary, such as the 1865 collection *The Manual of the Immaculate Conception: A Collection of Prayers for General Use, Including the Most Approved Devotions to the Blessed Mother of God.*[26] Because the proclamation affirmed a doctrine already tied to American Catholic identity, and because it resonated with broader trends in Catholic devotionalism, it represented, for many, a defiant stand against both Pius IX's political enemies and the daily personal affronts of American nativism.

American Catholics' propensity to connect their personal struggles to those of the pope and to embrace both the content and the means of the declaration was due, in part, to the ultramontane leanings of the American Church. "Ultramontanism" was an ecclesiastical philosophy that emphasized the spiritual primacy of the pope and the centralization of authority in the seat of Rome. The term was derived from *ultra montes*, Latin for "beyond the mountains," which, from a European perspective, denoted Rome's location beyond the Alps. In the nineteenth century, ultramontanism flourished as a popular movement characterized by a shared devotional culture that unified the worldwide Catholic community and solidified the role of the institutional Church as the mediator of spiritual life through officially endorsed devotions. American Catholics' ultramontane sympathies aligned them both with the increased papal power asserted in the pope's stand-alone declaration and the devotional context out of which the doctrine emerged and through which it was propagated.[27] American Catholics, who were already primed to connect their sufferings to Pius IX's, easily adopted his boldness as a model in their own stand against anti-Catholic violence and prejudice.

"Roma Locuta Est": Freedom of Conscience and Innovation

Protestant critics cited the proclamation as confirmation of Catholicism's fundamental antinomy to American freedom of conscience. They expressed outrage at the move of the doctrine from "pious opinion" to dogma, especially as they downplayed the role of institutional authority and theological creeds in their own religious lives. Religious populism, a movement that began in earnest in the eighteenth century and flourished in the nineteenth, undermined the fortunes of the Congregationalist establishment and, with its ties to England and its hierarchical structure, the Episcopal Church in the United States; it also stoked the flames of American anti-Catholicism.[28] Protestant opposition to the declaration, especially the charge that it brought an end to Catholics' freedom of conscience on an undecided issue and represented an improper assertion of papal power, was partly an outgrowth of this widespread democratic, antiauthoritarian rhetoric. At the same time, theological distinctiveness began to recede in importance as Protestant churches switched their emphasis from denominational particularity to a simpler, more coherent and appealing message.[29] The impact of these shifts was a renewed abjuration of creeds and doctrinal statements; the Bible alone was sufficient for understanding Christian doctrine, and Jesus the only focus of worship. This new "Jesus piety" created an evangelical consonance among theologically disparate Protestant groups. In contrast to this shared, simple, and affective Jesus piety, the Immaculate Conception doctrine appeared extrabiblical, overly complex, and irrelevant or distracting to a focus on Jesus.[30] Thus, in addition to being theologically discordant for Protestants, it was wholly out of tune with the mood of American evangelical piety.

Critics of the declaration repeatedly contrasted American freedom of conscience, which they tied to biblicism and democracy, with Catholic authoritarianism in pronouncing dogma. " '*Roma locuta est*,' and doubt is now heresy," railed Presbyterian theologian Henry Boynton Smith in an often-repeated line.[31] The pope's declaration of the dogma on his sole authority amplified Protestant fears that the Catholic Church was not merely stifling individual theological reflection, but being led by an activist pope whose personal power would grow unchecked, and whose command of his flock might pose a direct challenge to American democratic processes.

Underscoring the impact of Pius IX's stand-alone action in declaring the Immaculate Conception, the author of a Methodist tract entitled "Giant Pope" quoted from Pius IX's apostolic letter asserting his authority to decide dogma: "Wherefore if any shall dare—which God avert!—to think otherwise than as it has been defined by Us, they should know and understand that they are condemned by their own judgment."[32] Pius IX's letter emphasized the significance of the doctrine's move to dogma, underscoring that even though an ecumenical council was not held, the matter was authoritatively decided and the full magisterium of the Church was employed in the declaration. In quoting Pius IX, the tract writer highlighted both the elevation of the pope's authority and the restriction of lay Catholics' private judgment. Expanding his premise that this exercise of papal power by Pius IX was inappropriate and dangerous ("popery has [not] lost its appetite for blood"), he followed the quotation with lines cautioning against freedom of conscience taken from the papal encyclical *Mirari Vos*: "The absurd and erroneous doctrine or raving in defence of liberty of conscience, is a most pestilential error—a pest of all others most to be dreaded in a state."[33] Oddly, the tract's author attributed these lines (and by implication the encyclical *Mirari Vos*) to Pius IX, but they were actually penned twenty years earlier by his predecessor, Gregory XVI.[34] Whether the misattribution was accidental or deliberate, it strengthened his argument that Pius IX was a particular threat to Catholics' personal religious judgment (and possibly, by extension, their freedom to vote their own consciences as well).[35]

Protestant critics often tied arguments about the proclamation's restriction of liberty of conscience to claims about its "newness," "novelty," "suddenness," or late advent in history. A scornful editorial in the *National Era*, for example, exclaimed: "What an amount of credulity is required in the members of the Catholic Church, to believe unhesitatingly in this new dogma, now for the first time, nearly nineteen centuries after the existence of the Virgin Mary, declared to be a doctrine of the church, dissent from which must involve damnation!"[36] The threat of "damnation" was a dramatization of the doctrine's new status; however, the article implied that the doctrine itself, not just its status as dogma, was a recent invention. If the pope could declare this novelty, Protestant critics challenged, he could declare anything. The editorial continued: "It is upon occasions of this kind that we feel the value of our Protestantism, for, should all the Protestant Churches join with the Catholic in promulgating such a dogma as this we would not believe it, simply because there is no 'Thus saith the Lord' for it." The author's recourse to "Thus saith the Lord" indicated his belief that theological questions should be resolved by individual consciences and a literal, straightforward reading of the Bible. In this view, doctrinal stability was ensured not by apostolic succession or the magisterium, as Catholics maintained, but by the authority of the Bible. Thus, an *individual* free from authoritarian control—even, as this author makes clear, from the authority of "Protestant Churches"—could decide for himself what is foundationally Christian by turning to his own Bible. While Catholics would call this presumption the fodder of heresy, many American Protestants, based on a loose understanding of the Lutheran tenet of *sola scriptura* and influenced by the evangelical populism of the era, endorsed it as the only true safeguard of orthodoxy.

In response to Protestant demands for a "thus saith the Lord," some Catholic apologists cited relevant biblical passages in support of the doctrine, drawing on Old Testament passages they interpreted as prefiguring Mary, the Gospel narratives of the New Testament, and figurative passages from the book of Revelation. The most common was the plentitude of grace implied by the angel Gabriel's salutation of Mary in the Gospel of Luke (Luke 1:28). Other important biblical texts included metaphoric allusions to the Ark of the Covenant and descriptions of the bride from Song of Solomon. Other Catholic apologists asserted that the truth, propriety, and self-evident nature of the doctrine was so clear that direct biblical evidence was unnecessary. Bishop Neumann wrote: "If there were no other words of Holy Writ on this topic than these—'Mary, of whom was born Jesus who is called Christ'—(St. Matt. i, 16)—they would be amply sufficient."[37] Still others cautioned against entering into a theological debate with Protestants. By engaging the question of biblical evidence for the Immaculate Conception, they argued, Catholics forfeited the authority of the magisterium and tradition. Noted Catholic convert Orestes Brownson was particularly attuned to the underlying question of authority that the "bound consciences" criticism evoked. In his *Quarterly Review*, he reviewed an apologia for Catholic Marian theology written by the Reverend John Brande Morris. Brownson cautioned that Morris's goal, no matter how well executed, would lead

Catholics down a rocky path: "There is no Catholic dogma, taken apart from the authority of the church that is defensible. Deny or waive the commission of the Church from God to teach, therefore her presence as infallible teacher, and there is nothing that she teaches us of faith that a wise man will undertake either to deny or to defend. To waive that authority, and to descend into the arena to combat with Protestants, is to concede to them in the outset all they contend for, namely, the possibility of determining what is Christian faith without an infallible church."[38] Brownson emphasized that debate with Protestants must focus only on the location of authority. The very act of arguing the merits of a specific doctrine rather than citing the teaching authority of the Church was inherently Protestant. In his view, individual conscience must remain submissive to the authority given to Peter and his successors by Christ. This point of view admitted and accentuated the "bound consciences" of Catholics, and was therefore a difficult argument for many American Catholics who hoped that Protestants would perceive their faith as reasonable and their rational liberty as intact.

Instead of making similar arguments, most Catholics who responded to charges that the new dogma bound their consciences noted that the schisms, confusion, and division caused by Protestant "freedom" were inimical to true religion. Archbishop Kenrick, for example, suggested that doctrinal liberty regarding Mary's conception was a temporary and problematic state. He wrote, somewhat defensively, that "this liberty of sentiment thus tolerated and allowed did not imply a pledge that no definition of the doctrine in question should ever emanate; much less, an avowal that no such revelation existed which would authorize such a definition."[39] Rather than representing a positive state of "freedom of conscience," Kenrick held that the period of debate would soon be followed by the preferable state of certainty.

Despite conflicting viewpoints about whether and how to engage Protestants in theological debate, the proclamation did not appear to American Catholics as a diminishment of their freedom of conscience, the way it did to Protestant observers, but rather as an official approbation of their faith and devotional practices. Catholics understood that the feast of the Immaculate Conception had been celebrated for many centuries; that the doctrine enjoyed widespread acceptance; and that the pope's endorsement of it grew, in part, out of worldwide devotionalism and the encouragement of recent Marian apparitions. Archbishop Kenrick specifically acknowledged the role of devotionalism in the move toward the dogmatic declaration: "In the meantime, the pious sentiment has sunk deeper and deeper into the minds of the faithful, and the feeling of the whole Church is now so manifest in reference to this privilege of the Mother of our Lord, that dissent is no longer perceptible. This is no doubtful indication of the teaching of the Holy Ghost, who abides in the Church to lead her into all truth."[40] By "the meantime," Kenrick referred to the "indulged" period of open debate on the question of the Immaculate Conception, during which time "pious sentiment" in favor of the doctrine became entrenched. Though U.S. Catholics approved of the pope's action in declaring the dogma on his own authority, leaders such as Kenrick also framed it as arising not from Pius IX, but from and through the global Catholic community, guided by God.

Despite Protestant critics' endorsement of freedom of conscience and outrage over Catholics' loss of it, they failed to acknowledge broad lay Catholic support for the declaration. Critics overwhelmingly painted Catholics as naïve and credulous bystanders who were suddenly required to accept a new and bizarre teaching. The anti-Catholic polemicist and frequent *New York Daily Times* contributor Dr. John Cumming charged that the Catholic laity, "who are the victims, will soon be required to believe so much that they will rise in insurrection against the whole conspiracy, and assert for themselves that freedom from priestly domination which must precede their acceptance of a pure and noble faith."[41] Cumming disregarded Catholic familiarity with and support for the Immaculate Conception doctrine entirely. However, while painting American Catholics as pitiable sheep-like followers and "victims" was demeaning, critiques of the declaration that cited lost freedom of conscience often imagined Catholics as comembers of a broad American community in search of (Christian) truth and (democratic) freedom. Read closely, many Protestant critiques of the declaration validated Catholics' identities as "Americans" and included them as oppressed but fellow citizens. This was not unproblematic, but differed from more incendiary anti-Catholic propaganda that saw Catholic persons as irredeemable outsiders.

Episcopal bishop Arthur Cleveland Coxe exemplified this take on Catholic identity when he argued, in his introduction and notes to the U.S. edition of Laborde's anti–Immaculate Conception treatise, that American Catholics, like all Americans, prized their freedom of thought and would rebel against the new dogma. While Coxe may have been referring to lay control of parish boards of trustees, which had caused legal and ecclesiastical struggles in the American Church, he asserted, counterfactually, that all American Catholics opposed ultramontanism on principle: "When *ultra-*

montane notions have been imputed to the prelates and laity of the Roman communion in this country, they have been almost without exception denied and rejected with professions of abhorrence."[42] Catholics, he claimed, "especially in America," would support Laborde's critique of the doctrine as well as his freedom to protest its declaration. Whether Coxe was deliberately attempting to sway Catholic readers by ascribing to them his preferred opinions, or whether he was stating his sincere impressions of their views, he imagined that Catholics held much in common with other Americans.

The inclusion of Catholics as fellow "Americans," however, was predicated on their potential to react to the declaration (at least secretly or implicitly) with consternation, as Protestants did. When Catholic consciences heralded the declaration as an affirmation of their own sincerely held religious beliefs, Protestant critics did not call them "free," but ignorant and irrational. One Protestant Episcopal critic, for instance, equated clerical endorsement of the doctrine with fanaticism, writing that "the subjective 'feeling' in the breasts of the Roman clergy is soon, if it is not already, to be pronounced by their supreme Bishop, an objective and actual reality . . . Christian truth is subjected to the test of something within the human soul; a process which, however agreeable to mysticism and fanaticism, is essentially . . . infidel."[43] The author declared individual conscience (which is surely related to "subjective feeling" and just as surely resides "within the human soul") to be an untrustworthy source. In article after article, rhetoric trumpeting the power of "a free Bible and a free conscience" was not seriously applied to Catholics. In their formulation, freedom of conscience led to truth, truth was understood in Protestant terms, and, therefore, Catholic consciences that prompted other doctrinal conclusions were necessarily coerced, unreliable, or fanatical.

The reality that widespread Catholic devotionalism set the stage, if not the urgency, for the declaration was difficult to ignore, even for Protestant critics who wanted to assert Pius's agency in single-handedly deciding the dogma in order to emphasize Catholics' bound consciences. Thus, while some articles denounced papal agency in "inventing" the dogma, others railed against the popular devotional "excess" that led to its proclamation, and still others wavered jarringly between attributing agency and passive obedience to lay Catholics. Henry Boynton Smith was rare among Protestant critics in reconciling these seemingly contradictory positions by perceiving and clearly articulating the interrelationship of popular devotionalism, ultramontanism, and papal power. In his article "On the Dogma of the Immaculate Conception," he emphasized the role devotionalism played in bringing about the declaration, writing that the doctrine "gained in popular applause what it lacked in theological authority" and that the pope "just placed the crown upon the completed system of idolatry by the dogmatic declaration."[44] However, he also described the declaration as a moment of papal activism, writing of the doctrine: "For the last century and a half it had excited comparatively little discussion. . . . But the revival of the Papal claims in new vigour, the pressure of the ultramontane influence, . . . the necessary and consequent excitement of popular superstition, have pressed the matter to what is esteemed an authoritative and final decision."[45] Smith recognized both broad Catholic support for the doctrine and the declaration's assertion of papal power, reconciling them as characteristic of ultramontanism's nondemocratic but populist character. Despite this perceptive analysis, Smith did not see popular support for the doctrine as valid, disparaging Catholic devotionalism as "idolatry" and "superstition." Like many less astute critics, Smith labeled Catholics' support for the Immaculate Conception as the superstition of the "masses" rather than the free consciences of the "people."

A closely related tension arose in response to the timing of the doctrine's propagation. Those critics who emphasized the doctrine's roots in popular devotionalism often called it a holdover from a superstitious, premodern past, while those who emphasized papal activism called it a recent "novelty." Smith, for instance, wrote: "Such a decree at such a juncture proves that the day of Rome is past and her doom is at hand." And the *National Magazine* called the declaration "a preposterous attempt to maintain the superstitions of a past age." In contrast, Protestant critics who called the doctrine a recent invention elided all history between the earliest Christians and the nineteenth century, reinforcing biblicism by disregarding both the writings of the early Church fathers and the centuries of intervening theological reflection and practice. Cumming, for instance, wrote that "this novelty decreed by Pio Nono . . . if [it] be a vital article of the Christian faith the sleepy-headed Church of Rome has been nearly 1,800 years in discovering it."[46] Inverting the Catholic premise that apostolic succession ensured doctrinal stability, Cumming charged that the Church would "one day in its progressive developments arrive at the conclusion that 'God is great, and Mahomet is his Prophet.'"[47] However, unlike most critics, Cumming supported his claim that the doctrine was "innovative" not by ignoring the past, but by carefully mining the history of internal dissent.[48] Drawing on historical

Catholic sources that opposed the doctrine, Cumming charged that the declaration violated the second article of Pius IV's Tridentine Creed: "I will never take and interpret the Scriptures unless according to the unanimous consent of the Fathers."[49] He then listed quotations, taken from patristic commentaries, which he perceived as negating the doctrine, including Irenaeus's suggestion that Mary was guilty of an "untimely hurrying" of Christ at Cana; Tertullian's claim that Christ "with reason, felt indignant" at Mary's desire to speak with him while teaching; Origen's implication that Mary was "offended" by the Crucifixion and felt both unbelief and doubt; and Chrysostom's argument that Mary's behavior at Cana revealed "excessive ambition," a desire to "control" and "command" Christ, and "foolish arrogance."[50] None of these quotations was relevant to the Immaculate Conception debate, as negative interpretations of Mary's adult life had no bearing on the question of whether she was purified before, during, or immediately after the moment of her conception. But by presenting unflattering portraits of Mary from Catholic fathers, Cumming tried to undermine Catholic claims of doctrinal stability and point out that Catholics, too, had been troubled by biblical passages regarding Mary.

Cumming's approach was anomalous; in this period, most Protestants, including critics of the Immaculate Conception doctrine and Marian veneration, did not seek to discredit Mary's character. Instead, most went out of their way to avow her dignity and honor, and often cited their compliance with the biblical charge to "call her blessed" (Luke 1:48). Many Protestant publications and articles cited this verse, as well as Gabriel's salutation to Mary at the Annunciation, claiming that in challenging "Mariolatry," they did not dishonor Mary but honored her rightly. One example, from a tract called "The Worship of Mary" stated: "While Protestants are accused of putting dishonor on the virgin mother of Christ, let the Roman Catholic reader be well assured that this is quite a mistake, and shows great ignorance of our principles. We also honor the Virgin, and cordially believe the salutation of the angel, Luke 1:28: 'Hail, full of grace, the Lord is with thee: blessed art thou among women.'"[51] Cumming likely did not endorse the past critiques of Mary he cited; instead, he tried to destabilize the apparent unity of Catholic thought and open her to a variety of possible constructions. It was an ironic strategy, as his attempt to engage centuries of Marian theology also revealed the persistence of the Immaculate Conception and contradicted his insistent contention that the doctrine was a complete novelty. While most Protestant critics were less historically engaged, many similarly put themselves in the ironic position of simultaneously declaring the doctrine innovative and retrograde.

Catholic apologists were pushed by persistent Protestant criticism to respond to the problem of the doctrine's late advent (in ecclesiastical time). When Catholics reflected on the "timeliness" of the declaration, they were also responding to a tacit challenge: whether the pope's decision to make a bold spiritual statement was a *strategic* response to his political circumstances. Some Protestant critics raised the question directly, for example, a *New York Times* article astutely noted: "It seems singular, that the time when Pius IX was in exile at Gaeta, should have been seized upon to place ultramontanism at its culminating point, the pinnacle of all its hopes; but in point of fact at no other period in hundreds of years, was the Pope spiritually so free as then, or better able to place reliance upon the general dispositions of the Catholic nations towards his authority."[52] With Protestant opponents explicitly charging that Pius IX was countering diminishing temporal power with increased spiritual power, Catholic proponents of the declaration could not ignore the question of timeliness. Bishop of Birmingham, William Bernard Ullathorne, queried: "Who, then, could have faith and understanding, and yet ask why at length the doctrine has been defined?"[53] His question implied that some of his Catholic readers may have been raising or responding to these concerns. Likewise, Bishop de Charbonnel of Toronto responded to a similar challenge when he reminded his Catholic listeners that other privileges of Mary were not codified as doctrine until opposition forced clarification. Thus, he cautioned, doubt regarding the Immaculate Conception was just as heretical as doubt regarding other Mariological claims: "Therefore, to deny now, even mentally, the Immaculate Conception, would be the same sin of heresy as to deny the divine maternity of Mary, or her perpetual virginity, or her exemption from venial sin."[54] Charbonnel's solution, that increasing opposition prompted clarification, did not sufficiently resolve the problem. Both Protestants and Catholics understood that the doctrine was only controversial among some (few) Dominicans, separated Jansenist Catholics, and, more to the point, Protestants; it was not proclaimed during a period of increasing opposition, but increasing acceptance. The problem of the doctrine's modern definition also prompted an important internal Catholic conversation about whether theology (not just application) could be understood to change over time.

Some responded to the problem of timeliness by deflecting it. Bishop Hughes, for example, celebrated the suddenness of the declaration as a triumph for the Church, located the motivation for it in increasing unbelief, and refused to acknowledge the underlying question of papal motivation. In one frequently quoted sermon, Hughes declared the definition to be a sign that "the church is not dead, that the church is not unhealthy, that she still lives and reigns; and that she has seen the rise and ruin of empires and dynasties . . . and shall live to witness all the . . . vicissitudes of . . . human humanity."[55] These lines divorced the Church from its contemporary circumstances and placed the advent of the proclamation in the broad sweep of slow-moving spiritual time. He added: "But will any one say—will any Socinian [Unitarian] say—that because it was not defined, it was not believed? This would be absurd. . . . Before we believed by individual belief, it was a sentiment we were familiar with from our earliest traditions and feelings which we inherit from our fathers."[56] Tradition and "feelings," he asserted, contained and conveyed through the centuries the pious "sentiment" of Mary's Immaculate Conception. Dogma was not necessary where feeling continued unbroken. Hughes's argument, like Charbonnel's, turned on the premise that universal, implicit, unchallenged belief existed before doubt and opposition made it necessary to define the doctrine. The proclamation, then, was not an innovation, but the opposition was; hence, the appearance of historical support for it was delayed. Hughes's argument, however, had the same easily perceptible difficulties. If the opposition to the doctrine that had coalesced centuries before was, by and large, resolved by the nineteenth century, why declare it now? No matter how broad one's view of Church history, if the definition were a response to opposition, it seemed late in coming. And despite his reference to "Socinian[s]" (proto-Unitarian supporters of private judgment), it was not marginalized voices but many of the most revered doctors and theologians of the Church who had opposed the doctrine, undermining the premise that belief in the Immaculate Conception was universal and implicit in other theological formulations.

J. D. Bryant, another key apologist for the dogma, took a similar approach to Hughes, but used greater detail to establish his claims and made timeliness a central theme. In his book-length defense, he wrote (to an imagined Protestant critic) that the doctrine "is no novelty of the nineteenth century; and that the trivial sneer, 'I thought your Church never changed!' is a solemn and everlasting truth."[57] Glossing over the numerous objections to the doctrine by Church fathers, Bryant meticulously cataloged pro–Immaculate Conception sentiments. He relied heavily on the words "imply" and "inherent" in order to create what he called a "golden chain of testimony," asserting universal support for Mary's exemption from original sin, dating from "the remains of the Apostolic age, and the four centuries immediately succeeding" to the present.[58] He disingenuously called past opponents of the doctrine "dissidents" and rewrote the problem of historical dissent as an unbroken line of concord.

Other defenders of the doctrine admitted that past opposition arose from revered theologians, but circumvented the problem of discord by re-defining the Church—the site of unchanging universality of opinion—from the doctors of the Church to the lay devout. French author Abbé Matthieu Orsini, writing in the years preceding the declaration, conceded that the doctrine had been fiercely contested in the past and that its ascension was propelled by popular piety rather than approved theology. However, he maintained that the bottom-up spread of the devotion did not undermine its authority, but confirmed it. It was evidence of God's faithfulness in authoring consensus among the people and thus a sign that God was active in the Church. In a bold statement of the problem, Orsini wrote: "The adversaries of the immaculate conception glory in reckoning in their ranks St. Anselm, St. Bernard, St. Bonaventure, St. Thomas, Albert the Great, &c. Great as these names are, we must not allow ourselves to be dazzled by them . . . the belief in the immaculate conception of the holy Virgin prevailed in the end over the opinion of the great doctors of the middle ages; what the eagles of the schools had not seen was discovered to the unlearned."[59] His willingness to locate spiritual authority in the laity in order to circumvent the charge of innovation reveals the intractability of the problem for those who addressed it directly. Like Orsini, Ullathorne downplayed the charge of innovation by elevating the importance of lay devotionalism: "Mary had bloomed into the light out of the great heart of the church in prayers, devotions, festivals, and God had answered them by graces, protections, miracles; and that faith was all but formally defined. Pius IX has simply proclaimed that the Church believes what she does believe."[60] Situating theological continuity in the devotion of the people rather than in theological schools addressed but did not resolve the problem. Recounting the doctrine's history in a way that included hierarchical resistance to it revealed development over time and contradicted the Tridentine principle that doctrine was based on the "unanimous consent" of the fathers. Ullathorne allowed that some change had occurred, explaining somewhat cryptically "that light of truth leads to the rejection of profane novelties exterior to what is already believed and established, but hinders not such progress as successive explications of its own principles would give, whilst leaving those principles always one and the same."[61] Progress was a problematic word to employ, however, because truth was defined as uniformity of belief over time. Ullathorne's strongest claim was that the doctrine was not contradictory to what was believed in the past and that it was an elaboration of principles that were already held.

Other apologists for the doctrine accepted the difficulty created by past opposition and drew on contemporary Catholic theologians who suggested that doctrine could be legitimately understood in terms of development. These thinkers maintained that revelation is both progressive and reliable because of the gift of the Holy Spirit to the Church in the form of teaching authority: as God unfolds revelation through history, the Church's understanding may evolve. Seminarians debated whether development was a legitimate position and whether the modern declaration of the Immaculate Conception was an instance of development. The majority of U.S. Catholic leaders, however, rejected this approach. Francis Patrick Kenrick, Archbishop of Baltimore, offered a resolution to the problem of development in his pastoral letter of 1842:

> All the truths of revelation were taught by the Apostles, . . . and preserved always in the Church as a sacred deposit, from which nothing should be taken, and whereto nothing should be added. Nevertheless, even the great mysteries of the Trinity and Incarnation, . . . were not propounded from the beginning, in all their details and consequences. . . . The divine maternity of the ever Blessed Virgin was declared . . . yet no solemn and formal declaration was made of her exemption from that stain of sin which infects all the posterity of Adam. When attention was particularly directed to this point, the devout mind easily recognized a privilege . . . although some hesitated to admit such an exemption from the want of an explicit and formal declaration of it in the divine Scriptures, or in the writings of the ancient fathers.[62]

Kenrick prepared his audience for the doctrine's declaration and anticipated the charge of novelty. He affirmed that truth is unchanging and without development, while attributing the appearance of change to the Church's ongoing role in expounding the "details and consequences" of doctrine as the need arose. Kenrick suggested that the past opposition of

Church fathers to the doctrine had not been principled opposition, but caution due to a lack of direct scriptural and ancient evidence.

IN THEIR NEED to defend the dogma and its means of promulgation against Protestant critique, Catholics shared the experience of coming together to defend their Heavenly Mother. This reinforced their identity as a community that had been placed under the patronage of the Immaculate Conception. In responding to Protestant accusations of innovation and bound consciences, Catholics reflected on the role of the teaching authority of the Church, embraced Marian devotionalism, and affirmed a shared identity as a multiethnic community of Catholic Americans. This did not overcome ethnic and theological tensions within the American Church, but shared persecution and shared veneration of Mary were unifying experiences.

Likewise, in response to the Immaculate Conception declaration, American Protestants of various denominations shored up their identity as Protestants against the Catholic *other*. Accusing Catholics of novelty and authoritarianism, bound consciences and devotional excess, Protestants affirmed shared values: Jesus-centric piety, biblicism, individualism, and rationality. While Protestants decried the increased papal authority and activism signaled by the declaration, the Marian content of the declaration also caused unease. The doctrine's lack of biblical evidence was an irritant, but Catholic elevation of a female figure also provoked ire. In magazine articles and newspaper editorials, Protestants publicly debated the proper Christian attitude toward Mary: Should she be held as a model for all Christians or a model for women; as a transcendent figure or a representative disciple; as a parent of or a follower of Christ? A few minimized and limited Mary's role in response to the declaration's elevation of her. However, increased attention to Mary also popularized Marian themes and imagery among both Protestants and Catholics. Instead of rejecting or diminishing Mary, Protestants contested and claimed Mary, particularly as a way of buttressing Christian norms for women and mothers.

CHAPTER TWO

The Immaculate Conception and the Elevation of the Feminine, 1855–1860s

By favour of her immaculate conception, her pure and innocent actions were like those coats of snow which are silently heaped upon the lofty summits of the mountains, adding purity to purity, and whiteness to whiteness, till a dazzling cone is raised, on which the light darts playfully, and which forces man to turn away his eyes, like the sun.

—Abbé Orsini, *Life of the Blessed Virgin Mary*

In January 1855, a month after the Immaculate Conception declaration, the *New York Daily Times* printed a letter to the editor entitled "Rumors of Relics and Miraculous Madonnas Coming."[1] The anonymous writer described rumors "whispered about" that two "miraculous" statues of Mary would soon be arriving in New York. He linked the purported statues to the Immaculate Conception declaration, alleging that the Vatican was sending them to reward the "zeal with which the American prelates have sustained the new dogma, the Immaculate Conception" and, furthermore, that the statues themselves had affirmed the declaration, with "the winking Virgin sealing the truth of the dogma when announced by the moving of her eyelids, and the weeping Virgin by dropping a tear at the expression of all doubts on the subject."[2] While no Catholic sources substantiated the importation of the Madonnas or the alleged miracles, the *Times* noted that it would continue to pursue the story.

The letter's author characterized the recent Immaculate Conception declaration as an indication of a more active papacy. He declared sardonically: "With the promulgation of the new dogma, Rome seems to have determined upon pursuing a bolder policy . . . giv[ing] to her subjects in all lands the full benefits of all her sacred things."[3] He connected the "boldness" of the declaration to a more visible promotion of devotionalism's physical manifestations and supernatural claims. The title of the article, "Madonnas Coming," evoked immigration: Mary herself was arriving on American shores, riding the waves of Catholic immigration. An undercurrent of xenophobia is apparent, as is the connection made between papal power, immigration, and

Mary. In the letter's presentation of both the Immaculate Conception proc-lamation and the miraculous statuary, Mary symbolized the foreign and threatening aspects of Catholicism.

The editorial received several follow-up mentions.[4] In July, the *Times* printed the following brief, facetious note: "We do not yet hear of the com-ing of the Winking Madonnas. Were they not to have reached us before this? We trust they have not been wrecked."[5] This unnecessary bit of non-news mocked Catholic belief in the supernatural power of such statues by suggesting that they could not even protect the ships that bore them. In April, the publication of *The Life of St. Frances of Rome* occasioned another satirical comment by a *Times* writer: "This is a timely volume. If the winking Madonnas are to come over, the people may as well be prepared for them."[6] These follow-ups demonstrate the persistence of the story and the *Times'* casual derision of Catholic devotionalism. The *Times'* pairing of a biogra-phy of St. Francis with miraculous Marian statuary shows Mary's function as emblem of the Catholic community and object of anti-Catholic senti-ment. In comments like these, Mary signified Catholic otherness.

However, the primary focus of the editorial was Mary's sex: more than any other factor, the miraculous statues raised the specter of the female di-vine. The author provocatively suggested that "if these things are to take place . . . it will form a new era in the history of this City, which since its foundation has had no visible goddess to *adorn* its temples."[7] While Protes-tants often accused Catholics of worshipping a human woman, this letter made an explicit charge that Catholics viewed Mary as a "goddess." A god-dess is both divine and female, and in the coverage of the declaration it is clear that both aspects of Mary worried Protestants, with the problem of Mary's womanhood compounding and sometimes overshadowing that of her supposed suprahumanity. The threat of a goddess adorning the city's "temples" signaled more than just theological impropriety and excessive veneration of a human figure. It signaled the possibility of the female divine: the existence of a transcendent, worshipped woman.

The writer's sarcastic tone conveyed the discomfort elicited by the Im-maculate Conception proclamation and Marian devotionalism. In a post-script, the *Times* editor remarked: "At present we 'know nothing' of the matter."[8] This obvious nod to the anti-Catholic "Know-Nothing Party" placed the preceding commentary in the context of overt and endorsed hos-tility. The letter encapsulated the main elements of the Protestant response to the Immaculate Conception declaration: fear of Catholic immigration, accusations of increased papal control and activism, and, especially, disparagement of Mary in gendered terms. In responses to the proclamation, Protestants expressed alarm about a "female divinity," a "Heavenly Mother," or a "Catholic goddess." Midcentury debates about Mary were not only about theology but also gender.

MANY PROTESTANT AND CATHOLIC reactions to the Immaculate Conception focused specifically on Mary's sex and on the implications of the doctrine for models of womanhood. Feminist theologians have argued that constraints placed on Marian theology in the Second Vatican Council (1962–65) were a result of Protestant opposition to Mary's elevation, particularly as it coalesced in the nineteenth century in response to the Immaculate Conception proclamation, which Protestants saw as prioritizing Mary over Jesus. According to them, Protestants "dimly glimpsed the unintended threat to male supremacy" in the doctrine's focus on Mary's singularity and centrality to the salvation narrative.[9] A close examination of nineteenth-century Protestant responses to the Immaculate Conception declaration supports these assertions: in the many passionate denunciations of the doctrine published in these years, Mary's womanhood was often a central theme. The intensity of Protestant preoccupation with Mary's sex and gendering revealed their need for Mary to symbolize Christian womanhood in specific ways and their concern that the Immaculate Conception cast her in a role that would have problematic implications for American gender norms. Despite this, aspects of Immaculate Conception theology did resonate with Protestant desires; in particular, the supernatural purity extolled by the doctrine affirmed Protestants' own imaginings of Mary.

The Madonna of American popular culture was not a literal religious figure. Mary conveyed religious meanings for Protestants, but her imagery primarily appeared in nonreligious contexts such as living rooms, classrooms, art books, and magazines. Because there was little in-depth theological speculation about Mary by Protestants, the content of their characterizations of her was often derived from generalized and poorly understood Catholic theology. Implicit Catholic theological tenets were transmitted in and through images of Mary, but they were not acknowledged by the Protestants who propagated and interpreted them. Even in cases where Catholic meanings were overtly rejected, such as the Immaculate Conception, a complex series of real-world encounters, shared source material (art, biblical pericopes, cultural tropes), and dialog in print media created a convergence whereupon Marian characteristics were cemented as they were disputed. Thus, Protestant Americans often perceived Mary in implicitly Catholic terms—supernaturally pure, exalted above other humans, salvific—at the same time they rejected corresponding Catholic theological positions. Similarly, Protestants rejected the authority of Catholic tradition as a source for theology, but made claims about Mary's parentage, education, age at marriage, and other life incidents without noting their extrabiblical derivation from Catholic tradition.

Protestants vehemently opposed Catholic claims for Mary, in part because Catholic interpretations continued to shape the sets of meanings transmitted through her figure. The impetus behind the heated debates over Marian claims was not ecumenicism or an attempt to agree on correct theology; instead, Protestants' fought over her because their ongoing (and increasingly pressing) investment in using Mary as a metasymbol to encapsulate religious and cultural beliefs about gender was frustrated by associated theological claims that complicated the symbolic meanings of her figure.

While Americans were divided over the doctrine, both Protestants and Catholics drew on the exaggerated purity of the Immaculate Conception to reinforce the female domestic ideal, and both groups responded to an implicit challenge to American gender norms in the declaration's elevation of an autonomous female figure. Protestants adopted Immaculate Conception language and imagery while denouncing the declaration as threatening because of Mary's sex. Similarly, American Catholics celebrated the triumph for their "Lady," while also authoring apologies for the doctrine that constrained her relative power and authority as a female religious figure.

Mary Immaculate and Female Purity

The Immaculate Conception doctrine emphasized Mary's uncompromised purity by exempting her from the shared human inheritance of original sin and by asserting that there was never an instant—even at her own conception—when she was tainted with sin. The publicity surrounding the declaration and the explanations of its theology by both Catholics and Protestants drew attention to purity as a constitutive element of the Marian ideal. Female purity was also a crucial element in the ideology of separate spheres: the need to protect women from the corrupting influences of business and politics justified her enclosure in the home, while her ability to embody purity and resist sin enabled her to sacralize the domestic sphere and carry forward the Christian virtues Americans saw as necessary to a healthy society. While the spheres were never truly separate, and women in fact participated in many public and quasi-public areas of life (especially churches and reform societies), the ideology was advanced in magazines, advice literature, and domestic fiction.[10]

Protestant men and women embraced this model of womanhood, which emphasized purity and domesticity, to stabilize and counter economic change. In doing so, middle-class American women were neither passive recipients of a repressive gender ideology nor "heroines supporting unproblematic values."[11] While women, fulfilling idealized roles as wives and mothers, were portrayed as an ideological antidote to capitalism, in reality they were much more connected to the market economy than the domestic priestess role suggested. Domestic spaces did not exist in opposition to and as a haven from increasingly ruthless economic market spaces. Rather, women were aligned with and supportive of acquisitive (and divisive) economic goals. The belief that women were separated from and immune to the emerging market economy facilitated ongoing industrialization. Women were constrained by this domestic ideology that, to varying degrees, limited their movement, actions, and agency, but they also contributed to its creation in order to construct meaning and identity and to "consolidate middle-class control."[12] Thus, in embodying domestic femininity, middle-class women participated in the creation of a new economic order both by fulfilling an ideological role that mitigated cultural anxiety and by actively constructing symbolic spaces and categories that reinforced class distinctions.[13] Because the Immaculate Conception doctrine reinforced a key element of the female domestic ideal—purity—it resonated with these ideological commitments and was useful in emblemizing womanhood. Both Protestants and Catholics used Immaculate Conception imagery in this way, even as Protestants rejected the dogma as a theological position. This was evident in textual sources, in which Protestants imagined and described a supernaturally pure Mary, and in visual imagery, in which Protestants praised depictions of Mary as the Immaculate Conception and recommended other images of Mary because of their "pure" representation of her.

While Catholics understood the Immaculate Conception in various ways (e.g., as a validation of her mystical role as Ark of the Covenant and as an affirmation of the closely related doctrine of Mary's Assumption), many emphasized purity as its core message.[14] For example, Abbé Mathieu Orsini, writing about the Immaculate Conception in his *Life of the Blessed Virgin*

Mary, accentuated Mary's purity using romantic natural imagery: "Attracted towards good by a sweet and natural inclination, by favour of her immaculate conception, her pure and innocent actions were like those coats of snow which are silently heaped upon the lofty summits of the mountains, adding purity to purity, and whiteness to whiteness, till a dazzling cone is raised, on which the light darts playfully, and which forces man to turn away his eyes, like the sun. It has not been given to any second creature to present such a life to the sovereign Judge of men; Jesus Christ alone surpassed her—but Jesus Christ is the Son of God."[15] Inspired by Orsini's writings, American Catholic novelist and poet Eleanor C. Donnelly wrote a poem on the Immaculate Conception, "Maria Immaculata":

> 'Pure as the snow,' we say
> Ah, never flake fell through the air
> One-tenth as fair
> As Mary's soul was made for Christ's dear sake . . .
>
> The whitest whiteness of the Alpine snows
> Beside thy stainless spirit, dusky grows . . .
>
> There does not live, Virgin Immaculate
> In all the grassy haunts where lilies blow
> As white, as rare, as sweet a flower as thou.[16]

Written (as opposed to visual) Catholic depictions of Mary as the Immaculate Conception nearly always employed natural imagery of snow, lilies, or light to illustrate her purity.[17]

There was also a heightened emphasis on Mary's purity in midcentury American Catholic devotional materials.[18] Most of the prayers and devotions in these manuals focused on Jesus or Mary. Among Marian prayers and devotions, she was primarily depicted as either pure or protective. Purity was most emphasized in Immaculate Conception and Sacred Heart devotions, while protectiveness was emphasized in the rosary and in scapular devotions. Both furthered a high Mariology that prioritized Mary's spiritual apotheosis over her humanity.[19] Such devotions emphasized her difference from the rest of humankind; however, because purity was a constitutive element of "true" womanhood, the Church's emphasis on Mary's purity connected her to ordinary women at the same time it elevated her above them. The American domestic female ideal was beyond the reach of ordinary women, but its depictions were embraced by women in various forms and integrated into their gender identities. Marian versions of this ideal were also out of reach, but that did not necessarily reinforce a sense of distance from Mary; instead, many women embraced her as a model that affirmed their femininity. In this sense, she functioned as a religious sanction for their own attempts to embody a particular gender identity. While the ideal was generated by broad currents in culture and religion, and for some women must have seemed unattainable, undesirable, or external, many women embraced and perceived this ideal as their own.

Many Catholic texts, like Orsini's quoted previously, emphasized the fact that Mary was human in order to encourage women to see Marian holiness and femininity as potentially attainable. The prayers and religious practices cataloged in devotional manuals gave Catholic women tools that allowed them not only to embrace the Marian ideal of Christian womanhood but also to access an economy of grace that promised real transformation. Thus, the Marian ideal, while elevated, was made accessible and intimate.

Indeed, despite the doctrine's emphasis on Mary's supernatural purity and exemption from the common human inheritance of original sin, Catholics routinely recommended Mary Immaculate as a role model. Bryant, for example, concluded his book on Mary's Immaculate Conception by writing: "Let us, then, in conclusion, ascertain how her exalted merits may be most efficaciously applied to our souls. Is it by offering her a degree of devotion which exceeds what justly belongs to the creature, and from which she would shrink with displeasure and horror? . . . No, it is by imitating her holy example; in cherishing all the virtues of her consecrated life."[20] Like Orsini, Bryant concluded his remarks on a doctrine that elevated and exceptionalized Mary by humanizing her, reminding readers that her lived example was paramount. Significantly, Bryant held Mary up as a model to Christians of both sexes. He dedicated the book to Mary, the "most sweet and perfect model of humility, chastity, modesty, and of every grace," and adding that it was "most affectionately, most fondly, and most lovingly inscribed by the unworthy author."[21] In this dedication, Bryant placed himself among those in need of Mary's example. Elsewhere, he praised "our forefathers" who "marvelously" referred to Mary as "the type and model of purity and innocence," and asserted that Mary's "Immaculate Model of Chastity and every perfection" was given to Catholics ("her children in this corrupt and sensual age"). In doing so, he did not differentiate between Mary's male and female "children."

Many Catholic authors similarly claimed Mary as a model of Christian virtues for both sexes. Reverend Beatus Rohner, OSB, in his *Life of the*

Blessed Virgin, for example, repeatedly presented Mary's maternity as a particular model for mothers: "Mary was the mother in the home at Nazareth. Can it be possible that there exists any mother of a Christian family who does not venerate in a special manner the ever blessed Virgin, or does not take her and imitate her as an amiable and glorious model?"[22] Despite this example, he exhorted both men and women to relate their identity as Catholics to Mary's example, expressly noting that "for men," Mary was given as "a powerful intercessor and a sublime image and model."[23] He asked both men and women to imagine their own souls in relation to Mary's model of devotion: "Hence, too, should you, Christian reader, admire and reverence the body of the Mother of God, for it was the dwelling-place of a holy soul, and the ostensorium of Divinity. Forget not that your soul, too, though in a lower sense, is a temple of God."[24] Despite her sex, Rohner described Mary as a "powerful intercessor" and "model" for Catholic men, and presented the physical indwelling of the divine child in Mary's pregnancy as a metaphor for the Catholic of either sex whose body physically houses the Holy Spirit. The Catholic embrace of Mary's model for both genders contrasted starkly with Protestant understandings of Mary's role.

While Catholics saw Mary as a model to humanity in general and women in particular, Protestants associated Mary's purity with feminine virtues exclusively, not with the Christian life broadly understood. Protestant men were not advised to look to Mary as an exemplar of Christian discipleship, nor were they exhorted to Marian silence, meekness, or purity. If Protestants encouraged men to consider Mary, it was to deepen their admiration of a female ideal and to revere motherhood. Because Mary was not a devotional figure in Protestant religious life, when she was introduced it was primarily to give form to, sanctify, and promote a vision of pious femininity. For Protestants, it was important that both men and women perceive womanhood in these ways; thus, her figure was instructive to both sexes, although her model was intended only for women.

Protestants drew on the exaggerated purity of the Immaculate Conception in both visual and literary forms. One of the most salient of these forms was the Angel in the House. This recurring literary theme, which portrayed wives as meek, self-sacrificing angels, was more deeply indebted to Mary than many scholars have recognized. The English poet Coventry Patmore first used the phrase "Angel in the House" in his epic-length poem of that title, which he wrote and revised from 1854 to 1862.[25] The motif was thereafter taken up by many British and American authors. Literary scholars have often made the argument that the Angel in the House was a thinly veiled replacement for the Madonna, who met the same needs for Protestants that Mary met for Catholics.[26] The presumption has been that Protestants were opposed to Marian theology and imagery and thus did not draw on it. Instead, Madonnas were secularized into Angels in the House, which then began to permeate nineteenth-century literary culture.[27] However, Angel in the House images proliferated alongside and in conjunction with Marian iconography. The proliferation of Marian imagery in these same years shows that, rather than replacing the Madonna, the Angel in the House and Marian imagery reinforced each other.

Literary scholar Kimberly VanEsveld Adams builds a strong case that the Angel in the House motif was, in fact, *directly* derived from the Madonna as envisioned by English Catholics. In contrast to the prevailing view that the Angel in the House was a Protestant ideal "detached from Catholic forms of belief," she argues that Patmore and John Henry Newman were "directly or indirectly shaped by patristic theology."[28] Patmore and Newman were friends who were familiar with each other's writings, and Patmore described his feelings for Newman as "ardent and affectionate." Newman was fascinated with the Mariology of the Church fathers and, through their friendship, Patmore encountered the Marian ideals that shaped his vision of womanly perfection. He worked to convey those ideals in his poem, *The Angel in the House*. Shortly after completing it, he, like Newman, converted to Catholicism. After his conversion, Patmore reflected on his famous poem, concluding that he remained committed to its vision, which was fully supported by a Catholic understanding of womanhood.[29] Together, Patmore, Newman, and other writers popularized this domestic Madonna ideal, which became extremely influential in British and American literature. The Angel in the House evoked but did not directly invoke Mary. Nevertheless, the popularity of literary Angels in the House was a propagation of a distinctly Marian female ideal.

American Protestants were both fascinated and alarmed by Marian art and statuary, especially devotional art such as the "winking Madonnas" mentioned earlier. However, Protestant ambivalence toward Marian art did not hinder its growing popularity. While Protestants sometimes discussed Marian art reverently and appreciatively earlier in the nineteenth century, from the 1850s to the turn of the century, Marian imagery proliferated in magazines, gift and poetry books, and print reproductions. While Marian imagery was mostly absent in Protestant churches, except for Christmastime,

Titian, *Assumption of the Virgin*. From the Basilica di Santa Maria Gloriosa dei Frari, Venice (Scala/Art Resource, New York).

when her maternity took center stage, she was increasingly present in America's burgeoning visual culture. As museums and galleries opened in major U.S. cities in the 1860s and 1870s, they primarily sought to attain and display classic religious art by old masters—including Raphael, Murillo, Fra Angelico, and Titian—and as lithography and other printmaking technologies developed, reproductions of these works became best sellers. Representations of great Marian artwork became stock images for American print companies and had a particularly significant role in the early art curriculum of the public schools and the late-century kindergarten movement.

Some Americans reacted against the European provenance and Catholic theological underpinnings of religious art, initiating a conversation about whether new forms of distinctly American art, such as landscape painting, should supersede them. One critic, for example, answered the query "Can the old spirit and purity ever be revived?" with a definite negative: "No, they are incompatible with . . . this age; and religious art . . . is lost to the world forever. . . . We believe that in the development of the landscape art of the country we shall find the best substitute for, and the greatest resemblance to, the long lost art . . . as regards . . . honesty of purpose and religious emotion."[30] Despite the debate, and the embrace of landscape painting by many art critics, Americans' desire to situate themselves in a continuous Western cultural tradition and to use "high art" as a marker of status, taste, education, and religious refinement led them to embrace classic religious art.

An article titled "Objections against Chromos Considered," in *Prang's Chromo: A Journal of Popular Art*, published by the American print company, defended (with obvious self-interest) the reproduction of classic and religious art against those who demanded new American forms.[31] In answer to the query "Are we to have nothing but reproductions of dead ages?" the article emphasized that the best way for the American public to develop an appreciation for real, natural landscapes was not to acquire paintings of them, but instead to become culturally literate. "The truth cannot be too often repeated, or too earnestly dwelt on, that it is through history we come to Nature. Uneducated man has little appreciation of Nature in her fairest aspects." Critics of "the present antiquarian tendencies in art" should not undermine the value of such reproductions, the author argued, because they "educate popular taste." Mr. Prang's chromos, he continued, have finally created "in America . . . an art which is capable of giving a masterpiece of Murillo so that the critics in question would probably not know the difference."[32] Significantly, Murillo was selected as the exemplar of culturally elevating art. While Bartolomé Esteban Murillo painted a range of subjects, he was most famous for his Marian subjects; and, in the Prang collection, all Murillo reproductions were Madonnas.

From the 1860s on, printmaking techniques developed rapidly, each new process superseding its predecessor and increasing the number of art reproductions, illustrations, photographs, and other pictures available. Magazines also multiplied and included more illustrations and art reproductions. Prior to the advent of these technologies, the canon of high and religious art was viewable only by those who were able to afford the "European tour" of churches and art galleries abroad, those who could afford to collect art or moved in social circles with art collectors, or those who could purchase painstakingly engraved and reproduced art prints."[33] Mechanical printmaking made art available to other classes, exposing many Americans to religious and devotional art, among other subjects, and generating broad interest in art appreciation. Of these newly accessible reproductions, Marian images formed a basic and integral subset.

Despite the rapid increase in the availability of art reproductions, the writer of an *Appleton's Journal* article bemoaned what he saw as the limited range of European art being reproduced and encouraged the picture industry to strive for greater variety. In doing so, he enumerated the types of art prints that *were* commonly available: "While autotypes and photographs of the more popular paintings and sculptures of Europe are to be met with in every shop and . . . railway-station, there is a large class of very beautiful subjects that are rarely seen here, except by 'carbons' and photographs brought from Europe by private individuals. . . . 'Assumptions' by Titian and Madonnas by Raphael, are as frequent as pictures of Grant or views of Broadway, but scarcely anywhere can they find the faces which have stolen unawares upon their affections, and so unexpectedly have usurped the places of better-known pictures."[34] In his comments, he suggests that the broad appeal of the subjects chosen cater to this new middle-class market, not to the European traveler who (like himself) wanted to reminisce about his encounters with lesser-known artworks. His comments also underscored the prevalence of art reproductions, which were found in "every shop and railway station," while his examples of widely available images revealed the popularity of Marian subjects. The *Assumption of the Virgin* by Titian depicted Mary's assent to heaven, while Raphael's "Madonnas" most likely included his *Madonna and Child* and *Holy Family* groups, as well as his *Sistine Madonna*, unquestionably the era's most popular and widely acclaimed work of art.[35] The paintings that the author hoped would one day be made available and proceeded to list were also primarily religious works, including Marian subjects.

In the postbellum period, most art reproductions were imported from Europe; by the end of the century, however, there were several American companies producing prints, including Perry Pictures, Helman-Taylor, Louis Prang, Arts Study Pictures, and Currier & Ives. Most of these companies' catalogs included several to many Marian images, and almost all of them printed versions of the ever-popular *Sistine Madonna* or "Madonna Di San Sisto." Currier & Ives produced a catalog of popular and affordable lithographs that included at least 540 religious images, many of which were Marian.[36] Some of the Marian prints Currier & Ives produced in the 1850s and 1860s were clearly directed to a Catholic audience; for example, prints of the "Sacred Heart of Mary" or the "Infancy of the Virgin" were likely intended for Catholics. However, Madonna and Child and Holy Family prints such as the "Infant Savior with Mary and Joseph" had a broader appeal, as is clear from the many magazines, home decorating books, and kindergarten publications that recommended these companies as affordable sources for purchasing such images.[37]

Beginning in the 1860s, educators emphasized art appreciation as an important facet of the education of young children. This was partly due to the increased availability and affordability of reproductions of historically significant artwork. Prang capitalized on this market, calling his chromolithographs "the democracy of art," and promoting them for schoolrooms and Sunday school classrooms. The first issue of the company's magazine, *Prang's Chromo: A Journal of Popular Art*, included testimonials supporting such uses by well-known figures. Famous American biographer James Parton emphasized the affordability of Prang's reproductions, which allowed class boundaries to be crossed: "It has been a favorite dream with me for years, that the time would arrive when copies of paintings would be multiplied so cheaply, and reduced so correctly, as to enable the working-man to decorate his rooms with works equal in effect to the finest efforts of the brush."[38] He praised Prang's achievement of this goal, writing: "The works which are issued by your house, which have often and long detained me at the picture-shop windows in Broadway, show me that my dream is coming true." Harriet Beecher Stowe also endorsed Prang's chromos. She was

Currier & Ives, *Ascension of the Virgin/Na.Sa. de Transito*, ca. 1848. One of the many images of the Virgin Mary in the Currier & Ives catalog. From the Library of Congress, Washington, D.C. (Gale Research, Detroit).

quoted in the magazine as praising their quality, which filled her with "patriotic pride that such work, at last, is done in America," and recommending them for Sunday school classrooms.[39]

Since these were promotional materials, they have limited reliability in ascertaining broader responses to these images. While it is clear from the continued publication of Marian art reproductions that they were selling well, it is harder to find resources to evaluate the public's reception of these images. An excellent set of sources, however, are the educational journals where the use of art reproductions in classrooms was explicitly discussed. Women's magazines also ran articles on the use of art reproductions in decorating homes to create moral and educational environments for children. In one typical example, Mary Nearly argued in a *Ladies Repository* article for the superiority of visual images over books in educating children, and noted their success in the "famous kinder-garten system of education." As evidence, she shared that her eleven-year-old nephew was familiar with classic Marian art: "Oh, Auntie," he announced one day, "I have just seen a lady who is the very image of Murillo's Madonna."[40] She attributed his art education to the arrival of a Prang reproduction of the painting, which she hung on the wall without explanation or instruction. "I noticed Arthur looking at it often in the pauses between his lessons," she shared, adding that he spent weeks using an encyclopedia and art dictionary to study it, and finally, "his dark eyes sparkling with a new revelation," he proclaimed, "'Oh! auntie, I know all about Murillo and the "Madonna" now!'" In this and many similar vignettes, familiarity with a canon of classic art was presumed to be integral to children's education, both in terms of historical and cultural knowledge and aesthetic development. However, the idealized subject matter, including the idealization of womanhood and motherhood transmitted by Marian subjects, was also prized in the education of both boys and girls.

By the late nineteenth century, photographs, sentimental images, and art reproductions were offered side by side at equivalent rates in print catalogs and department stores. The sentimental maternal ideal was expressed through a variety of forms, including staged Madonna and Child–style photographs and reproductions of *Madonna and Child* paintings.[41] Describing this new and, for some, disturbing blurring of "high" and "low" culture, scholar of visual culture Katherine Martinez writes: "Countless different art reproductions of paintings depicting Mary plus pictures of mothers holding babies, many simply titled *Madonna*, were staples of the commercial picture industry. Consumers could purchase copies of Madonnas by Renaissance

Irene Jerome Hood, *Self-Portrait*, ca. 1892–1900. Hood reclines under a large reproduction of Raphael's *Sistine Madonna*. The room is identified in another photograph as "Muller's Home, Denver." From the Colorado Historical Society.

painters such as Raphael or Madonnas by more modern painters such as von Bodenhausen, as well as contemporary photographs of women cuddling infants titled *Madonna*."[42] While the cult of domesticity that had developed over decades may have popularized this romanticized maternal image, the prevalence of Marian and Marian-derived motifs must be accounted for, especially because an association between Mary and Catholic identity also grew during the same decades. Martinez and other scholars who have acknowledged the sheer number of Marian images in late-century visual culture have generally attributed the impetus for their popularity to the motherhood movement. Maternal associations, such as the League of American Mothers and the National Congress of Mothers, were formed as early as the 1820s, and grew in number and influence throughout the century. In these groups, women created a distinct vision of motherhood that emphasized their role as transmitters of Christian culture and as salvific figures, living out engendered ideals to save their children, husbands, and the nation.[43] The flourishing of such groups undoubtedly contributed to the popularity of Madonna and Child images. However, Protestants did not only embrace maternal images, but reproduced a wide range of Marian images. Depictions of solitary Madonnas, Mary with an angel or angels, Mary's being crowned, and Mary enthroned (including the Immaculate Conception, Assumption, Annunciation, Coronation, Mary as Queen of Angels, and Mary as Queen of Heaven), were all widely available in print catalogs, magazines, gift books, and department stores.

Protestant consumption and reproductions of images of Mary without her Son, or images in which the infant Jesus is present but Mary is in a non-maternal posture, calls for further explanation. When books and articles treating Marian art are taken into account, it becomes clear that Marian imagery was not just a means of promoting sentimental maternalism but also an important way of grappling with shifting gender norms more broadly.

No "MOTHER of Grace and Mercy": Protestant Censure of Mary's Elevation

As women were increasingly associated with piety, some Protestants reacted against the perceived increase in female religious influence by encouraging men to reassert their authority in the Church. These anxieties led to attempts to masculinize Jesus and to incorporate more men into the Church through avenues like the 1857–58 "businessman's revival." The revival was comprised of Americans all over the country, of every major Protestant denomination, and of varying classes; however, leaders of the revival and the media characterized it as primarily involving urban businessmen, hence its appellation "businessman's revival." The increased leadership of Protestant laymen, as opposed to clerics, in the revival and afterward in the Young Men's Christian Association (YMCA) movement and the United States Christian Commission (a Civil War men's ministry) came at the deliberate expense of women's inclusion and visibility.[44] The interpreters of the revivals were engaged in a rhetorical reversal: "In a sense, they turned the ideology of separate spheres on its head to portray male religious superiority. Instead of worldly men and pious women, revival accounts conveyed the opposite impression."[45] The semiotics of the revival reveal that anxiety about Protestant feminization, and attempts to counter it, were already under way by midcentury. Movements like Men and Religion Forward in the early twentieth century (an initiative that aimed to increase male participation in Protestant churches of various denominations) were therefore not novel, but the culmination of half a century of Protestant laymen's activity, ranging from the provision of physical and spiritual support to Civil War soldiers, to the creation and development of the YMCA (which promoted Christian conversion and discipleship as well as physical exercise and sportsmanship), to the proliferation of laymen's organizations in the postbellum period.[46]

These efforts were contemporaneous with Protestants' increasing use of Marian imagery to conceptualize and express Christian womanhood. At the time of the Immaculate Conception proclamation, Protestants were already experiencing and reacting against the feminization (real or perceived) of their churches. There was a tension between the need to reinforce the female role as the seat and protector of Christian piety and the need to move her out of the way to allow men to reassert leadership in Protestant churches. In light of this internal tension, and their desire to employ Mary to communicate the religious dimension of separate spheres ideology alongside other less demonstrative tropes—like the domestic priestess, Angel in the House, and, toward the end of the century, queen of the home—Protestants were especially concerned about Catholic Marian veneration. While the purity of the Immaculate Conception resonated with Protestant imaginings of Mary, other implications of the doctrine challenged them. From a Protestant perspective, Immaculate Conception theology emphasized Mary's transcendence and implied the worship of a female figure, triggering the same fears of woman-centered religion as the feminization of American Protestantism. As non-Protestant others, Catholics were easy targets to isolate and denounce. Thus, Protestants sometimes redirected anxieties about women-filled pews, clerical disestablishment, and the shifting role of religion in public life onto Catholics. While Protestants idealized woman's purity and piety, and Mary was a reassuringly traditional figure to convey this ideal, they resisted a prominent religious role for a powerful female figure. In their responses to the Immaculate Conception declaration, Protestant critics asserted that they objected to the doctrine's elevation of a human figure over the divine figure of Jesus, but a close reading of their rhetoric suggests that Mary's sex was a crucial problem.

Anglican minister Reverend Michael Hobart Seymour produced one of the clearest and most influential expressions of Protestant censure of Mary's elevation in his widely read book *Mornings among the Jesuits at Rome*.[47] *Mornings* was published in 1849—the year the Holy See announced its resolve to decide on the Immaculate Conception doctrine—in both New York and London, and subsequently reprinted in the United States in 1850, 1855, 1856, and 1860. The book merits close attention because of its highly gendered critique of Catholicism, its preoccupation with the role of Mary, and its lasting influence on Protestant perceptions of Catholicism in the decades following its publication.[48] While Seymour was Anglican and Anglicans had a distinct and complicated relationship to Catholics, the saints, and Mary (especially in these decades), Seymour consistently used the word "Protestant" in the text to characterize his point of view and he supposed himself to be speaking to and for a broad Protestant readership with a shared set of concerns about these subjects.

Mornings was a self-styled travelogue that recounted Seymour's conversations with Roman practitioners and defenders of Catholicism. While the text employed some of the conventions of travel writing, and Seymour did go to Rome, conversations and events in the book were carefully composed to refute Catholic thought and practice. And while travelogues were often preoccupied with the *foreignness* of foreign lands and were often anti-Catholic, *Mornings* was more of an outsized propaganda piece than a typical travelogue. Throughout the book, Seymour juxtaposed Mary and Jesus, critiquing their relative positions in the affections of their Catholic devotees. His primary argument was that devotion to Mary precluded devotion to Christ. In a typical passage, he wrote: "It seemed to me that all tended to the honor of Mary rather than to the honor of Christ; and this seemed to me to be carried to such an extreme that I felt in my calm and sober judgment that the religion of Italy ought to be called the religion of Mary rather than the religion of Christ!"[49] Seymour set up a spiritual competition between Jesus and Mary for the hearts and prayers of the Catholic populace, using the phrase "religion of Mary" as a near-constant refrain in the text. He charged Italian Catholics with idolatry, writing: "The praying to her more frequently than to him bore the complexion of idolatry—as lowering him and exalting her,"[50] and continuing, "[it is] still more saddening, even to the point of fear and trembling, to hear the Savior practically dethroned from his High Priesthood and Mediatorship . . . on the ground of so awful an error as that Mary is . . . more ready to hear than Christ."[51] Through attention to Mary, Seymour contended, Jesus was diminished. While he acknowledged that Catholics differentiated between veneration and worship, and restricted worship to the triune God, he asserted that "the mass of the population, and of the children, were both incapable of understanding [the distinction] and of observing it."[52]

Mornings featured carefully scripted dialogues between Seymour, the author/narrator, and his Catholic opponents, followed by summary comments directed to the reader. These scenes merged the conventions of first-person travel memoirs with the didactic dialogues and parenthetical asides of nineteenth-century novels. What was most remarkable about the interactions he narrated, however, was their lack of theological content. Instead of the theologically revealing conversations Seymour proposed to relate, he instead described encounters that show him almost literally accosting Catholics with his unexamined biases.

This was particularly true of conversations intended to reveal Catholic "Mariolatry." Seymour identified Marian theology and veneration as one of the main obstacles to reconciliation between Protestants and Catholics; yet, in the text, Seymour rarely engaged or challenged Marian theological tenets. Instead, he repeatedly related his personal fears about Mary's prominence. In one exchange with a Roman Jesuit, he cited his perception that Mary's figure loomed over Christ's in paintings that explicitly depicted her as his *mother* as evidence of Catholic idolatry: "I reprobated the practice of representing Mary as the chief or principal figure in the picture, and Jesus Christ being introduced as a subordinate figure—as a figure that was merely accessory to hers, a sort of appendage to her, as if he was introduced merely to show that the figure of a female was intended as the figure of Mary—as if, there being innumerable female figures in such pictures, figures of various saints, it was necessary to introduce the child Jesus to show that this female figure was intended for Mary. . . . I expressed myself strongly against this practice as an awful dishonor to Christ. It was making God the creator a mere secondary to a creature."[53] In this passage, Seymour charged artists and their patrons with the creation of literal statements of their subject's relative value. Nearly all respected art critics and art historians of the time, including Anna Jameson in her influential texts on religious art, clearly distinguished between representational and devotional images. Representational images depicted biblical or sacred events, while devotional images encapsulated doctrines or functioned as icons, transmitting key attributes of a religious figure. Seymour's misconstrual of the conventions of devotional art was unsophisticated but not atypical—many other commentators and several of the book's reviewers concurred with his arguments. Ironically, the image of God as a helpless infant entrusted to human care is intrinsic to the Christian narrative. Yet rather than engaging Christian theology, Seymour described being repelled by images of the infant Jesus in the arms of an adult woman/mother. Instead, he preferred, and added that the "Protestant mind" also preferred, to dwell on "Christ in the maturity of his manhood."[54] Seymour depicted his Jesuit opponent as agreeing with his critique of Marian art: "He again expressed himself as disapproving of such pictures, saying that, although others approved of and liked them, yet he did not think them altogether justifiable."[55] Befitting his propagandistic agenda (and transparent narcissism), Seymour generally depicted his opponents as rationally ceding the merits of his arguments, but stubbornly refusing to convert to his opinions.

In a subsequent encounter, Seymour engaged another Jesuit in a conversation about Mary's womanhood and motherhood that explored whether Mary should be held up as a model for Christians to emulate. In this debate, Seymour's Jesuit opponent described Mary as the one "selected by God to bear his Son in her womb," presenting her, in her act of submitting to God's will and becoming the vehicle of the incarnation, as a model of human devotion. Seymour rejected this description of her unique mode of devotion as "substituting some fanciful ideas respecting her for the remembrance of his death, and sacrifice, and atonement as a safeguard against sin."[56] Seymour again polarized Jesus and Mary, asserting that attention to Mary's role displaced the remembrance of Jesus. Dismissing Mary's inarguably female act of devotion as "fanciful," he held up Jesus's own acts as the only acceptable model for Christians.

In response to Seymour's dismissal of his argument that Mary could not represent all Christians in her *fiat*, the Jesuit countered that, at the very least, Mary could represent Christian *women* in her compassionate and sacrificial motherhood.[57] He suggested that "the great encouragement to the devotion of ourselves to the Virgin Mary" arose from the way that Mary, as a mother, facilitated the devotion of Christian mothers, specifically how "mothers praying to her who was herself a mother, with all the sympathies of a mother, were heard and answered; that such prayers for children in sin, or in danger, or in sickness, were heard and answered."[58] Mary's sex and her maternity made her an important resource for Christian women and mothers, whose life experiences were mirrored and affirmed in hers. Again, Seymour rejected his contention. Jesus, he asserted, offered sufficient compassion for all Christians and his acts were the only relevant acts of sacrifice and mercy.

In this exchange, Seymour dismissed the problem, raised by his Jesuit opponent, of the exclusive masculinity of God and Christ, denying that this could be an obstacle for Christian women. He also expressed ambivalence about women's power in childbearing and motherhood. His opponent, failing to secure Seymour's agreement on any point, eventually conceded Seymour's argument, defensively mitigating Mary's importance by stating: "The Holy Virgin is never honored above Christ, nor as equal to Christ, but only as His mother, who has a mother's influence over him; and thus all the homage and worship paid to her is really a homage and a worship to Him, inasmuch as it is only as His mother that it is offered to her."[59] Declaring that Mary's motherhood did not place her over Jesus but under him, the Jesuit affirmed Seymour's position, that Mary was merely a mother who had only a "mother's influence." By placing this restraint on the value and authority of motherhood in the Jesuit's voice rather than the narrator's, Seymour reinforced the unreasonableness of portraying Mary as a real heroine for Christians. Even Mary's ardent supporters, Seymour suggested, conceded that motherhood does not equate to real authority or preeminence. The conversation overall, however, reinforced the equation of the figure of Mary with motherhood. During the course of the conversation, the participants expressed different perspectives about motherhood and women's authority and proper role, but both linked their feelings about motherhood to their perception of Mary's value and importance.

At the conversation's close, Seymour again placed Jesus and Mary in direct competition. His Jesuit opponent defended the Catholic populace against the charge of Mariolatry by explaining, finally, that Mary seemed more approachable than Jesus because of her humanity, her suffering, her womanhood, and her motherhood, especially to sinners whose consciences led them to fear Jesus. In response, Seymour exclaimed: "'Afraid of Jesus!' . . .

'Afraid of Jesus, who died for them—who showed his love in dying for them, and yet not afraid of Mary, who never professed or showed any love for them!'"[60] Rather than concede that Mary may be a less intimidating figure for some, Seymour countered that Jesus's acts of love and sacrifice made him approachable despite his masculinity and divinity. To heighten the contrast, Seymour denied that any action of Mary's revealed love or mercy. In the context of the conversation, in which Mary's willingness bodily to receive the divine child and relinquish him to God's tragic will was repeatedly discussed, this statement denied the value of Mary's specific acts and model of devotion. When Jesus triumphantly wins Seymour's constructed competition as "more attractive, more loving, and more merciful," the reader is left wondering if God is trumping humanity or if masculinity is trumping femininity. By the end of the conversation, divinity and masculinity are closely allied.

The vast majority of American reviews of *Mornings* were enthusiastic, promoting the book as a reliable compendium of authentic Catholic positions. A review in *Littell's Living Age*, which contained nine pages of excerpts from the book, "strongly" recommended it, calling it "one of the best and most authentic accounts of the present teaching of the Church of Rome . . . together with remarks upon some of its leading errors, showing considerable acuteness."[61] A few reviewers, however, expressed reservations about the authenticity of Seymour's account and his motivation in writing. One questioned whether the book had a polemical agenda, and asked who this unknown English cleric was: "We do not say that the book is not what it professes to be, or that the author is not an unimpeachable witness, we merely ask before receiving it as testimony, some vouchers of its worth in that respect."[62] Another reviewer also recognized the propagandist bent of the book, pointing out that Seymour was a Low-Church advocate in the Anglican Oxford controversy.[63] He wrote that "the whole . . . has the air of a design to counteract the growing *respect* for Rome, and to damp the growing sympathy, and to re-assure the wavering."[64] However, despite his concerns about the potential biases of the author, the reviewer was swayed by Seymour's descriptions of his Jesuit opponents and their arguments, writing that "the injudicious conduct of the Romish leaders is the greatest enemy the Church now possesses, and is the surest bulwark the Anglican church has against her proselytes."[65]

Despite the occasional cautious review, the book was widely accepted as an accurate account of the theological arguments of the most learned Catholics in Rome.[66] Passages from *Mornings* were consistently cited on a variety of subjects as evidence attesting to the weakness of Catholic thought. For example, several years after the book's publication, the author of a *Princeton Review* article entitled "Is the Church of Rome Idolatrous" used passages from *Mornings* to substantiate charges of Roman Catholic idolatry, calling quotations from the book the "actual belief of many Romanists."[67] Seymour's concerns about Marian devotionalism and Mary's sex and maternity were particularly influential. The reviewer from the *Princeton Review*, for example, affirmed Seymour's arguments about Catholic "Mariolatry" and responded with his own gendered critique. Like Seymour, he objected to the role of Mary, and particularly Marian art, in the devotional life of Catholics. "We feel strongly inclined to the opinion," he wrote, "that for this prevailing preference of Mary to Christ, the Fine Arts are in a great deal responsible."[68] He prefaced a selection of lengthy quotations from the book with the observation that "the growth of Mariolatry is painfully brought to view in these pages."[69] And commenting on Seymour's discussion of Marian art, he added his own judgment that "the most revolting length to which the practice has been carried is the representation of Mary administering chastisement to her child, by way of illustrating his subjection to his parents. How is it possible for people whose only books are such pictures as these, to take up any other idea than that of the permanent inferiority of Jesus?"[70] Like Seymour, the reviewer preferred to dwell on Jesus's manhood, not his childhood subjection to his mother.

Seymour and his reviewer may have been influenced on this point by a well-known 1844 anti-Catholic tract called *Mariolatry; or, Facts and Evidences Demonstrating the Worship of the Blessed Virgin Mary, by the Church of Rome* by Reverend Thomas Hartwell Horne and Samuel Jarvis that contrasted biblical passages with the writings of many Catholic authors.[71] Under the subheading "Parental Authority over God the Son," Horne places Philemon 2:9–10, which reads in part, "At the name of Jesus every knee should bow," opposite a quotation from St. Bonaventure's *Crown of the Blessed Virgin*: "Therefore, O Empress and our most benignant Lady, in right of [being his] mother, command thy most beloved Son our Lord Jesus Christ, that he deign to raise our minds from longing after earthly things to heavenly desires." Horne objected to the "right" of "command" Mary had over Jesus as his mother, a theme that was taken up and elaborated by Seymour and other Protestants. The *Princeton Review* specifically cited the impending Immaculate Conception declaration as evidence of "Mariolatry," writing that "we may add [to Seymour's evidence] the infatuation of the present pope, Pius IX, whose whole soul seems to be much more taken up with having the Immaculate Conception of the Virgin formally established as the doctrine of the Church, than with the personal administration of his dominions."[72] The reviewer connected the declaration with the pope's political struggles, but assumed it was causative—a source of distraction—rather than compensatory, an attempt to counterbalance lost political authority with increased spiritual authority.

The popularity of *Mornings* in the United States reinforced the perception that Marian veneration was at the heart of the Catholic-Protestant divide, while Seymour's descriptions of Italian Mariolatry were commonly cited as evidence for previously held judgments about Catholicism. Because the book preceded the declaration by six years, it directly influenced the Protestant response to the Immaculate Conception declaration. Many Americans who did not read it may have encountered its premises in one of its many reviews, excerpts, or citations. Protestant critics of the declaration, on the whole, shared Seymour's preoccupation with Mary as a female religious figure and the implications of her elevation for gender norms. Critics emphasized her sex in their arguments against the Immaculate Conception and other Marian tenets, strategically opposing the terms "him" to "her," "father" to "mother," and "man" to "woman." For example, in the article "Is the Church of Rome Idolatrous?" cited previously, the author repeatedly contrasted Mary to Christ, emphasizing their respective sexes through the use of italics, capitalization, and repetition. In one passage he wrote, "If we are to come unto God by Christ *himself*, then we are not to come by his *mother*," "in the 'Confiteor' his mother is addressed *three* times *before* him," and "again the mother takes precedence of her Son, the Son of God."[73] He also contrasted Mary's maternity to the paternity of the masculine God: "Jesus Christ taught us to pray to our Father which is in heaven, but when did God ever direct us to pray to our Mother in heaven, and to ask her to show herself to us?" and "The Bible says that God is the FATHER of mercies, but it is silent about any MOTHER of grace and mercy."[74] While the author's stated intent was to argue that veneration of the human figure of Mary distracts from the worship of God, he repeatedly contrasted maternity to paternity, rather than humanity to divinity. The power of his rhetoric lay in its gendered content: the apparent absurdity of suggesting that a mother have precedence over her son, or the existence of the feminine divine (note his capitalization of a "heavenly Mother," "a Mother of grace and mercy"). The author's emphasis on gender shifted his ostensibly theological critique to base mockery and bias.

While many Protestant critics of the declaration echoed Seymour's arguments, some employed them for different ends. In a notable response to the declaration published in the *New York Daily Times*, Paris correspondent Frank Goodrich, using the pseudonym Dick Tinto, called Catholicism, "Madonnaism," and suggested that Marian art was the main cause of idolatrous Marian veneration. However, rather than finding this repellant, he claimed it was an attractive, even seductive aspect of Roman Catholicism. His article, "Madonnas and Madonnaism," denounced Marian veneration in France and other Catholic countries using many of Seymour's exact arguments.[75] Goodrich wrote that, "it may safely be said that the galleries of Italy present but two grand divisions of paintings; those that are Madonnas and those that are not. Which is the biggest half I cannot say." That Catholicism was primarily Marian, he asserted, was clear from the profusion of Marian imagery and the veneration of these images by her devout. Like Seymour, Goodrich claimed that Marian worship distracted from or substituted for worship of God. "I . . . do not exaggerate," he wrote, "when I say that throughout . . . every country where the Catholic is the exclusive religion of the people, for one knee bent to God, thousands are bowed before the shrines of the Virgin." Also like Seymour, Goodrich was troubled that the figure of Mary overshadowed the infant Jesus depicted in her arms. In illustration of this latter point, he related a conversation he claimed to have overheard in Paris between two art patrons, one of whom, an American Protestant, upon viewing a Madonna by Raphael declared: "The Savior ought never to be represented as an infant!"[76]

However, unlike Seymour, Goodrich charged that the Catholic hierarchy's promotion of Marian spirituality, what he termed their "policy of Madonnaism," was a deliberate strategy to win converts. In his view, the popularity of Marian veneration, among both men and women, was primarily due to Mary's sex and maternity: "A woman—a mother of God and man—with human sympathies and divine attributes is indeed a most attractive deity. Only let the heart incline to belief and how many are the sad and dark hours of life in which the soul would instinctively carry its cares and its burdens to the foot of her altar." He affirmed that it was natural and "instinctive" to find comfort in Mary, and called Mary as "a divinity, a goddess, an object of worship," the "trump card of the Catholic Church." According to

Goodrich, Catholicism was Marian because Mary was an inherently appealing, nearly irresistible, religious figure. Thus, he charged, the Immaculate Conception declaration was primarily a strategic decision intended to "purif[y] the fame of their chief divinity from the taint of original sin . . . [and] to exalt, perpetuate and intensify her worship."[77] He accused the Vatican of deciding the Immaculate Conception and promoting Marian veneration with the specific intent to lure converts by offering something against which Protestants could not compete: a feminine and maternal divine figure.

In particular, he affirmed that Mary fulfilled the genuine religious needs of women. Unlike Seymour, he did not suggest that Jesus should or could function similarly. Goodrich called the image of a divine Mary "seductive especially to the softer sex—to the mother, the daughter, the sister, the woman!" He sympathized with their desire for her, calling it "lovely." However, he warned that it was extrabiblical and that it resulted in "idolatrous worship, inasmuch as adoration belongs only to God." Such idolatrous Marian veneration, he warned, would become a significant religious movement in the United States if Catholic immigration continued unchecked, or if religious art continued to be embraced. He exhorted his readers to prevent this eventuality by examining the content of religious art: "Don't admire a thing simply because it's a Raphael!"[78] Where Seymour displayed unease, even misogyny, toward the female elevation and power evident in Marian art and Immaculate Conception theology; Goodrich revealed instead a fascination with and attraction to idealized constructions of womanhood and motherhood. His response to the declaration showed the concordance between Immaculate Conception theology and the era's idealization of domestic womanhood. Instead of Seymour's charge that Marian elevation represented disorder and a "foreign" set of cultural norms propagated by feminized men, Goodrich found Marian veneration so appealing to Americans and consistent with their values that he feared for the male Jesus and the male God's ability to successfully compete.

Other responses took the contest between mother and son further, employing Mary and Christ not just as engendered religious figures whose veneration had implications for societal gender norms, but as emblems that literally engendered the Catholicism and Protestantism they represented. Henry Boynton Smith, for example, in his 1855 *Methodist Quarterly Review* article "Dogma of the Immaculate Conception," emphasized Mary's sex and worried that Catholic Marian veneration superseded worship of the male godhead. He established the typical dichotomy between Mary and Christ, with attention to one diminishing attention to the other. "Effigies of the mother and Son become frequent," he wrote, "as sacred symbols, and supplant the cross. Christ begins to recede and his mother to come into the front rank of popular veneration." However, he extended the problem of their respective sexes, writing that "the nations . . . need an almighty helper, and the Papacy gives them a deified woman."[79] Christ, through his masculinity, was powerful and active, "an almighty helper"; while Mary, the "deified woman," was a false and weak alternative.[80] He characterized the Immaculate Conception declaration as a key moment of Mary's eclipse of Christ and the ascent of the feminine.

Deriding Catholicism as retrograde, Smith asked: "Is this the gospel for this nineteenth century of strife and infidelity? Has Rome changed? Is superstition extinct? Is the Roman Church the Church of Christ or of Mary?" He argued that the modern age required masculine strength to combat "strife and infidelity" and suggested that Marian veneration evoked past "superstition."[81] By offering Mary instead of Jesus to the faithful, he suggested, Pope Pius IX was creating a feminine rather than masculine Church and thus weakening its ability to act in the world. Situating the declaration as a pivotal moment in world history, he concluded: "The heart of the conflict of Europe . . . is the question between Romanism and Protestantism . . . between reason and faith, on the one side, and superstition against reason and Scripture on the other."[82] In this gendered dichotomy, Smith aligned modernity, reason, faith, scripture, power, masculinity, and Jesus with Protestantism; and superstition, irrationality, weakness, humanity, femininity, and Mary with Catholicism. For Smith, like for many Protestant critics, Mary typified Catholicism, while Jesus, her spiritual "opponent," represented Protestantism. However, in his rhetoric, Protestantism was not masculine just because it rejected a significant religious role for Mary, but because it embodied culturally constructed masculine characteristics. Likewise, Catholicism was not feminine just because it embraced a significant religious role for Mary, but because it embodied culturally constructed feminine characteristics. Goodrich and Smith, like the majority of Protestant critics of the declaration, omitted theological engagement with the doctrine, while devoting pages to gendered analyses.

Fears about, and voyeuristic imaginings of, transgressive Catholic sexual practices and domestic relationships had been key themes in anti-Catholic propaganda throughout the nineteenth century. This propaganda sensationalized the prominence of Mary, the demasculinization of robed and celibate priests (and, contradictorily, their supposed predatory hypersexuality), and the enclosure and eroticization of women religious.[83] While anti-Catholicism, on its surface, "seem[s] to have little to do with domestic religion," Protestant theologians who emphasized domesticity also "promoted the creation of a pure 'American' nation."[84] Horace Bushnell and Lyman Beecher, for example, explicitly linked their domestic ideologies to their anti-Catholicism. In reaction to the Immaculate Conception declaration, Protestants rhetorically contrasted a feminized Catholicism to a modern, rational, masculine Protestantism. And as Protestants' own concerns about the numbers and role of women in their churches led to efforts to masculinize them, at least rhetorically, Protestants displaced their anxieties about gender onto Catholics, painting them as a feminized other.

Travel Writing and Marian Art

While Seymour's book was anti-Catholic propaganda masquerading as travel writing, other Protestants also reflected on and debated the appropriate religious role for Mary and appropriate responses to Marian art in the popular genre of travelogue and European tour literature. In this literature, the tension between Protestants' desire to utilize Mary as an exemplar of womanhood and their desire to shore up their identity as American Protestants by disparaging Catholic Marian veneration was manifest. The European grand tour was only accessible to wealthy Americans, but there was a broad audience for magazine articles and books describing these experiences. The standard itinerary included famous Catholic churches and cathedrals, as well as museums and galleries full of religious art. In literary accounts, an American Protestant narrator typically described his or her encounters with religious art, hitherto only seen in reproductions, and firsthand impressions of European Catholicism, which differed in many respects from its more familiar urban-American form. While these writings often conveyed the narrator's anxieties, judgments, or sense of alienation from Catholicism, most also voiced awe and appreciation for religious art. One author wrote: "When Americans travel in these older countries, they first become aware how young their native land is . . . but show any Yankee . . . the *Sistine Madonna*, and see if the *Io Anche* of fraternal emotion does not fall from his half-unconscious lips."[85]

One popular example of this genre was the 1860 travelogue *Echoes of Europe; or, Word Pictures of Travel*, written by E. K. Washington. In the book,

Washington described viewing Marian artwork in European museums in detail. His publisher called this "a marked peculiarity of the work ... the *subjective* elucidation of the most important works of art in the world."[86] However, while Washington might have been particularly skilled at it, his approach was not unique. Like many Protestant travelogue writers, Washington grappled with the Catholic theological content of artworks and the prominence of Mary. "As a Protestant you object, of course to the whole thing," he wrote, "and think this religion is too sensuous; and that they ought to look behind the thing to the thing signified. But ... all people should survey all things from the standpoint of others. Catholicism twines in many soft and pleasing tendrils around a heart. Where there cannot be sunlight, the moonlight may do very well. Protestantism is a larger leap of mind; but we must not despise 'the day of small things,' nor think that 'wisdom will die with us.' "[87] Washington repeated the common disparagement that Catholicism was more sensuous than Protestantism; however, while "rational" Protestant theology may be superior, Catholic forms—art, music, poetry—were sufficient to convey religious truth. It was fairly typical for travel writers to express admiration and surprise at Catholic forms of Christianity abroad, and to take a similar tone of grudging admiration.

In the same vein, Washington repeated standard Protestant objections to Catholic Marian theology, but he closely analyzed Mary's presentation in art in a way that showed emotional and possibly religious engagement. One of the paintings Washington encountered was Murillo's *Immaculate Conception*, which he called the "real gem of the Louvre" and declared finer than any Marian subject painted by Raphael or da Vinci.[88] He praised Murillo's depiction of Mary as possessing "innocence," "lofty serenity," and "a holiness." She seemed to him "almost girlish" though "wearied and broken." The traits Washington admired—serenity, youthfulness, and holiness—were typical Protestant preferences in Marian art. Attention to and praise for Mary's "holiness" belied Protestant theological emphasis on her shared humanity, yet revealed a desire for her to epitomize the purity of the true womanhood ideal.

Washington explicitly sought this female ideal in Marian art, writing that "originally the *idea* of the Virgin was a beautiful one, and is so in reality. She is thought to have been perfectly sinless, pure as Christ. ... She is always perfectly beautiful, often in sorrow for her son."[89] He dismissed the Catholic belief in her perpetual virginity, asserting that the "direct intimations of Scripture" proved that she was a mother more than once, but he praised the idea of a sinless virgin mother nevertheless, singling out paintings that evoked a holy, pure, and sinless Mary. Washington, like many of his contemporaries, found the *Sistine Madonna* the most personally meaningful representation of the Virgin: "It is impossible to look at it as a painting. The art is very great, but there is more than art there."[90] He described regarding the painting in person as a spiritual experience. It both "commands and entrances," he wrote: "You go away and look at others: this mingles with every thing. You return: it is alone, and glorious, and tranquillizing, and lovely." In describing the painting's depiction of Mary and the infant Christ, he wrote: "You would think unexhausted heaven breathed from those faces.... The Virgin's eyes have all that the most lovely female's eyes could express, when suffused with soul and holy, sinless regard." Washington's descriptions were not devotional, nor were they free from theological critique, and yet they revealed a spiritual engagement with the Marian ideal: her sinless femininity, her elevated womanhood, and her divine and compassionate motherhood.

Similarly, an 1867 travel article, "Painting and Painters in Italy," invited readers to imagine themselves touring the great masterpieces on display in Italy.[91] The author praised the faith and devotion that underlay the great religious art of Italy, expressing gratitude that the greatest developments in painting occurred at a time when "theism was the ruling thought," which led the "noblest achievements" of art to portray "distinctively Christian subjects." Marian art figured centrally in his reflections. He echoed the widely held belief that Raphael's *Sistine Madonna* and his *Seated Madonna* (*Madonna della Seggiola*) were "generally regarded as the best" Madonnas ever painted. He described Mary in the *Seated Madonna* as possessing "calm maternal joy," and having "eyes full of ... pure deep thought and pensive wonder."[92] Like Washington, he prized Mary's maternity and her serenity, which he tied to her intellect and capacity for reflection. He dwelled on Mary's expression in the painting, writing that it appeared she was "saying in her heart, 'My soul doth magnify the Lord' while with caressing tenderness she lays her cheek to the child's and clasps it to her bosom." After praising both the technical achievements of the painting and the spiritual content transmitted through the figure of Mary, the author condemned Catholic theology, stating that "the picture expresses most perfectly the Roman Catholic idea of the immaculate Mother, which is the germ of the Mariolatry of that church." Taken in context, however, the sentiment was not entirely negative. Though he linked Raphael's *Seated Madonna* to the Immaculate Conception doctrine and condemned Marian veneration as "Mariolatry," his tone

Raphael, *Madonna della Seggiola*. This painting was variously called the "Seated Madonna" or the "Madonna of the Chair." From the Galleria Palatina, Florence (Scala/Art Resource, New York).

was strangely upbeat. The painting was a "most perfect" expression of an idea that is not necessarily offensive in itself, but the germ of the problem—the cause, but not the equivalent, of "Mariolatry." He went on to extol the female ideal expressed in the painting, praising the concept of "ideal womanhood and purest Motherhood," despite his reservations about idolatry. He wrote: "All the attributes of perfect womanhood are wrought into the picture of the Mother . . . according to the artist's pure and classic ideas of woman's nature and of female beauty." The author equated his own expectations of the content of "perfect womanhood" with Raphael's, and perceived it in, or projected it onto, the painting. The female ideal was, in his opinion, fully achieved in this "pure and classic" representation.

In addition to praising characteristics such as serenity, maternity, thoughtfulness, and wonder in Raphael's *Seated Madonna*, the author of "Painting and Painters in Italy" also approved of Mary's attitude of self-abnegation: "It is not the charm of physical contour or of coloring that attract you, though these are perfect, but the *higher fascination of sentiment*, of spiritual beauty, virgin purity, and maternal self-abandoning affection."[93] He viewed Mary primarily as a vehicle for conveying an abstracted ideal of womanhood. Dismissing the technical achievement of the painting as secondary, he praised the spiritual virtues of the subject. Encountering it was not a devotional experience for the author, nor a purely aesthetic one, but it triggered a "higher fascination of sentiment." That is, the visual representation of Mary was emotionally moving.

However, he ended the article ambivalently, contrasting his approbation for the female ideal realized through Mary with his discomfort with Catholic theology as he understood it. He concluded: "It is not strange that such ideal womanhood and purest motherhood should attract adoration; that such a picture should be worshiped where the people are taught that there are two mediators instead of one, and that the divine Son forgives sins reluctantly, if at all, only at the intercession of the human, immaculate Mother." He asserted the typical Protestant objection that attention to Mary diminished Christ. Yet, despite this rhetoric, there was a clear undercurrent of approval in the article. After the author's praise for the "higher fascination of sentiment" evoked by the painting, the reader was primed to agree that it was "not strange" that Catholics valued and were inspired by Marian womanhood.[94]

Another article published in the same magazine three months later also wrestled with the role of Mary as a cultural figure and a part of Western cultural inheritance. Repeatedly drawing connections between Marian art and Marian music, as it was performed abroad, the article described the *Stabat Mater*, a medieval Marian poem chanted or sung as a hymn.[95] Like "Painting and Painters in Italy," the article critiqued but then excused "Mariolatry," similarly portraying it as an excess of legitimate and admirable sentiments. Directly comparing the *Stabat Mater*'s value to that of the *Sistine Madonna*, the author encouraged Protestant readers to appreciate it in a similar way, allowing the Catholicity of the work to be mitigated by its cultural value and inspiring content. The author encouraged readers not to "overlook the truth which underlies almost every error of the Roman Church, and gives it such power over the pious feelings of her members." Remarkably, the author of this article reiterated a typically Catholic argument that Marian worship did not denigrate from the worship of Christ. He wrote: "As in the inimitable Madonnas of Raphael (especially that of Dresden) it is, after all, the glory of the Divine Son which is reflected in every feature and emotion of the human mother." His affirmation that Mary's glory was a reflection of Christ's—that she mirrored him, rather than competing with him—was an unusual claim for a Protestant writer to make. He then affirmed the Catholic tenet that Mary represented the Christian Church as a whole: "Mary at the manger and Mary at the cross opens a vista to an abyss of joy, and of grief such as the world never saw before. Mary stood there not only as the mother, but as the representative of the whole Christian church, for which the eternal Son of God was born an infant in the manger, and for which he suffered the most ignominious death on the cross." Again, this was a surprising statement coming from a Protestant writer. Despite the author's unusual concessions, the article typified Protestant attitudes, which claimed not only religious art (and music) as their legitimate cultural heritage, but also the Marian ideal itself. He objected to what he called the Roman Catholic habit of "pious contemplation upon the mother first, and only through her upon the Son," but encouraged Protestants to reclaim the *Stabat Mater*. In these articles and many others, Protestant writers expressed not merely heightened feelings but a sense of being overwhelmed with emotion in the presence of Marian art.

For example, the biographical article on Francis Lieber (see the introduction) described his strong emotional reaction to the *Sistine Madonna* while traveling in Europe. His biographer described his experience of being "overcome by his feelings" in order to praise his innate sensitivity and show the formative influences that led him to become a humane political philosopher and keen observer of American society.[96] Similarly, a travel essay from the *Southern Literary Messenger* (which also reprinted the Lieber article) emphasized the emotional impact of the *Sistine Madonna*. This author, traveling in Bavaria, expressed his disappointment with Munich's art museums because he found nothing there that "spoke to the feelings with the power and pathos which the *Madonna di San Sisto* exerts"—nothing that, like the *Sistine Madonna*, "the memory would keep as a treasure forever."[97]

Such hyperbole was common in Protestant descriptions of the subjective experience of viewing Marian art. However, Protestants remained ambivalent about Mary's role and prominence in Catholicism and sometimes critiqued each other's fascination with Marian art. For example, in 1868 Andrew Peabody published a well-received travel book called *Reminiscences of European Travel*, which described his deeply emotional, even devotional, responses to viewing Marian art abroad. A review of the book, published in *Overland Monthly and Out West Magazine*, criticized Peabody for his spiritual engagement with Marian art.[98] The reviewer dismissed Peabody's responses as demonstrating "the delight of a divinity student rather than the criticism of the arts," and charged that he "revels in . . . Madonnas and saints, with an enthusiasm . . . that partakes more of theology than aestheticism." In *Reminiscences of European Travel*, Peabody contrasted the emotion evoked by Marian art with contemporary rationalism, which he blamed for his era's failures.[99] The reviewer objected to such evocative claims, particularly Peabody's statement that the *Sistine Madonna* "lifts the soul into an ecstasy of praise and adoration, [and] cannot be unworthy of the Divine wisdom and love." While many Protestant writers were moved by the *Sistine Madonna*, the boundary between a moving encounter with Marian art and a devotional or *Catholic* one was delicate, and in *Overland Monthly*'s opinion, Peabody transgressed it.

In travelogues, Americans explored their conflicted feelings toward Catholic culture and power outside of the American context. Travelers and travel writers confronted Catholicism as a cultural and religious progenitor to their own faith, art, and music traditions. Condemnation, mockery, desire, and appreciation alternated in this literature that offered vicarious experiences of Europe and shaped Americans' understandings of the Old World. Despite frequent censure of Catholic theology and practice, Protestant travel writers appreciated Marian art as part of a desired cultural heritage, and a female ideal transmitted through (or projected onto) images of Mary.

The tension between admiring and chastising Catholic depictions of Mary ran through this literature. In the most negative readings, Mary was derided as the Catholic "goddess." Many Protestant travel writers compared her "worship" by Catholics to the cults of Greek, Roman, and Egyptian goddesses in articles with titles like "The Pagan Element in France" and "Corruption of Christianity by Paganism."[100] By calling Mary a goddess, and then asserting that she was more prominent or more frequently prayed to than the male godhead, Protestants rhetorically moved Catholics outside the Christian canopy and derided them as both pagan and feminized. The frequent appearance of the "goddess" epithet in the wake of the Immaculate Conception declaration revealed that many Protestant critics saw the doctrine as promoting a female religious figure who was autonomous and powerful in a manner that the True Woman was not. Thus, many Protestants imagined that Mary's elevation was a threat to American gender and domestic norms, and linked Catholic veneration of her with disordered gender roles, even though American Catholics did not readily admit or make use of such potential.

"One So Lowly": Womanhood and Domesticity in Catholic Responses to the Declaration

Catholic veneration of Mary had the potential to foster alternative, empowered models of womanhood, but this potential remained largely dormant despite Mary's elevation in the Immaculate Conception declaration. Through the end of the nineteenth century, Protestants were significantly more likely than Catholics to use Mary to bolster arguments for woman's rights and egalitarian marriage. It seems ironic that, among American Christians, the community that actively venerated a powerful, female religious figure was *less* likely to use her to challenge restrictive gender norms than the community that actively campaigned against granting her a significant religious role. However, since anti-Catholicism was often expressed as slanderous attacks on Catholics' domestic and sexual behavior, U.S. Catholics contending against such hostility defended their status as "good Americans" by asserting that they actually surpassed non-Catholics in their conformity to American gender norms.[101] Because Protestant critics objected to Mary's elevation in the Immaculate Conception declaration, Catholics explicitly downplayed any aspects of Marian theology that might have challenged American social norms.

In defending the Immaculate Conception, U.S. Catholics faced not only the traditional theological critiques of the past, but those concerns most frequently raised by U.S. Protestant critics: timeliness, development, and bound consciences (discussed in chapter 1) and gendered critiques about the relative positions of Jesus and Mary and Mary's role and authority. The potential of the doctrine to elevate the status of women was not merely a projection of Protestant fears. The Immaculate Conception placed Mary in a unique and transcendent position: it posited that in all of human history only one person, a woman, was purified by God at the moment of her conception, escaping the stain of original sin. The text of the apostolic constitution *Ineffabilis Deus* affirmed: "The Blessed Virgin Mary in the first instant of her conception was preserved exempt from all stain of original sin by a *singular* privilege and grace granted by God."[102] The text accentuated Mary's distinction from all other persons in light of this privilege, as well as in her role as Christ-bearer, opening the way for Christ's work of salvation through her cooperation. Additionally, the text quoted biblical passages that underscored Mary's uniqueness, including Genesis 3:15, in which God placed enmity between the serpent and the woman.[103] Traditionally, Catholic theology understood "the woman" in this passage to prefigure Mary and read it as signifying a metaphysical struggle between Mary and the devil, emphasizing Mary's agency in the salvation narrative. Thus, in *Ineffabilis Deus*, the doctrine's theological explication (and in her dramatic coronation at the ceremony), Mary's exceptionalism and her agency in the human salvation were emphasized.

However, nineteenth-century U.S. Catholics did not expect high honors for Mary to be generalized into rights or privileges for her sex. As we have seen, Catholics were more likely than Protestants to hold Mary up as a model for all Christians, male and female, rather than portraying her solely as a role model for women. Thus, her agency, power, and exceptionalism were more likely to be discussed as figuring the Church as a whole or all Christians, than women qua women. However, some Catholics writing on the subject of female domesticity in advice manuals or articles about marriage and motherhood did suggest that Mary provided a particular example to women and mothers. These writers connected Mary's life experiences, *as a woman*, to those of everyday women. Because of this connection, Catholic women may have felt that the declaration—which justified Mary's singular grace in being conceived without original sin by citing her role in bearing Christ—increased the religious significance and dignity of their own vocations as mothers. Catholic defenders of the dogma emphasized that Mary's example did sanctify maternity, but did not imply any correspondent increase in woman's sphere or agency. Beginning in these years, Protestant "maternalists" would argue for increased social and political power for women on the basis of their roles as mothers. Catholics did not make similar arguments until the early twentieth century. Instead Catholic writers used Marian motifs to reinforce a traditional, domestic ideal of woman-hood, speculating that Mary's home life conformed to nineteenth-century American ideals and exhorting laywomen to model themselves on this do-mestic vision of Mary.

In response to Protestant criticism and possibly their own concerns, many Catholic apologists for the Immaculate Conception directly confronted the empowering potential inherent in the doctrine. In many apologetic works, authors propounded high Mariological claims, for instance, celebrat-ing the Immaculate Conception as a singular honor distinguishing Mary from all other humans or making triumphalist predictions for her powerful geopolitical interventions in the wake of its declaration, and then immedi-ately bounded the implications of such claims. In doing so, many directly cited concerns about Protestant censure or disordered gender norms. Ullathorne, for example, acknowledged Protestant opposition to the doctrine, employ-ing the concept of humility—a predominantly feminine virtue—to temper the implications of Mary's elevation: "And the appearance of that blessed one, illuminating by her immaculate light the unclean gulf of original sin, is greeted with clamours and cries from the enfeebled sects of Protestantism. It is as if they had been struck by a terrible blow. Pride is offended that one so lowly should be so great, and that humility should be so supremely exalted. Nature, poor fallen thing, is indignant and disgusted in its self-sufficiency at such a revelation of grace, and the spectacle of its anger is as painful as it is instructive to contemplate."[104] Ullathorne grounded the potentially chal-lenging aspects of Mary's exaltation in her manifest weakness. According to him, the elevation of Mary, which Protestants perceived as too high, per-haps even higher than Jesus, should be understood as an affirmation that she was intrinsically lower than him. In a theological context in which pov-erty was wealth and humiliation was glory, he argued that Mary's glorifica-tion should not be seen as a threat to male supremacy, but as a confirmation of it. In effect, God made so much of her because she was so little: her youth, her femaleness, and her submission to God were emblematic of her lowliness.

Taking a similar approach, Rohner linked Mary's humility to her role as a mother. He wrote: "Suffering and sacrifice win for every mother an exalted position in the family, a sublime place in the estimation of all good men. Ac-cording to our views, disinterested self-sacrifice takes the most exalted posi-tion: it stands higher than power or dignity, wealth or influence."[105] Rohner redefined honor and exaltation as self-sacrifice and suffering. Like other

Catholic apologists, he used a "last shall be first" argument to mitigate or deny the gender implications feared by Protestant critics. Mary's exaltation, according to these writers, did not indicate female strength, pride, or elevation, but lowliness and humility—nonthreatening virtues.

Redemptorist priest Joseph Wissel placed a stronger emphasis on Mary's independent agency, writing: "All that God can and is willing to grant to man, according to His infinite power and mercy, is placed in the hands of Mary for her free distribution." In making this statement, Wissel promoted a traditional claim for Mary that originated in St. Alphonsus's *Glories of Mary*.[106] However, using a similar "last shall be first" argument, he undercut his strong assertion of the potency of Mary's will by domesticating the heavenly realm: "This agrees perfectly with her office as Mother. For the mother has free dispensation of the treasures of the house on behalf of her children. . . . Nor does this in the least derogate from the honor and authority of God . . . as little as it derogates from the authority of the father of a family, to allow the mother to provide the children with all that they need, and one whom the children call for all that they want."[107] Wissel balanced his affirmation of a traditional high Mariological claim with his desire to protect patriarchal power and conform to American gender norms. His statement responded to an implied challenger—the invisible Protestant critic—who asserted that such theological claims for Mary *did* derogate from the authority of God. Wissel negated Mary's potency as the dispenser of divine grace by reversing its implications: rather than modeling domestic relations on heavenly ones, Wissel modeled Mary's relationship to God on American domestic standards. By comparing Mary's subordination to an emphatically male God with the subjugation of wife to husband, Wissel neutralized the potential for female power exemplified in Mary's spiritual mediation. Wissel assured the reader that the male godhead, like the male householder, was not threatened by power benignly bestowed on a dependent, subordinate female. In these apologetic works and others, high Mariological claims were reaffirmed but also reconceived in nonthreatening terms.

There was, however, one important exception. Ullathorne was unique among English-speaking defenders of the Immaculate Conception both for his willingness to embrace the high Mariology of the dogma without limiting its implications and for his lyrical and respectful treatment of motherhood and the female body. While he did maintain the paradoxical premise that Mary's power arose from her radical humility, he emphasized Mary's literal power and agency. Ullathorne may have been atypical in this respect because he was writing in the British rather than the American context. While Mary's role was equally contested in England, where the Oxford movement was gaining ground and Catholic religious freedom was curtailed by legislation, the trajectory of early feminism and the relationship between female domesticity and national identity took a different path there. Mary played a specific and well-defined role in the Tractarianism controversy in England. In the United States, as I discuss in subsequent chapters, Marian imagery was used interchangeably with other maternal imagery to retain, promote, and reinterpret persistent "republican motherhood" themes. However, because in Europe, and particularly in France, Mary was associated with monarchism, her figure primarily indicated political and religious identities in England and was not used to symbolize and reinforce a domestic female ideal.[108] Ullathorne's British context may have allowed him more room to affirm Mary's power without being constrained by the implications of these claims for women's social roles. Still, Ullathorne was the most widely read and frequently cited apologist for the Immaculate Conception doctrine in the United States, and his impact was significant.

In one particularly striking passage, Ullathorne reversed the typical gendered rhetoric that emphasized the derivative nature of Mary's power by affirming instead that the glory of the male patriarchs, and Jesus himself, was derivative of *her*. He wrote: "Abraham, Jacob and David are so great, because Mary is to be their daughter. When they have given birth to her, they have accomplished that for which they were appointed, and the line of David disappears from history. She is the sum and complement of all those preparations. Christ is the Son of David, and the Son of Abraham, because He is the Son of Mary. And she embraces the Son of God as her child, whom they embrace but as a Son through her."[109] In Ullathorne's analysis, Mary herself was the culmination of the royal line of the Old Testament. Rather than placing Jesus as the telos of the line of David, he asserted that the line culminated with her: after Mary's birth, David's royal line "disappears from history." Ullathorne did not describe Mary as a mere vessel for a male line, but as the reason the line existed. He portrayed Mary's agency in bearing the Christ child as momentous, maintaining that her cooperation with the divine and her complete purity formed the only possibility for the incarnation of the divine. While Mary "embraces" her son, male figures may only embrace him "through her."

In this passage, Ullathorne asserted the primacy of the maternal bond over patrimony—a position that could easily have been extended to contemporary gender norms. Feminist scholars have found "ambiguity for androcentric gender definition" in such Marian theology.[110] The Marian conception narrative has a dual potential: she may be viewed as a tool for the male God to incarnate the male divine child, or she may be viewed as a woman conceiving and bearing the divine (humanity's salvation) beyond human male domination or control. By stressing, in extended and poetic passages, that Mary bore Jesus without the contribution of a human male, Ullathorne evoked such "independent integrity" and articulated the radical potential of the Immaculate Conception doctrine rarely acknowledged by other nineteenth-century Catholics.[111] In his account, Mary's maternity is dominant over paternal lines and necessary to the incarnation. "Christ is the Son of David, . . . because He is the Son of Mary."[112]

Many Catholic writers drew on Mary's bodily intimacy with Jesus during pregnancy to defend the theological necessity of her absolute purity, and thus her Immaculate Conception. In a traditional formulation, apologists compared her to the Ark of the Covenant, arguing that God's requirements for the purity of the vessel that would contain him remained unchanged through the centuries. If the ark had elaborate requirements in order to create a pure accommodation for the divine presence, how could Mary's body, they asked, which also physically enclosed the real presence of God, have ever been "a slave to the devil" marked by original sin? While this argument was common enough, Ullathorne's version transcended the typical brief, abstract expressions of it found in other texts. Ullathorne showed a deep respect for, even a fascination with, motherhood. In one passage he wrote: "He was formed by the Holy Ghost of her flesh. And His blood, that saving blood which redeemed the world, was taken from her heart. And whilst the Godhead dwelt bodily in Him, He, for nine months, dwelt bodily in her. And all that time He breathed of her breath and lived of her life. All that time the stream which nourished the growth of life in Jesus flowed from the heart of Mary, and at each pulsation flowed back again and re-entered His Mother's heart, enriching her with His divinest spirit. How pregnant is that blood of His with sanctifying grace, one drop of which might have redeemed the world!"[113] Ullathorne dwelt lovingly on the physicality of pregnancy and the connection between the mother and her child. He indicated that an ontological change occurred in Mary because of the intimacy of her contact with Jesus during her pregnancy, making her sacramental reception of the divine unique in human history: "The sacraments spring from the Body of Christ, and that very Body is the greatest of the sacraments. But the Body of Christ sprang from Mary. Yet she receives the fruits of the sacraments before they are instituted, in a manner altogether pre-eminent."[114] Ullathorne placed more emphasis than his contemporaries on the physical origins of Jesus's flesh and blood out of Mary's, describing both a physical and spiritual union between them forged during her pregnancy.

Most significant, Ullathorne did not attempt to limit Mary's privileges and ascendency by making concessions or comparisons to patriarchal models. Ullathorne's Mary was not the generously blessed but subordinate and dependent figure that Rohner and Wissel described, but an active agent who presided over the unfolding of the gospel. "In short," he concluded, "the Immaculate Conception of Mary is a summary of all the truths of the Gospel, displays all the graces of her Son, strikes down the countless errors, and puts sin, and the author of sin, beneath her stainless feet."[115] While Ullathorne was considered the prime authority on the Immaculate Conception, and lines from his text were often cited in Catholic writings and sermons, no American Catholic apologists copied his striking descriptions of Mary's maternity or his unqualified affirmations of Mary's transcendence and power. Despite its potential, Ullathorne's *Immaculate Conception of the Mother of God* did not trigger alternative Catholic gender theorizing in the period. It was not until the end of the century that some Catholics, particularly female Catholic novelists, began exploring the liberatory potential for women in high Mariological claims.

IN PROTESTANT RESPONSES to the declaration, Mary was increasingly employed as an avatar of the Catholic faith. Even in moderate or theologically engaged Protestant responses to the declaration, Catholicism was often rhetorically feminized as the "religion of Mary." This was due, in part, to a desire to shore up a vision of a rigorous, masculine Christianity against fears of feminization within Protestant churches. American Catholics also deliberately strengthened the association of Mary with their religious identity. They drew on traditional Marian constructions to emphasize their Heavenly Mother's status as the emblem and patroness of the U.S. Catholic community in order to create unity among Catholics of disparate national origins; to bolster a vision of supernatural Marian intervention leading to the community's success in America despite ongoing persecution; to participate in the global Catholic community and support the exiled pope through shared devotionalism; and to partake in the spiritually vibrant devotional culture emerging around worldwide Marian apparitions.

However, despite the boost the Immaculate Conception declaration gave to the rhetorical use of Mary as a symbolic stand-in for Catholicism, Protestants ultimately remained ambivalent about ceding Mary's figure to this use. Their conflicting desires to retain Mary as an exemplar of Christian womanhood and to refute her veneration by Catholics (as well as their conflicting desires to use religious "high art," much of which was Marian, to legitimate class status and to reject the European Old World and its symbols as anti-American) led to deep, ongoing tensions. In the early decades of the twentieth century, Mary became unambiguously "Catholic," and was less available to Protestants as a source to eulogize maternity and typify transcendent womanhood. But in the mid- to late nineteenth century, Mary's traditional signification of maternity and her multivalence made her essential to both U.S. Protestants and Catholics coping with rapidly changing gender norms triggered by industrialization and the emergence of modern markets.

Thus, in the decades following the Immaculate Conception declaration, Mary grew increasingly pervasive in Protestant-produced visual and literary culture. This was due, in part, to Protestants' use of Mary to resolve their own debates about gender. Later, as the woman's movement gained prominence, the combination of Mary being maternal and highly powerful made her a site for the renegotiation of women's public agency. Catholics freely drew on Mary as both a religious figure and a model of idealized womanhood; however, as Catholics grew in number and Marian devotionalism was increasingly entrenched in Catholic religious life, Protestants had to disassociate Mary from Catholic theological claims in order to continue to use her imagery. One important step toward this disassociation was the writing of art critic Anna Jameson, who, in her book *Legends of the Madonna*, deliberately reclaimed Mary as a Protestant religious and cultural figure.

CHAPTER THREE

The WOMAN Highly Blessed

Marian Art and Anna Jameson's "Great Hope," 1850s–1870s

I wonder sometimes why it is that we so continually hear the phrase, "a virtuous woman," and scarcely ever that of a "virtuous man," except in poetry or from the pulpit.

—Anna Jameson, *Commonplace Book*

In August 1855, just a few months after warning of the imminent arrival of two "miraculous" statues of Mary in a sarcastic and pointedly nativist editorial, the *New York Daily Times* reported the inauguration of an actual Madonna and Child statue in a Manhattan Catholic church.[1] The installation of the life-size, colorful statue during a three-day celebration of the Immaculate Conception declaration at the Church of the Most Holy Redeemer warranted a full article, with a more respectful tone. However, the *Times* reporter speculated that the large audience at the ceremony, which included military companies, religious societies, and "heretics," was drawn by curiosity about whether "the rumor [is] true that one of the winking Madonnas said to have been recently imported here would make her *debut* on the occasion."[2] While the referent of "heretics" was not specified, the reporter was probably facetiously alluding to the presence of Protestants at a Catholic service. He acknowledged that the statues' "miraculous" nature was merely a rumor, albeit a rumor that captivated the public and drew a significant crowd.

The *Times'* coverage of the rumors and the installation shows that Marian art was both fascinating and alarming to its readership. The coverage also revealed and reinforced the connection between Marian art and the Immaculate Conception declaration, the inspiration for both the statues' "miracles" and the celebration at Most Holy Redeemer. (The editorial on "miraculous Madonnas" claimed that the statues winked and wept in response to the affirmation or denial of the Immaculate Conception dogma.) Newspapers and magazines perpetuated the "miraculous Madonnas" motif long after the coverage of the statues' alleged importation ceased. "The winking and nodding Madonnas have of late years become standing jokes in the newspapers of Christendom," explained a contributor to the *National Magazine*.[3] More than a decade later, a *New York Times* article suggested that a wooden bust of Shakespeare would protest charges of Germanic ancestry for the bard and might "like a winking Madonna . . . express its indignation in portentous frowns."[4] In such articles and asides, detractors derided Catholic willingness to embrace the supernatural in material forms: the trope of the "winking Madonna" signified Catholic credulity.

The press also propelled a broader identification of Catholics with Marian art. The *Times'* own editorials about the rumored statuary helped draw the crowds to the inauguration of Most Holy Redeemer's Madonna and Child statue that the paper then reported on. And after the widespread coverage of the Immaculate Conception proclamation ceremony, culminating with the coronation of a statue of Mary, the devotional role of Marian art was debated. The American press also devoted significant space to reporting on the Marian apparitions that were occurring in Europe. These often spurred medals, statues, or other visual depictions, which were sometimes also noted. Media stories like these perpetuated the association of Marian art with Catholic distinctiveness. They examined Marian art in Catholic devotional contexts: the "miraculous" statues were supposedly heading to Catholic churches in Baltimore and New York, while the Madonna and Child statue was installed in a Manhattan Catholic church. Because of their devotional purposes and religious context, the press presented these Marian artworks as spectacle. The Protestants who were said to have gathered at Most Holy Redeemer hoped to glimpse something—the miraculous, mass credulity, or simply idolatry.[5]

The press treated Marian art in nondevotional contexts quite differently. An article published in the same paper three years after the statue's installation at Most Holy Redeemer notified the public that an *Immaculate Conception* painting by the seventeenth-century Spanish painter Bartolomé Esteban Murillo would soon arrive in a New York City gallery.[6] The reporter encouraged readers to take advantage of this opportunity to see the painting and enthusiastically declared that Murillo's tribute to the Immaculate Conception would "elevate public taste." Theologically, Murillo's *Immaculate Conception* was just as tied to the suspect doctrine as the "miraculous" Marian statues, yet its arrival in New York City was heralded as an opportunity not to be missed.[7] While these articles also dealt with the importation of Marian art, their destinations were markedly different: the statues were heading to churches, while the painting was to be delivered to a Manhattan gallery.

Notices of the impending arrival of "Murillo's Celebrated Picture, The Conception" began to appear in January 1858. These notices praised the painting as a "wonderful picture" and "one of the finest works of the great Spanish Master."[8] The exhibit, which charged an admission of twenty-five cents, continued through March, with ongoing notices in the *Times*. The *Times* also ran a full-length article describing the painting's history and significance.[9] The author first lamented America's lack of artistic achievement (a common refrain in the period), and suggested that the "rising classes" could be transformed by exposure to high art or art reproductions. The arrival of Murillo's *Immaculate Conception* in the United States, he opined, showed an encouraging upturn in "public taste." He plainly categorized the painting as a work of high art rather than as an artifact of Catholic devotion. It "merits in every way the distinction thus accorded to it," he wrote, and is "unquestionably the finest original painting of its class ever brought to this country."[10] He described the painting in detail and encouraged readers, "for the sake of the poetic value of the picture alone," to "embrace this opportunity of teaching themselves a precious lesson."[11]

The "poetic value" and "precious lesson" were not, presumably, the dogma of the Immaculate Conception. Rather, the author commended the technical achievement of the painting and the value of the figure of the Virgin herself, whom he described as "refined," "spiritual," and "tender." Such spiritual and emotional engagement with the content of Marian art was not atypical for Protestants; art critics and other writers often commented on Mary's spirituality (or purity, or transcendence) and her womanly tenderness (or sympathy, or gentleness, or compassion) when describing paintings of her. Despite broad Protestant discomfort with the Immaculate Conception doctrine, the *Times'* writer recommended the painting to his readership in full awareness of its theological content, which he discussed cogently in the article. At no point did he deride the painting or its theological premise, although he did assume that his readers would be unfamiliar with the underlying theology.

The final mention of the exhibition came in March, when the painting's departure was noted with sadness, but the "good fortune" of the arrival of yet another Murillo was simultaneously announced. The new arrival was not named, but its location in a gallery on the East side of the city was specified. The contrast between the fawning coverage of Murillo's *Immaculate*

Bartolomé Esteban Murillo, *Immaculate Conception of Soult*. This is one of several paintings by Murillo referred to as "Assumptions" in the nineteenth century. Their status as "Assumptions" or "Immaculate Conceptions" was debated. From the Museo del Prado, Barcelona (Scala/Art Resource, New York).

Conception and the mocking and nativist coverage of the Madonna statues is striking. The artworks' media likely played a role, as American Protestants were often less censorious of religious painting than statuary (a traditional site of veneration).[12] The renown of the artist also influenced the coverage; Murillo and Raphael were among the most reproduced of the great masters. However, the primary factor that shaped Protestant reactions to Marian art was context, as another article about an *Immaculate Conception* painting demonstrates.

A few years after the exhibition of the Murillo paintings in New York, the Church of the Company of Jesus (*Iglesia de la Compañía de Jesús*) in Santiago, Chili, tragically burned, killing between two and three thousand people. *Harper's Weekly* ran a voyeuristic and demeaning article describing the accidental burning of the church.[13] The congregation had been holding a monthlong celebration of the anniversary of the Immaculate Conception declaration and many candles were lit in Mary's honor. The sanctuary was filled to capacity for the service, with thousands of women and few men (a detail the reporter emphasized, suggesting that he saw Marian devotionalism as a feminine practice). The reporter dwelled on a reproduction of Murillo's *Immaculate Conception*: "Over the altar was an image representing Murillo's Madonna of the Immaculate Conception, her feet resting upon a crescent, which, being illuminated became a crescent of fire . . . catching into a blaze the flimsy transparency above, and stretching upward toward the tinsel and gauze with which the roof was decorated, . . . till a sheet of flame surmounted the kneeling multitude below."[14] The author claimed that the attending priests selfishly locked themselves in a back room to "prevent escape in that direction—looking out for the safety of a few gewgaws of their own." According to the *New York Times*, the priests who were present for the service did escape, some carrying "treasures" with them, along with approximately five hundred others, before the exits became blocked by bodies. While the *Times* article was sensationalistic and showed anti-Catholic bias, the contention by the *Harper's* writer that the priests intentionally prevented escape revealed strong anticlericalism. He drew attention to Murillo's *Immaculate Conception*—glowing with fire and presiding over a scene of chaos, devastation, priestly hypocrisy, and homicidal cruelty—in order to discredit Marian devotionalism. By locating Mary above the tragedy, figuratively "watching" it unfold, he accentuated her powerlessness as a religious figure and the impotency of devotional art. This was a core iconoclastic theme: the idol cannot save. The contrast between these articles demonstrates how fully the context of Marian art shaped Protestant responses to it. That a reproduction of a Murillo was hung in a church rather than an urban art gallery signaled Roman Catholicism, Marian veneration, and the Immaculate Conception dogma rather than the elevation of public taste.

THE AMERICAN DESIRE to reclaim religious art and to use Marian art to transmit a female ideal was in tension with the increasing use of Marian imagery to signify Catholic identity. This could be neutral, as when the American Catholic hierarchy made the Virgin Mary as Our Lady of the Immaculate Conception patron saint of the United States, or derogatory, as when Protestants used "winking Madonnas" to mock Catholic credulity, but either way, Mary was increasingly viewed as an avatar of American Catholicism. Anna Jameson, author of several popular art histories and other books, helped resolve the dissonance created by these dual strands of response. She helped popularize Marian imagery in the United States by framing Mary as a potent symbol rather than as a religious actor. While Jameson did not ignore theology, she promoted Mary as an inspirational figure and an emblem of womanhood—traditional, Christian, yet decoupled from Catholic dogma. Her 1852 book *Legends of the Madonna* helped readers navigate the myriad images of Mary then available in European (and increasingly American) galleries, museums, books, and print catalogs. She gave her audience tools to categorize Marian subject matter; judge paintings' religious, moral, and aesthetic merits; and appear well informed. The latter was especially useful for the burgeoning class of Protestant Americans who were beginning to emphasize cultural literacy as an indicator of socioeconomic status and who sought to claim Old World art and music as part of their own cultural heritage.

Jameson's books fell out of favor precipitously in the early twentieth century. Modern scholars have generally overlooked her contributions to Victorian thought, art history, and early feminism. Yet she unquestionably popularized religious art in England and America, and with *Legends of the Madonna* played a key role in mitigating American Protestant iconoclasm and advancing Mary's figure as a symbolic site for reimagining womanhood, maternity, and domesticity. Her recommendations of specific artists (e.g., Raphael and Murillo) and compositions (e.g., Immaculate Conception and Queen of Heaven) directed Americans toward these subjects. At the same time, her clear preference for powerful and independent (rather than sentimental or domestic) scenes promoted the reinterpretation of Mary as a liberatory figure. Jameson's story and the story of the ascendency of religious and Marian art in the nineteenth century are deeply entwined.

Sacred and Legendary Art

Anna Jameson was a lifelong Anglican, born in Ireland and raised in Whitehaven, Cumberland. She traveled widely throughout Europe and Italy, and also lived for a time in the United States and Canada where her husband was chief justice of the province of Upper Canada. She published fifteen major books (including books on literature and poetry) as well as dozens of essays and lectures between 1826 and 1864, establishing herself as a popular art historian and intellectual. While some of her contemporaries—and later scholars—have underestimated the caliber and importance of her work, she achieved widespread esteem as an art expert and as an engaging and provocative speaker. During her life, she was one of a handful of pioneering female intellectuals and her sex was often noted in discussions of her work.

After her troubled marriage to Robert Jameson disintegrated in 1837, she left Canada and returned to London alone. She supported herself and her unmarried sisters through her writing and continued to do so after the death of her husband, who excluded her from his estate. Due to financial constraints, she continued to write and market her work late into her life. As a significant author, she received a government pension of a hundred pounds a year (a circumstance noted disparagingly in *Appletons' Journal*, which listed her among other well-known English "literary people" such as "Tennyson, Carleton the novelist, Southey, William Howitt" as enjoying a "royal bounty" unheard of in the United States, "this happy land of simple republicanism.")[15] The instability of her financial circumstances prompted her to write and speak on behalf of women's economic independence, including increased job opportunities for women and married women's property rights. In her later years, Jameson became a mentor and friend to a group of younger Englishwomen writers and reformers, and participated in the establishment of the reform-minded periodical *Englishwoman's Journal*. While she was not a suffragist, her success as a serious art critic, her advocacy for women's labor, and her association with the periodical positioned her as a high-profile member of the English woman's movement. Jameson spent the final years of her life traveling between England and Italy, where she was part of an expatriate community, "for which the Brownings provided one of the more constant cores and around whose edges swirled an ever fluctuating stream of British and Americans."[16]

Jameson's series of guides to religious art, *Sacred and Legendary Art*, comprised the two-volume *Sacred and Legendary Art* (1848) as well as *Legends of the Monastic Orders* (1850), *Legends of the Madonna* (1852), and *The History of Our Lord* (1864), published posthumously with additional work by Lady Elizabeth Eastlake. The series became a standard reference in art history and criticism, and *Legends of the Madonna* became the touchstone work on Marian art. The series remained popular from its first printing through the early decades of the twentieth century. *Legends of the Madonna* alone was reprinted thirty-nine times in ten editions from 1852 through 1904 in both England and the United States, and was reissued several times in subsequent years. Twenty-nine U.S. reprints were published in Boston and New York before 1904. This was especially impressive because the books' costliness, due to length and illustrations, was noted by fans and critics alike.

Despite its size and length, *Sacred and Legendary Art* became popularly associated with American tourists abroad. Henry James portrayed a character in his novel *The American* as hopeless and unsophisticated by depicting him encountering European art through the mediation of Jameson's books. Travel and art writing were enmeshed in this period before art history and art criticism fully emerged as separate genres.[17] In the volumes of *Sacred and Legendary Art*, Jameson occasionally fell back into the travel-writing style she had developed in her 1834 book *Sketches at Home and Abroad*, conversationally inviting the reader to imagine himself in a foreign art gallery surrounded by patrons. However, the *Sacred and Legendary Art* series was categorically different. In these books, Jameson grouped artwork thematically, not by geographical location or even period, and she provided historical, biographical, and theological contextualization of artwork. The originality of her approach was widely noted by reviewers. Even so, part of the appeal of the books was their vicarious experience of the larger world of European museums, art, and culture. The books were read and popularized in the context of an increasing market for both art and travel writing that was tied, in part, to hopes that class boundaries in America were permeable and that intellectual and aesthetic "correctness" held the key to developing an educated, cultured, and cosmopolitan public self or, at least, "improving" lower classes to prevent vice. While its Catholic context was problematic, great Western religious art had both class and moral implications. Jameson's books developed their reputation as travel guides precisely because she succeeded in framing religious art in a familiar (to English and American Protestants) cultural idiom that was both informed and religiously sensitive. The magazine *Crayon* highlighted these aspects of Jameson's appeal: "To be competent to travel is tantamount to the best of education. . . . To be truly educated 'to go to Europe,' is to be prepared to know something more of mankind than can be learned in the pages of poetry and romance. . . . As one of the best works, therefore, to assist the mind in such an education, as well as to lighten its labor by rendering it capable of enjoying Art, we have to recommend the work . . . *Sacred and Legendary Art*."[18] The reviewer went on to praise Jameson's competency and common sense: "The greatest lover of Art, like the greatest artist, is one whose range of feeling is the most comprehensive, and whose judgment is mingled with deference and charity. Such a person we conceive Mrs. Jameson to be. Of all writers on Art in these days, she seems to us to be one of the truest and most instructive; none have given us so full an idea of the relation of common sense to Art." The reviewer contrasted Jameson's "judgment," by which he meant both aesthetic and religious (theological) judgment, to her "deference and charity," allusions to the absence of anti-Catholic polemic in the book. He illustrated his point by quoting Jameson who, in *Legends of the Madonna,* cautioned against "narrow puritanical jealousy which holds the monuments of a real and earnest faith in contempt." By including that quotation, he implicitly noted, and allowed Jameson's words to deflect, the underlying issue of Protestants valuing and appropriating pre-Reformation (and, therefore, Catholic) religious art. The line was meant to shame Protestant iconoclasts and polemicists and to affirm Catholic faith as "real" and valuable despite theological difference. Whether read negatively, as James did, or positively, as this reviewer did, the books' success as travel guides stemmed from their thoroughness, readability, and above all, their conscious reclamation of religious art for contemporary tastes and spiritual needs. Despite Jameson's stated goal of "translation," she was scrupulous in her attempts to place works in their original theological and cultural contexts.

Jameson strove to represent Catholic history, theology, and devotionalism fairly in the series. She neither advanced Anglo-Catholicism's high Mariology (as a devotional stance) nor deferred to sectarian or iconoclastic criticism. Instead, she drew on her extensive research, her frequent travels to European museums and galleries, and her own theological reflection to create a distinctive *moral aesthetic*: a set of Christian yet nonsectarian standards for evaluating religious art that included technical skill, fidelity to Catholic tradition and biblical sources, and technical contribution to the progress of art; as well as more ephemeral criteria such as beauty, spiritual uplift, dignity, transcendence, nonmaterialism, and simplicity. These normative standards mixed art critical, art historical, theological, and subjective approaches, allowing sometimes arbitrary and didactic pronouncements to undermine her well-researched, critically engaged, and innovative writings. Despite its inconsistencies and limitations, her approach was widely embraced by Protestant readers because it enabled them to evaluate, appreciate, and be spiritually moved by religious and Marian art without betraying Protestant theological strictures.

Critics consistently acknowledged the need for this approach and its originality. An 1853 biographical article on Jameson and the body of her work praised her ability to contextualize art and bridge the Catholic-Protestant divide. The author quoted the same line from *Legends of the Madonna* that the *Crayon* reviewer cited about Jameson's avoidance of "narrow puritanical jealousy" and then continued: "In this field is finely displayed her remarkable critical prowess . . . her judicial temperateness, which so happily avoids whatever is captious. . . . Mrs. Jameson is no rash zealot in anything she handles—critical, theological, or aesthetical. Be it true or not, that that the way to Rome is through Geneva, she, at least, abides at a salubrious distance from both."[19] As these lines exemplified, Jameson was not read as an apologist for Catholic theology, but her ability to convey Catholic thought without interjecting Protestant criticism was widely recognized and valued. This evenhandedness contributed to her contemporaries' perception of her work as reliable and modern. For example, the famous art critic, collector, and newspaper editor James Jackson Jarves, who promoted Italian art in America and contributed the first major collection of Old Masters to an American museum (the 1871 sale of 119 Italian primitives to the Yale University Art Gallery), expressed admiration for Jameson's books. He was highly critical of most of art critics and historians, but of Jameson he wrote: "Mrs. Jameson's numerous volumes on the motives of Christian art, interestingly compiled from authentic sources, evince the purity of taste of their author, and an equal pietism while leaving their readers unbiassedly [sic] to form their own inferences."[20]

Similarly, a review of the 1861 edition of *Legends of the Madonna* in the *New Englander and Yale Review* judged that Jameson had "done a service for all true lovers of art, in the preparation of this book."[21] The reviewer continued:

> Copies of many of the most celebrated paintings of the Madonna are now everywhere common in this Protestant land. But what is the number of persons who remember that they grew slowly under the hands of men who never began their labors till they were rapt in the highest state of poetic and religious excitement! . . . Mrs. Jameson tells us that the idea which the mediaeval painters sought to develop in their representations of the Madonna was "an impersonation in the feminine character of beneficence, purity, and power, standing between an offended Deity and poor sinning and suffering humanity, and clothed in the visible form of Mary, the mother of our Lord." The conception was erroneous, to be sure; but, as a matter of fact, it prevailed through all the Christian and civilized world for nearly a thousand years. . . . Hence it is perfectly idle for any one to attempt to judge of these great works of art till he has in some measure learned to "comprehend the dominant idea lying behind and beyond the mere representation."[22]

Reminding readers that religious art developed in a Catholic devotional context, the reviewer praised Jameson for promoting understanding and overcoming distrust of religious art. Piety, he suggested, was to be commended, especially in regard to religious art. And despite the underlying "erroneous" theology, Marian art should be judged not by aesthetics, but by its success at achieving its original purpose, that is, transmitting a female ideal of "beneficence, purity, and power." These comments exemplify the consensus of most of her contemporaries. Some judged her to be too sympathetic toward Catholicism while others assumed that she must have been judiciously holding back a Protestant theological critique, but most commented approvingly on her thorough and respectful treatment of the theological basis of religious art.

Later scholars were more critical. As the genres of art criticism and art history developed, academic standards were formed, and trained (male) experts moved disciplines into the twentieth century, many dismissed Jameson's contribution. Despite her judicious treatment of religious art, Jameson's moral aesthetic led her occasionally to make highbrow dismissals of works of art. She was rooted in her own milieu and could fail to reflect critically on the criteria she employed. Her sometimes didactic tone led to her work's fall from favor in the early decades of the twentieth century. Others called her work derivative, like John Steegman, who wrote in 1950 that "she was rather a compiler than a thinker."[23] But in 1983, Adele Holcomb brought Jameson back into consideration in her article titled "Anna Jameson: The First Professional English Art Historian," in which she demonstrated that Jameson's research was careful and exhaustive, that she was the first English-speaking writer to catalog types, images, and themes used in conjunction with the Virgin Mary, and that she did not write about art in order to propose an "absolute and exclusive standard of excellence," or express nostalgia for the past like most of her peers.[24] Jameson, she noted, also frequently broke with other art critics, putting forth original analyses that contradicted established opinion and challenged details, including curator's labeling of subjects. Since Jameson published most of the *Sacred and Legendary Art* volumes before her contemporaries—including Ralph Waldo Emerson, John Ruskin, and Dante Gabriel Rossetti—published their major works on religion and art, it is clear that Jameson led the way in this conversation.[25]

In spite of her achievements and rigorous work, Jameson was self-effacing, expressly denying her competency and belittling the value of her scholarship in the introductions to her books and in public comments. Some of the criticism Jameson received, both during her lifetime and subsequently, stemmed from a literal acceptance of these disclaimers. For example, an 1864 article described her books as "elegant and instructive," but not serious scholarship: her "knowledge of the objective history of art," the author wrote, was neither "very accurate nor very profound."[26] In substantiating this charge, he cited Jameson herself: "To do her full justice, we will borrow one of her own elegant sentences to describe the part she wished to fill. The Introduction to the 'Sacred and Legendary Art,' concludes in the following words: 'Let none imagine that in placing before the uninitiated these unpretending volumes, I assume any such superiority as is here implied. Like a child that has sprung on a little way before its playmates, and caught a glimpse through an opening portal of some varied Eden within . . . runs back and catches its companions by the hand and hurries them forwards to share the new-found pleasure, . . . even so it is with me—I am on the outside, not the inside, of the door I open.' "[27] Jameson authored these lines in an attempt to deflect censure of her scholarship and of herself as a female scholar. However, in doing so, she cooperated with those who wanted to devalue her contribution.

Jameson discouraged serious engagement with her work through her use of an intentionally "female" voice in her writing. She reflected on this in a letter to a friend, noting that she had neglected to sufficiently feminize her writing style in an article she had written for the *Athenaeum* and "regretted 'assuming the masculine character.' "[28] She likely meant that she was too direct and forceful in giving her opinions in the essay, but the comment reveals that she was aware of and strategic about the role her sex played in the reception of her scholarly work. Her explicit and implicit strategies to avert sexist attacks may have helped the public accept her as a female intellectual; however, it also led critics and peers to underestimate the significance of her work. Whatever her public tone, she was not unsure about her intellectual rigor or the merit of her work. In her private correspondence, she revealed a deep desire for recognition and an awareness of the perilous path she trod as a female intellectual.

Jameson's Religious Thought

Jameson acknowledged that she found *Legends of the Madonna* particularly difficult to write. She aimed to treat Catholic Marian theology thoroughly and respectfully, and to win sympathy for Marian themes in art without alienating her Protestant audience. "It is selling very well," Jameson wrote to her close friend Ottilie von Goethe, "but I suppose neither Protestants nor Catholics will approve."[29] In the preface, Jameson asked readers for sympathetic understanding: "With regard to a point of infinitely greater importance, I may be allowed to plead—that it has been impossible to treat of the representations of the Blessed Virgin without touching on doctrines such as constitute the principal differences between the creeds of Christendom. . . . Not for worlds would I be guilty of a scoffing allusion to any belief or any object held sacred by sincere and earnest hearts; but neither has it been possible for me to write in a tone of acquiescence, where I altogether differ in feeling and opinion. On this point I shall need, and feel sure that I shall obtain, the generous construction of readers of all persuasions."[30] Jameson's plea for forbearance was surprisingly direct. In Britain, where Jameson wrote *Legends of the Madonna*, both Roman and Anglo-Catholic interest in Mary was increasing, intensifying Reformists' and Low Anglicans' alienation from her. An English Catholic journal, the *Rambler*, connected the increase in Marian devotion to the growth and success of Roman Catholicism in England. After cataloging growth in both numbers and fervor, the editor asked: "Who could have foreseen some twenty years ago that the devotion to our Blessed Lady would have extended and intensified itself in the Catholic community of this country in the way and to the degree that we have lived to witness?"[31] He commented that Marian devotion in England had previously been curtailed "from deference to Protestants"—for example, by omitting the Litany of Loretto from prayer books—but was now unabashedly practiced. One must wonder, he wrote, "at the present frequency, publicity, and universality of her invocation."[32] Mary was pivotal for the politics of Christian identity in midcentury England. High Church Anglicans like Keble and Newman heightened Mary's importance through their writings and sermons, while anti-Tractarians resisted her as a symbol of Anglo- and Roman Catholicism. Some historians have put Mary at the center of British anti-Catholicism, like one who wrote: "British Victorians consider[ed] Mary the personification of all that was most alien and monstrous in Roman Catholicism."[33] However, Tricia Lootens, in *Lost Saints*, demonstrates that there was a more complex dynamic of attraction and rejection of Mary among Britons, concluding that "there was nothing simple about nineteenth-century English fascination with and resistance to veneration for the Mother of God."[34]

Writing *Legends of the Madonna* as an Anglican to a transatlantic, primarily Protestant audience in this context was fraught. By asking for forbearance toward Catholic Marian theology and by admitting her own engagement with Mary as a spiritual figure, she acted boldly; and, as her livelihood depended entirely on her writing, she took a considerable risk. Jameson never departed from her Anglican upbringing and considered herself a member in good standing of the Church throughout her life. However, in the few brief religious reflections she recorded, she distanced herself from Anglican orthodoxy and reconceived various doctrines into abstracted spiritual tenets that harmonized with her personal values. This flexible, nondoctrinaire approach underlay the evenhanded treatment of religion that was apparent in her books. In her 1854 *Commonplace Book*, a compendium of thoughts, quotations, and autobiographical material, she included a brief account of her childhood religious instruction in which she clearly distinguished the religion that she was taught from the religion that "was growing up" in her heart. She declared the former to have been an "indoctrination" given through the medium of "creeds and catechisms" and the "*letter* of the Scriptures," while the latter was a "sentiment of faith and adoration."[35] "Taught religion," was extraneous, but heartfelt faith, which she associated with her mother, prayer, beauty, and goodness, was more deeply rooted. Jameson called the standard religious instruction of her childhood confusing and claimed that she was "truly heterodox" in her youth.[36] In other writings,

Jameson put forth a theological vision of the autonomous individual responding freely to a loving God. Religion, in her view, harmonized the individual's ethical convictions and life experiences with supernatural reality; true religion should not require uneasy acquiescence to doctrines or self-negation. This perspective prompted her to renounce dogmatism and cultivate respect for, as she put it, "any belief or any object held sacred by sincere and earnest hearts," an important aspect of her scholarly work.[37]

According to Jameson, human spiritual needs mirrored the divine reality they echoed; that is, humans crave the God that *is*. Religion was, she wrote, "the comprehension and acknowledgement of an unseen spiritual power and the soul's allegiance to it."[38] Most religious striving, even heterodox, was motivated by legitimate spiritual longings and approximated, however poorly, the reality of God. The existence of a good God and Savior Christ were, therefore, corollaries of the persistent needs and hopes of humanity. Likewise, some form of the feminine divine was also necessitated by intrinsic human longings. With regard to this need, and its satisfaction in the figure of Mary, she wrote: "Everywhere it [Mary] seems to have found in the human heart some deep sympathy, deeper far than mere theological doctrine could reach—ready to accept it; and in every land the ground prepared for it in some already dominant idea of a mother-Goddess, chaste, beautiful, and benign."[39] If the human heart longed for a feminine form in religion and the equal realization of the feminine in the supernatural realm, then, she argued, there must be a reciprocal feminine aspect to the divine. Divinity must reflect the human balance of masculine and feminine, or more accurately, humanity's duality must mirror a more complete and integrated divine reality.

Jameson described pagan goddesses as prefiguring Mary. She explained that "these scattered, dim, mistaken—often gross and perverted—ideas which were afterwards gathered into the pure, dignified, tender image of the Madonna, were but as the voice of a mighty prophecy, sounded through all the generations of men, even from the beginning of time."[40] The collective cry for a feminine aspect of the divine must reflect some supernatural reality. Mary, in Jameson's view, was an expression of this spiritual longing and its concomitant spiritual reality. Whether theological claims made about Mary were literally accurate or not, there was something true, on a deeper level, about Marian claims.

Jameson's enthusiasm for sacred art and music, the symbolic utility of the saints, and the value of tradition, led to speculation that she was sympathetic to the Oxford movement. And a close reading of *Legends of the Madonna* reveals that despite her promise to distance herself from Catholic doctrines in the introduction, she rarely followed through in the text. Instead, she gave either sympathetic or dispassionate, but in either case fair, accounts of Catholic Marian theology, without inserting Protestant counterclaims or critiques. Despite the speculation her apparent sympathy toward Catholicism generated, Jameson carefully distanced herself from the Oxford movement. In her *Commonplace Book*, published the year after *Legends of the Madonna*, she deliberately constructed a public identity as a broad-minded, non-Tractarian Episcopalian. In it, she responded to unnamed critics who suspected her of Anglo- or Roman Catholic leanings. The book contains her most direct and candid statements about Roman Catholicism, but also her most critical. Perhaps because she was writing with her critics in mind, the book is more censorious of Roman Catholicism than her personal correspondence.

Early in the *Commonplace Book*, Jameson quoted St. Thomas's *Discourses on St. Paul's Epistle to the Corinthians*: "The Christian religion was, in fact, a charter of freedom to the whole human race."[41] Ironically, Jameson used this quotation from a Roman Catholic theologian to denounce his faith. The quotation, she wrote, represented "the true Catholic spirit—the spirit and the teaching of Paul—in contradistinction to the Roman Catholic spirit, the spirit and tendency of Peter, which stands upon forms, which has no respect for individualism except in so far as it can imprison this individuality within a creed, or use it to a purpose."[42] Thus, she asserted her distance from Roman Catholicism at the outset of the book. Of the many culturally salient critiques of Catholicism then popular, Jameson chose to emphasize Protestant individuality and freedom over Catholic conformity, forms, and creeds. This was a typical setup, but one that particularly resonated with her own theological priorities.

In another reflection on Catholicism in the book, Jameson recounted a conversation with a friend regarding the conversions of mutual acquaintances to Roman Catholicism. Jameson approvingly quoted her friend's comment that "the peace and comfort which they had sought and found in that mode of faith was like the drugged sleep in comparison with the natural sleep: necessary, healing perhaps, where there is disease and unrest, not otherwise."[43] In the context of the period's virulent anti-Papism, this quotation revealed Jameson's willingness to consider Roman Catholicism a legitimate expression of Christian faith. However, her patronizing tone also exposed the limits of her sympathies.

In her personal correspondence, Jameson displayed a more nuanced and conflicted attitude toward Roman Catholicism. She admitted that she saw the Catholic faith as regressive and antimodern, but also as a repository of beauty, powerful symbolism, and high ideals that could potentially remedy the spiritual maladies of her age. In a letter to Lady Byron in 1847, Jameson wrote: "It is in Rome that one can best understand how people have become Roman Catholics, but of all places in the world it is the place where one is least tempted to turn Roman Catholic."[44] Her historical and theological research and her travels in Italy created an objective distance from, as well as a deep attraction and affinity with, her subject. In her letter to Lady Byron, Jameson further explored these contradictory feelings: "The study of art, by enabling me to trace all the steps by which imaginations became representations and allegories and symbols became facts, lays bare a good deal of the construction of this religion—I see how certain things have been built up in men's belief—and while I am farther than ever before in my life, from all capability of entering into this belief, I have more and more sympathy with its effects—more and more comprehension of its past and present power—a deeper and deeper conviction that this power must, like the ancient mythology merge into poetry—You will see this, I think, all thro the book I am now writing—it may—if I succeed, do something for the cause of true art—but certainly it will not aid the cause of superstition."[45] Jameson wrote this letter as she was finishing the first volume of *Sacred and Legendary Art*, but the passage explicated the underlying methodology of the series as a whole. Her distinction between the forms of religion and the reality of faith is also evident here. Jameson felt herself too pragmatic and independent to desire a "papist" worship experience, but her private spiritual life included some abstracted and idealized Catholic forms. She hoped her writings would elevate public taste and regenerate culture by providing a transformative set of ideals and symbols. However, in order for Catholic forms to be useful, they had to be transformed, as she put it, into "poetry"—that is, to be made transcendent, abstracted, deinstitutionalized, and nondogmatic.

Jameson was not a Tractarian, and did not advocate Marian veneration within the Anglican Church, yet she made Mary central to her literary project and personal spirituality. The Oxford movement brought a literal reinstitution of Catholic ideals and symbols into the Anglican Church; Jameson was not interested in that goal. The utility of Catholic forms, she believed, came not from their reinstatement, but from their secularization. As with "ancient mythology," the divorce of Catholic forms from actual belief and worship would free them to meet the needs of contemporary culture. In Roman Catholicism, Jameson sought a usable past, not a present faith. And, like many of her generation, she also sought authenticity.

Jameson explained her marked preference for medieval over later Renaissance art in terms of immediacy of experience. In doing so, she participated in the spirit of the Oxford movement, as well as the broader "nostalgic medievalism" of the time, while rejecting its institutional forms.[46] Unlike the leaders of Anglo-Catholicism, her affinity for Catholic art, music, and theology did not lead her to hope for their reincorporation as religious experiences; instead, she mined them for images, meanings, and symbols that she offered up to society in diffuse and palatable forms.

"The WOMAN Highly Blessed"

For Jameson, the Madonna was one of the most fruitful and personally resonant of these Catholic symbols. "In spite of errors, exaggerations, abuses," she wrote, "this worship [of Mary] did comprehend certain great elemental truths interwoven with our human nature." This was a bold statement, especially for her Protestant readers. It affirmed that Roman Catholicism contained, in its extrabiblical tradition and worship, important elemental, human truths. Jameson proceeded to declare these truths to be "involved perhaps with our future destinies."[47] Mary was not, in her view, an expression of a past, retrograde faith, as many of the Immaculate Conception critics declared, but a forward-looking solution to social problems.

When she detailed her vision for humanity's "future destines," she connected them explicitly to woman's inclusion and social contribution. "The coming regeneration," she wrote, the "complete and harmonious development of the whole human race," was inextricably tied to "the establishment, on a higher basis, of what has been called the 'feminine element' in society."[48] By "higher basis," Jameson referred to a spiritual reality. The feminine element in society, she argued, must be reflected, upheld, and elevated by a feminine spirituality; religion must reflect the gendered duality of humankind in order for society to flourish. Mary, Jameson concluded, cleansed of the inappropriate Catholic dogma that bound her, could become a catalyst for the progress of civilization.

"And let me at least speak for myself," Jameson concluded. "In the perpetual iteration of that beautiful image THE WOMAN highly blessed— *there*, where others saw only pictures or statues, I have seen this great hope standing like a spirit beside the visible form; in the fervent worship once universally given to that gracious presence, I have beheld an acknowledgement of a higher as well as gentler power than that of the strong hand and the might that makes the right—and in every earnest votary, one who, as he knelt, was in this sense 'pious beyond the reach of his own thought,' and 'devout beyond the meaning of his will.' "[49] In this passage, Jameson made her most daring and most personal claims for the Madonna. Mary was not merely a historical figure to Jameson, nor a devotional one; Mary was the "great hope," the counterforce to the masculine in society. Mary's votaries inadvertently participated in the larger project of honoring the feminine by passing down the symbol of the "woman highly blessed" to future generations. Though Jameson dismissed the theological validity of their faith, she affirmed their piety as a meaningful affirmation of a transcendent and salvific female ideal. Her willingness to treat the longings of her own heart as legitimate spiritual needs, needs which must necessarily be met by a loving God, freed her to move beyond dogmatism and affirm the longings of other "earnest hearts." Jameson entwined her feminism, spirituality, and social thought in this reinterpretation of the Madonna.

However, Mary was not herself a literal divinity in Jameson's view, but a powerful and inspiring symbol of the feminine component of the divine. Because she tied religious legitimacy to persistent human desire, she had to account for the growth in Marian veneration and proliferation of Marian imagery over time. In the introduction to *Legends of the Madonna*, she explained: "Christ, as the model man, united the virtues of the two sexes, till the idea that there are essentially masculine and feminine virtues intruded itself on the higher Christian conception, and seems to have necessitated the female type."[50] Jameson argued that Marian veneration was not inherent in Christianity, but developed in response to new spiritual needs, but this did not mean that it was illegitimate. Before the separation of virtue into masculine and feminine expectations, she contended, Christ sufficiently represented both genders and all virtue. After Christ was masculinized and particular virtues became associated or disassociated with men, a need for the feminine element grew. This need, she believed, led to the proliferation of Marian imagery and devotion, which revealed the spiritual reality of the feminine aspect of the divine. "I firmly believe," she wrote in the *Commonplace Book*, "that as the influences of religion are extended, and as civilization advances, those qualities which are now admired as essentially *feminine* will be considered as essentially *human*."[51]

While maintaining that Marian virtues should be emulated by both sexes, Jameson affirmed that Marian devotion was particularly important to women. Compared to other civilizations and religions, she claimed, Christianity had elevated the dignity of womanhood by creating a civil society where women were honored and protected. In her view, Mary was integral to this achievement. Unlike some other leaders of the woman's movement, such as Elizabeth Cady Stanton who contended that Mary's status and characteristics did not elevate the position of women in Christian societies, Jameson posited that Mary had supported women's ongoing struggle for dignity and justice.[52] God, she explained, following Augustine, had ensured that Christ was born of a woman in order to give hope to women as well as men, "Christ . . . was born of a woman only, and had no earthly father, that neither sex might despair; 'for had he been born a man . . . yet not born of woman, the women might have despaired of themselves.'"[53] Jameson maintained that failure to honor Mary ultimately frustrated God's intention of bringing women, through a female actor, into the divine mystery of salvation. To ignore Mary's contribution to the Gospel story left women in "despair." Neither sex, she reminded her readers, "shall be base before God." Jameson thus positioned her history of Marian art not merely as an aid to understanding the Western art tradition but as an attempt to make Marian iconography spiritually relevant to non-Catholics.

Marian Types and Characteristics

The story of the Magi was particularly important to Jameson because she saw it as an acknowledgment by representatives of non-Christian cultures of the ascendance of Christianity in the form of a woman and a child. She contrasted the "savage lands" from which the Magi came, where "innocence had never been accounted sacred, where society had as yet taken no heed of the defenceless woman, no care for the helpless Child; where one was enslaved, and the other perverted," with the dawning Christian society where "righteousness prevail[s] over deceit, and gentleness with wisdom reign for ever and ever!"[54] The Magi, she wrote, were "called up to worship the promise of that brighter future . . . under the form of womanhood and childhood." Jameson described their visit as initiating a period of Christian progress; however, she maintained, the full implication of the narrative had not yet been realized. The true elevation of women and children was "reserved for other times, when the whole mission of that Divine Child should be better understood then it was then, or is *now*."[55] In those last three words, Jameson critiqued her own time and place for failing to esteem womanhood highly enough. The Magi's reverence of Mary began a cultural transformation, Jameson argued, and continuing to revere the female in the form of Mary continued this work and remained integral to its fulfillment.

Jameson argued that Mary rose to prominence in Christianity because she represented abstracted, idealized womanhood, not because she served a crucial theological role. The transcendent, powerful, abstracted images Jameson categorized as "Devotional Subjects" conveyed the strength and dignity toward which women could strive; while the ordinary, domestic, naturalistic images categorized under "Historical Subjects" conveyed Mary's connection with ordinary women. Jameson needed Mary to be both a heroine and a sister to women. Yet even though Jameson praised both types of images, she especially valued "high" images of Mary, such as the Immaculate Conception, the Misericordia (in which Mary is portrayed "as patroness and protectress . . . who stands with outstretched arms, crowned with a diadem . . . her ample robe, extended on each side . . . while under its protecting folds are gathered worshippers and votaries of all ranks and ages"), and the Heavenly Queen.[56] When reflecting on what she termed the "divinization of Mary" in the Middle Ages, Jameson neither endorsed nor condemned the development. She argued that in the Middle Ages, the "theological type," that is, attributes borrowed from Mary's soteriological role, came to overshadow the scriptural and moral types, attributes that described her humanity.[57] Jameson called this theological type of Mary "very beautiful and exalted."

The specific traits Jameson praised in Marian art held constant between devotional and historical subjects. Whatever the category, Jameson admired renderings of Mary that showed strength, depth, and Christian virtue, those that she described variously as dignified, chaste, noble, tender, mild, intellectual, active, gentle, powerful, strong, humble, prophetic, human, divine, knowing, sad, and peaceful. She repeatedly faulted acclaimed works for portraying Mary too weakly or too passively. For instance, Michelangelo's *Virgin* failed to meet her standard because though "grand in form," she was "too passive . . . She looks down and seems to shrink."[58] Jameson sought out works that portrayed an active, dignified, self-possessed Madonna. She lamented that the "majestic ideal of womanhood" realized in Marian art from antiquity to the Middle Ages had been reduced in the post-Raphaelite period to "merely innate prettiness, or rustic, or even meretricious grace."[59]

Piero della Francesca, *Madonna della Misericordia*. One of several Misericordias praised by Jameson. An ink sketch of this painting appeared in Jameson's *Legends of the Madonna*, 30. From the Pinacoteca Comunale of Sansepolcro, Tuscany (Scala/Art Resource, New York).

She also condemned images of Mary that emphasized physical beauty, those that she called long-limbed, studied, inflated, tawdry, bashful, and meretricious; as well as those that portrayed Mary as stern, dogmatic, passive, undignified, weak, fearful, excessively young, or emotional.

Jameson embraced what she saw as the elevation of Mary in the development of the doctrine of the Immaculate Conception. She expounded on the doctrine, attributing its development to a larger, gradual transformation of Mary's "tender woman's wisdom" into "supernatural gifts." "And thus," she explained, "step by step the woman was transmuted into divinity."[60] She refrained from interjecting a theological counterargument. Instead, she wrote: "How . . . [precious] to him [Christ] was that temple, that tabernacle built by no human hands, in which he had condescended to dwell . . . Such was the reasoning of our forefathers; and, the premises granted, who shall call it illogical or irreverent."[61] Quickly sidestepping polemic by admitting different "premises," Jameson evaded Protestant criticism of the doctrine, asserting its basic logic and reverence. She also subtly bridged the Catholic-Protestant divide by reminding Protestant readers of their debt to Christian history—Catholic teachings were the beliefs of "our forefathers." By her choice of words, she revealed that she approved of the transformation—not necessarily of Mary into divinity, but of "the woman" into divinity. She attributed the elevation of Mary to her inherent feminine gifts. Mary's "tender woman's wisdom," a trait that she shared with other women, led votaries to ascribe supernatural qualities to her. By honoring her, her devout honored the essence of womanhood—and, by extension, all women. This line of reasoning brought Jameson's argument full circle: the exalted "theological type" of Mary affirmed the fundamental worth of ordinary women.

Along with her stated preference for more independent and powerful representations of Mary, Jameson admitted her particular affinity for Mary as Queen of Heaven. In the preface to *Legends of the Madonna*, Jameson praised the paintings of the medieval artists who brought to life Dante's vision of Mary as Queen of Heaven, calling their successes not merely aesthetic, but both religious and poetic triumphs:

> In the Paradiso of Dante, the glorification of Mary, as the "Mystic Rose" and Queen of Heaven—with the attendant angels, circle within circle, floating round her in adoration, and singing the Regina Coeli, and saints and patriarchs stretching forth their hands towards her—is all a splendid, but still indefinite vision of dazzling light crossed by shadowy forms.

The painters of the fourteenth century, in translating these glories into a definite shape, had to deal with imperfect knowledge and imperfect means; . . . and yet—thanks to the divine poet!—that early conception of some of the most beautiful of the Madonna subjects—for instance, the Coronation . . . has never, as a religious and poetical conception, been surpassed by later artists.[62]

In Jameson's exultant description, Mary, as Queen of Heaven, formed the center of an adoring group of men and angels. And Mary's Coronation was, in Jameson's estimation, among "the most beautiful of the Madonna subjects."

In another passage, Jameson eulogized the seventh-century "Greek type" of Mary, "most sacred Queen and Mother, Virgin of Virgins," writing: "The form under which we find this grand and mysterious idea of glorified womanhood originally embodied, is wonderfully majestic and simple. A female figure of colossal dimensions, far exceeding in proportion all the attendant personages and accessories, stands immediately beneath some figure or emblem representing almighty power."[63] The queenly Mary that Jameson celebrated was a powerful representation of the female ideal. Her "colossal dimensions" and right to rule, sanctioned by a symbol of "almighty power," presented an inspiring vision of womanhood that was decidedly not domestic, sentimental, or maternal. She describes several artworks that fit her ideal, beginning with the oldest, the mosaic of Mary from the Chapel at San Venanzio, whose hands are uplifted in prayer and who wears a clerical pallium.[64] Jameson did not attempt to mitigate the high Mariology of these paintings, but clearly relished the transcendent, powerful, and queenly vision of womanhood expressed through Mary.

Jameson most clearly expressed her desire for Mary to represent the feminine divine when she enumerated her criteria for a successful Marian painting, writing that "the Church, from early times, had assigned to her, the supernatural endowments which lifted her above angels and men; all these were to be combined into one glorious type of perfection." After this statement, she asked: "Where shall we seek this highest, holiest impersonation? Where has it been attained, or even approached?" Jameson did not defend why this should be an appropriate rubric for Protestants to employ, although she implied that works of art should be judged by the achievement of their original intention. Instead, she enumerated reasons that Marian art failed, paintings where the ideal Mary could not be found: "Not, certainly, in [images of] the mere woman, nor yet in the mere idol; not in those lovely

Cimabue, *Madonna of the Holy Trinity*. One of the paintings Jameson described as "noble enthroned Madonnas which represent the Virgin as queen of heaven and of angels." An ink sketch of this painting appeared in Jameson's *Legends of the Madonna*, 65. From the Church of the Trinity, Florence (Scala/Ministero per i Beni e la Attività culturali/Art Resource, New York).

creations which awaken a sympathetic throb of tenderness; nor in those stern, motionless types, which embody a dogma; not in the classic features of marble goddesses, borrowed as models; nor in the painted images which stare upon us from tawdry altars in flaxen wigs and embroidered petti-coats. But where?"[65] Here, Jameson argued that "we"—that is, she and her readers—must seek and approve of Marian art that attained the full Catholic type of Mary, including the "theological type." Her lofty language, how-ever, revealed that Marian art that achieved a "glorious type of perfection" was important to her not only because it was faithful to its creator's theo-logical context, but because it had the socially transformative power she described earlier. Jameson approved of paintings that represented high Catholic Mariology because they resonated with her own goals of propagat-ing images of Mary that could be reinterpreted as representing the feminine aspect of the divine.

Jameson identified Raphael's *Sistine Madonna* as the most complete real-ization of her Marian ideal. In describing the painting, she emphasized its depiction of Mary's spiritual power: "There she stands—the transfigured woman, at once completely human and completely divine, an abstraction of power, purity, and love, posed on the empurpled air, and requiring no other support; looking out, with her melancholy, loving mouth, her slightly di-lated, sibylline eyes, quite through the universe to the end and consumma-tion of all things."[66] Jameson's ideal Mary was not at all domestic, but an elevated, "transfigured woman," almost Christlike with full divinity and full humanity, literally floating in space. Jameson called her an "abstraction," an ideal representation of female power, female purity, and female love—elements that, she contended, society needed. Jameson's claim that the fem-inine divine was crucial to humanity's future was echoed in her interpretation of the painting: Mary saw "through the universe to the end and consumma-tion of all things." In her vision, abstracted womanhood was a benign and powerful element that existed over and above the earth, seeing the universe through to its telos.

Significantly, when describing the *Sistine Madonna*, Jameson did not re-mark on Mary's maternity. The painting depicts Mary holding the infant Christ, but Jameson's commentary omitted references to Jesus or mother-hood. Instead, she emphasized the painting's realization of Mary's qualities of independence, transcendence, and spiritual vision. She did not exclude maternity from her conception of the Virgin and discussed it in passages throughout the book, but it was not central to her Marian ideal.

In her *Commonplace Book,* she also acknowledged the importance of maternity in conceptualizing Mary. However, unlike many of her peers who characterized motherhood in terms of suffering, self-sacrifice, and devotion, Jameson tied motherhood to strength: "When we place before us the highest type of manhood, as exemplified in Christ, we do not imagine him as the father, but as the son; and if we think of the most perfect type of womanhood, we never can exclude the mother."[67] In this account, Mary's idealization of womanhood was deeply linked to her maternity. However, by paralleling Mary's motherhood with Jesus's sonship, she provocatively associated the female ideal with parental authority, while the masculine ideal was associated with reverent submission.

In her discussion of Holy Family paintings, which depict Mary with Jesus and Joseph, Jameson also sought a prominent, active role for Mary. She contended that Joseph was altogether out of place in theological art and that his introduction into representations of the Madonna and Child "could not possibly have occurred before the end of the sixteenth, or the beginning of the seventeenth century."[68] Jameson derided the religious art of the postmedieval period and considered Joseph's presence unseemly, adding dryly that "the introduction of Joseph rather complicates the idea." It clearly complicated her own goals in reclaiming and promoting Marian art. In historical scenes of the Holy Family, however, Jameson allowed that "his presence is natural and necessary." However, she maintained that Joseph always must be subordinate to Mary. In her view, he could be depicted engaged in work, but he should never be the prime actor in the scene. So, for example, she criticized Joseph's prominence in the famous painting *Le Raboteur* by Annibale Caracci: "It represents Joseph planing a board, while Jesus, a lovely boy about six or seven years old, stands by, watching the progress of his work. Mary is seated on one side, plying her needle. The great fault of this picture is the subordinate and utterly commonplace character given to the Virgin-mother: otherwise, it is a very suggestive and dramatic subject."[69] Jameson required Mary's spiritual primacy—a theological premise—to be apparent in depictions of historical scenes. Since she was generally very careful to distinguish between the two types of religious art, it was unclear (perhaps deliberately so) whether her requirement for Mary's primacy over Joseph was supposed to represent their relative spiritual status symbolically or represent their earthly relationship literally.

Jameson must have been aware of the symbolic import of such images. Since, for many Christians, the Holy Family was a model for family life,

Raphael, *The Marriage of the Virgin*. A stone etching of this painting, which Jameson described as one "everyone knows," appeared in her *Legends of the Madonna*. She praised its youthful depiction of Joseph and the lily that bloomed on his staff in Mary's presence, 161. From the Pinacoteca di Brera, Milan (Scala/Art Resource, New York).

Jameson's preference for paintings that depicted Joseph as subordinate to Mary implicitly challenged female submission in marriage. Only in Holy Family paintings could she insist on the primacy of the wife over the husband without hesitation or apology, and yet these images were uniquely influential in modeling normative marital relations. Even Catholic theologians with high Mariological commitments held that Mary would have demonstrated humility and submission not just to God but also to her husband. Jameson, however, did not acknowledge or expound on the implications of her requirement that Joseph be subordinate to Mary in naturalistic, domestic scenes.

Such ambiguity was typical of Jameson. She often put forth radical claims in subtle and obscure ways and used abstract rather than concrete language that allowed for varying interpretations. She advocated for the expansion of women's rights while simultaneously trying to minimize the potential for her words to inspire radical positions. In her "Statement on the Position of Women," Jameson strongly supported equal legal rights for women, writing: "I believe that the gospel of Christ recognizes mankind, male and female, as one body, one church, both sexes being *equally* rational beings with improvable faculties, *equally* responsible for the use or abuse of the faculties entrusted to them, *equally free*, to choose the good and refuse the evil, equally destined to an equal immortality; and I insist that any human and social laws which are *not* founded in the recognition of this primary law, are and must be false in the general principle, and in the particular application and in result, equally injurious to both sexes."[70] However, despite explicitly rejecting any social law that discriminated against the equality of women, she opposed woman suffrage. Further on in her "Statement," she argued for a separate spheres model of gender norms and against the participation of women in civil government: "The natural and Christian principles of the moral equality and freedom of the two sexes being fully recognized, I insist that the ordering of domestic life is our [women's] sacred province indissolubly linked with the privileges, pleasures and duties of maternity, and that the exclusive management of the executive affairs of the community at large belongs to men as the natural result of their exemption from the infirmities and duties which maternity entails on the female part of the human race."[71] Lest her use of maternity as the criteria by which women should be barred from civil roles exempt nonmothers (like herself), she extended the argument: "And by maternity I do not mean the actual state of motherhood—which is not necessary nor universal—but the maternal organization, common to all women." While some of her contemporaries in the early woman's movement were beginning to make maternalist arguments, grounding their calls *for* woman's participation in public life on their common maternity and the ethical perspective it developed, Jameson made motherhood the obstacle. In this "Statement" and in her other writings, she argued forcefully against the existence of "male and female virtues" and for equal rights before the law on the basis of common humanity, common aptitude, and common intellectual potential, only to then dismiss the real-world implications of these claims. Perhaps her keen awareness of her public image, her need to continue publishing her writing, and her desire for respectability as a moderate intellectual warred with her desire to advocate for women.

IN ONE OF HER many asides, Jameson called Mary "the chosen vessel of redemption, and the personification of all female loveliness, all female excellence, all wisdom, and all purity."[72] Jameson envisioned Mary as the "great hope" for women and for society. By "translating" Mary into an accessible spiritual symbol for Protestants, she hoped to create a powerful female ideal that could transform cultural expectations for women. Yet she located that hope in the future, after Christian spirituality had shifted through the reincorporation of Mary and the degendering of Christian virtue. In some ways, she succeeded in achieving her goals: *Legends of the Madonna*'s lively writing, accessible scholarship, and religious objectivity led to its great popularity—and with it, the broad distribution of Jameson's standards for correct and successful Marian art. Her books were routinely cited in discussions of religious art, and her standards often went unchallenged. It may be possible that Madonna and Child paintings would have grown popular in these years without the stimulus of her books due to their ability to represent sentimentalized motherhood, growing interest in the Western art heritage, and renewed interest in Mary triggered by the Immaculate Conception declaration and global Marian apparitions. However, it is unquestionable that Jameson played a key role in popularizing solitary images of Mary and steering English and American publics toward stronger, theologically higher Marian subjects. She especially popularized Immaculate Conception and Queen of Heaven images—motifs that were theologically untenable for Protestants and did not support a sentimental maternal ideal. For a few decades after the publication of *Legends of the Madonna*, nearly every article about Marian art quoted Jameson's descriptions and analyses as authoritative. One representative example, an 1882 magazine series on "Christianity

Hans Holbein the Younger, *Madonna des Buergermeisters Meyer*. A stone etching of this painting appeared in Jameson's *Legends of the Madonna*. Jameson commented that "in purity, dignity, humility, and intellectual grace, this exquisite Madonna has never been surpassed, not even by Raphael; the face, once seen, haunts the memory," 102. From the Hessisches Landesmuseum (Foto Marburg/Art Resource, New York).

and Art," included the comment "Next to the *Sistine Madonna*, thinks Mrs. Jameson, is that of Holbein," without indicating Jameson's first name or the titles of her books, which were presumed to be commonly known.[73]

Jameson's vision of Mary in *Legends of the Madonna* was by turns bold, subtle, and contradictory. However, the possibilities inherent in Mary that made her so meaningful a symbol to Jameson also made her a useful figure for nineteenth-century Americans grappling with the social role of women. Mary could represent a restrictive female role in her silence, obedience, domesticity, and maternity; and, at the same time, a powerful, expansive female role in her suprahumanity, queenship of heaven, and motherhood of God. Jameson brought forth all these aspects of Mary in her book, and steered readers toward the most empowering forms. Likewise, Americans could cloak empowering and sometimes radical claims for social change in Mary's reassuringly traditional figure. Both Protestant and Catholic authors drew on Marian models of womanhood to endorse female domesticity, resist shifts in gender norms, and, later, oppose the New Woman. At the same time, Catholic and Protestant authors also used Mary to expand female power within and beyond the domestic sphere. Thus, while her vision for a future Christian society that embraced Mary and the feminine aspects of the divine may not have come to pass, Jameson did achieve her stated goals of popularizing Marian imagery and promoting the figure of Mary as a site for reconceptualizing gender. Her pioneering work shifted America's visual landscape and also contributed to the use of Marian imagery in literature, especially by non-Catholics. Chapter 4 closely examines two novels that used Marian themes to grapple with changing gender norms and the appropriate role of women.

CHAPTER FOUR

Revitalizing Church and Culture

The Marian Heroines of Anna Dorsey
and Alexander Stewart Walsh, 1880s–1890s

They needed sorely . . . pilot and beacon; some one to inspire as well as to exemplify all that is best in womanhood. The need was patent, but the remedy but dimly discerned.

—Alexander Stewart Walsh, *Mary: The Queen of the House of David*

One other point about the Marian devotions and apparitions of the nineteenth and twentieth centuries deserves to be underlined: women are at their center. . . . The revival of pilgrimages to Marian shrines . . . perhaps represents a resurgent female principle defying "male" iconoclasm.

—Sally Cunneen, *In Search of Mary: The Woman and the Symbol*

In a climactic scene in Anna Dorsey's 1887 novel *Adrift*, an orphan converts to Roman Catholicism after finding herself alone in an unfamiliar city, seeking refuge in an empty Catholic church, and discovering there a statue of Mary enthroned, cradling the infant Jesus in her lap. While young Amy had never been in a Catholic church before, she identified the statue as the "Heavenly Mother" that a caring Catholic friend had told her comforting stories about when she was little. Seeing the statue of Mary in the church, Amy longed to run to her, but imagining that the figures were real, stood immobilized by the sacred vision. "Here they were at last! Oh God! How the child's simple heart leaped with joy at having found Mary the Mother of Jesus. . . . She knew them by what she had heard and figured them in her own mind. Oh, if she might only go and lay down at the feet of that tender Mother! But she dared not move, and stood gazing, gazing, until darkness veiled them and she thought they were gone."[1] As night fell, Amy reclined on a pew and slept, safe in her Catholic sanctuary from the dangers outside. Dorsey described the church's interior in detail, lingering on the sumptuous materials and sacred imagery: the stained glass windows, the rich and tasteful fabrics and metals, and the soothing presence of saints and angels in the artwork:

Softly the tinted hues bathed the marble image of the Virgin Mother and her Divine Babe; softly it fell, like a royal mantle, upon St. Joseph of the wise soul and golden silence; while, flowing from both sides, the glowing rays met and folded as in an embrace the great altar with its carven tabernacle, covered with patterns of fretted gold, its costly candelabra of precious metal, its lofty tapers, its vases and flowers; . . . Still Amy slept; *adrift* so long, she had at last found a haven of sweet peace—guided to it, doubtless, but by devious and painful ways, by the Angel to whose keeping she had been given in charge . . . those rich banners of blue, and crimson and green, whereon the images of Mary and her SON, where the forms of patron saints, of holy men and holy women, were painted, amidst borders of gold and cunning embroidery, which hung against the fluted pillars.[2]

Like other Catholic writers of the period—especially other converts—Dorsey emphasized the aesthetic power of Catholic sacred spaces to comfort and guide individuals to religious truth. As Amy slept, she became an extension of the Catholic space: "The child, reposing so motionless in the narrow pew, looked like one of those lovely effigies in which the sculptor's art has wrested half the triumph from death by preserving in precious marble, beauty too rare to be obliterated by dust and forgetfulness, which one sometimes sees on the tombs of the old, storied cathedrals of Europe." With this somewhat morbid description, Dorsey situated American Catholic spaces in the broader temporal and geographical arc of Catholic architecture, subtly asserting the ancient and global reach of the Church. When Amy awoke early the next morning, her first thought was of the enthroned Madonna: "She opened her eyes with a start . . . and was about to spring up to see if the 'great white throne,' the Virgin Mother and the fair Angels were there or if it had been all a dream."[3] Evoking the great European cathedrals, Dorsey anchored her heroine in the aesthetic landscape of Catholicism, a landscape of "holy men and holy women" over whom the enthroned Virgin presided. When Amy was discovered by a caretaker and taken to the parish priest, she indicated her desire to convert to Catholicism and come to know that Mother. In Dorsey's narrative, the church interior, statuary, and the reassuring presence of the Heavenly Mother, who can only be fully known in the Catholic faith, all worked together to spur her heroine's conversion.

Like Amy, the heroine of Alexander Stewart Walsh's historical novel *Mary: The Queen of the House of David and Mother of Jesus* entered a Catholic church, encountered a statue of Mary, and immediately thereafter converted. Set at the end of the Crusades, Walsh's book centered on the conversion of Miriamne (a form of the name Mary) from Judaism to Christianity as a result of the efforts of a proselytizing priest who recounted in detail the life of Mary, the Blessed Mother. Like Dorsey, Walsh described his heroine's first moments in a Catholic sanctuary and encounter with a statue of Mary in sumptuous detail:

> At the east she beheld a silver altar, . . . just back of the altar, in a light that made the face of the presentment more beautiful, she discerned the image of a woman, splendidly robed and jewel-crowned. For a moment she thought she was looking upon one living, for the crowned woman was so beautiful, so much a part of the place and seemed so inviting. . . . Just then, with little persuasion, she could have run toward the woman, back of the altar, and plead [sic] for sympathy. The feeling was momentary. Little by little the truth dawned upon her, and she thought, "this represents the beautiful Mary. . . ." The moonlight within the maiden's soul began to change into dawn. She gazed and gazed, and as she was so engaged, her thoughts took wing for heaven and her soul cried within itself as a babe for its mother. She knew not her way, but she knew she needed and yearned for a guide as pure as heaven and as serious as God.[4]

In this remarkably similar scene, Walsh's heroine encountered a figure that she first interpreted as an apparition of Mary, to whom she longed to run, only to realize that she faced a statue. Miriamne, like Amy, was mesmerized, comforted, and inspired by the spiritual presence of Mary, and like Amy, responded to her as a longed-for mother. Both scenes vividly described a Catholic church interior, and both used royal imagery for Mary: Dorsey's Mary was enthroned, while Walsh's was "jewel-crowned." Finally, both scenes were pivotal moments in their respective texts, catalysts for Mary-centered conversion experiences. However, while Anna Dorsey was a Catholic convert and well-known novelist, Walsh was neither. He was a well-respected New York City Baptist minister, and *Mary: The Queen of the House of David* was his only published work.

ON THE SURFACE, Walsh's decision to write a Marian historical novel seems peculiar. One might expect the high Mariology evidenced in the text to have elicited censure, or at least comment, from Protestant critics; yet it did not. From its publication, *Mary: The Queen of the House of David* was recognized and reviewed as a treatise on womanhood. By the 1880s, Marian imagery had an established, culturally accepted function as signifying idealized womanhood. Just as the context of Marian artwork primed Protestant viewers' responses, Walsh's status as a Baptist minister and the book's introduction by well-known Presbyterian minister Reverend T. DeWitt Talmage primed the book's audience to read it as a meditation on womanhood, not on Catholics or Catholic theology. While the high Mariology in the text should have been theologically troubling for many Protestant readers, it was not because concerns about woman's role in society were so pressing and Walsh's solution so compelling that the text's Catholic context and premises were overlooked.

There is no evidence that Walsh was familiar with Dorsey's books or with the domestic novels written by other Catholic writers like Mary Sadlier. And as *Mary: The Queen of the House of David* was published mere months after *Adrift*, it could not have been directly influenced by it. The two novels differed in style (domestic fiction versus historical romance), geographical and historical setting (early nineteenth-century America versus medieval Europe and the Holy Land), and intended audience (American Catholics versus American Protestants), but they employed markedly similar Marian themes and contained several nearly identical scenes. They shared a central theme: an impossibly pure heroine whose fully formed heroic femininity, grounded in Marian spirituality, was salvific to those around her and society at large. Their gender ideals and Marian conceptions of womanhood were also surprisingly similar; each critiqued non-Catholic Christianity as overly masculine, emphasized Mary's importance in attracting converts, and elevated Mary as an archetype of female holiness and a source for expanding women's sphere and agency. While *Queen of the House of David*'s setting predated the Reformation, Walsh's Jewish characters functioned as pseudo-Protestants, rejecting or misunderstanding Catholic Marian devotionalism in exactly the ways that American Protestants might. Christian characters explained the importance of Mary to their Jewish opponents and, indirectly, to Walsh's presumed Protestant readership. Through this conceit, Walsh did not advocate for readers to embrace Roman Catholicism, but rather to recognize that Marian spirituality was a legitimate part of their own Christian heritage. Finally, both authors critiqued American gender norms—indirectly and anachronistically for their fictional historical settings—lamenting women's economic and physical vulnerability, especially in marriage. These critiques were consistent with woman's movement rhetoric; however, rather than calling for suffrage (which would have been extremely anachronistic and was not the intention of either writer), both Dorsey and Walsh suggested in didactic passages that *churches* must revitalize society by redefining conceptions of womanhood and protesting injustice. Each author suggested that by embracing a simultaneously elevated (romanticized) and more egalitarian vision of womanhood, modeled on Mary, and by supporting women's education and expanding women's roles to encompass more influential, ministerial engagement with society, the unjust treatment of women could be remedied. While both made some fairly radical claims, especially about marriage, and decried the masculine normativity of Protestant churches and American society, neither ultimately challenged men's political hegemony. Despite the gulf between their religious contexts, Dorsey and Walsh each turned to Mary to fashion a Christian response to changing gender norms, and they found nearly identical solutions. These similarities reveal, if not a theological convergence between U.S. Catholics and Baptists, a set of parallel strategies for employing Marian themes to address the late-century "Woman Question."

Anna Hanson Dorsey

Anna Hanson Dorsey was a prominent American Catholic writer. She was a prolific novelist whose work—which spanned the second half of the nineteenth century and reflected the many shifts in Catholic life in those decades—profoundly influenced the course of American Catholic fiction and helped to frame the conversation about the place of Catholics in American life. She also reached a large readership by writing for several Catholic magazines and newspapers. She wrote most frequently for the *Boston Pilot*, an Irish American newspaper to which she was the single most prolific contributor (rivaling her peer Mary Sadlier).

Dorsey mothered five children while publishing more than forty novels. In most respects, her career was overwhelmingly successful: she was well connected to important figures in the U.S. Catholic establishment, was officially recognized by Pope Leo XIII for her contributions to American Catholicism, and received the University of Notre Dame's Laetare Medal for accomplishments in the arts and sciences in 1889.[5] However, she continually struggled for adequate compensation. Especially after her husband died in 1852 at the age of forty-three, Dorsey faced several financial hardships. She ceased publishing new fiction during the Civil War, in which she lost her only son, a Confederate soldier in his early twenties. After the war, with many family members to support and no male wage earner, she began writing again in earnest, establishing a lasting relationship with *Ave Maria* magazine.

The early decades of Dorsey's career were devoted to writing stories and novels that would establish the respectability of the Catholic community in the United States and assimilate new Irish immigrants. While Dorsey was not Irish, her long relationship with Boston's *Pilot* (1848 through 1860) gave her an influential and trusted voice in the Irish Catholic community. She came from a prominent Episcopal family, directly descended on her father's side from John Hanson, one of the signers of the Declaration of Independence and the first president under the Articles of Confederation. Her family was not wealthy but was well connected, with publically known abolitionist sentiments. Her father, William Hanson, left the Episcopal Church to become a Methodist minister and the first chaplain to the U.S. Navy. He was also a prominent member of the American Colonization Society. Dorsey's status as a convert and her family's social connections made her work for the *Pilot* particularly valuable. As one biographer noted, Dorsey's contributions "lent this Irish and Catholic periodical a voice of steadfast respectability, one with important historical links to America's founding families and with close contemporary ties to its Anglo-Protestant hegemony."[6]

In interviews and personal correspondence, Dorsey expressed her desire to show new Catholic immigrants how to acquire the taste and refinement necessary to attain social status in the United States, while still maintaining a distinctive Catholic identity. Unlike Mary Sadlier, who was antiassimilationist and whose relationship with the *Pilot* was shorter-lived, Dorsey focused on building bridges between Protestants and Catholics. This strategy was also evident in her books: she developed sympathetic Protestant characters and she often portrayed Catholic characters reflecting on how they might appear to Protestants. Many American-born Catholics appreciated her mission, which they hoped could effectively blunt some of the reaction against Catholicism caused by mass immigration of poor Catholics, while many immigrant Catholics themselves were hungry for just this kind of advice.[7]

In addition to modeling refined upper-class manners, Dorsey's novels contributed to the larger project of mediating between Catholic subcultures and the surrounding culture. As a genre, Catholic domestic novels worked to create a Catholic version of American gender norms and models of female domesticity. In a nativist climate, conforming to prescriptive gender norms allowed anxious immigrants to prove their compatibility with

American values. Catholics aspired to set themselves apart as ideal Americans in their family structures, just as they did in their patriotism. While this was initially an assimilationist strategy, eventually Catholics' embrace of more traditional gender norms and past models of domesticity would become a proud sign of Catholic distinctiveness. Like other Americans who struggled with the "Woman Question," American Catholics became preoccupied with defining womanhood late in the century. "In 1875, articles about women were relatively rare in Catholic publications, with the exception of an occasional essay on the religious life of nuns or domestic servants," explains one historian, "but by the late 1880s . . . Catholic magazines and newspapers featured a variety of articles about women from a range of backgrounds."[8] In context, Dorsey's emphasis on the "true womanhood" of American Catholic women was not merely a rebuttal to nativist attacks on Catholics' supposedly disordered gender norms, but was, like Walsh's, a creative contribution to the ongoing public conversation of a society experiencing rapid shifts in gender expectations.

Dorsey's early project of envisioning a Catholic domesticity that reflected the values of refined, Anglo-American culture would define her entire career, as would an emphasis on Mary as a devotional figure and a model for women. Marian themes ran through all her novels and she habitually placed her books under Mary's patronage.[9] Even before her conversion to Catholicism, Dorsey was interested in the Madonna, and some of her early published poems contained Marian imagery. While Dorsey's interest in the Madonna was likely a factor in her later conversion and while she wrote about characters whose attraction to Mary drew them to the Church, allusions to Mary by Protestant poets were not uncommon and not necessarily signs of impending conversion. Also, while Dorsey's father became Methodist, Dorsey's upbringing was Episcopalian and, as such, may have included more attention to Mary than Reformed or Evangelical Protestant contexts would have.

Probably more significant to Dorsey's religious path was her fiancé Lorenzo's conversion to Catholicism a year before their wedding. After her marriage to Lorenzo, Anna maintained her Episcopal identity for several years, raising her firstborn in the Catholic Church, but not joining herself until 1840. In Dorsey's semiautobiographical novel *Old Gray Rosary*, the narrator described obstacles to the heroine's conversion that may have mirrored Dorsey's own experience: "Human respect . . . had so long held her in thrall, whispering that the world would say; 'she had become a Catholic only because her husband was one'; appealing to her not to pain the heart of a fond father, not to separate from her race and kindred, not to place herself in the power of a religion which demanded constant humiliation, and made human reason subservient to Faith."[10] Ultimately, the character, like Dorsey herself, followed her husband into the Catholic fold.

Another factor in Dorsey's conversion may have been her perception that Catholicism was uniquely affirming to women. In many of her novels, she emphasized that the Catholic Church was the *woman's* church: a space where women's spirituality was affirmed, where women were honored as saints and Mary venerated, and where women were shielded from exploitation and harm. Because of her emphasis on female purity and sentimental domesticity, and possibly because of her Catholicism, scholars have not viewed Dorsey as a protofeminist author, but her vision of Mary as a locus for women's spirituality and as a model of autonomy and dignity exceeded that of many other domestic novelists.[11] Dorsey's solidarity with other women and awareness of the challenges they faced as women was clearly evident in her writings. She repeatedly protested women's subordination in marriage, the blocking of married women's vocations to serve the Church and the world, and the physical and sexual abuse of wives and girls. While she did not endorse women's suffrage, she did envision an enlarged role for women in both the Church and in society. Dorsey proposed that attention to Mary as an exemplar of female agency and autonomy, and veneration of Mary as a site of devotion would powerfully transform victimized women and a society that did not value women's contributions.

Anna Dorsey's *Adrift*

Adrift is a 640-page apologetic and didactic novel written in third-person narrative mode. The narrator frequently addresses the reader directly to build tension or to drive home a moral warning. There is no distance between the narrator and the author, which creates a sense of earnestness and increases the moral import of key scenes, as Dorsey pleads with the reader for compassion and action. Catholic periodicals gave *Adrift* universally positive reviews and it remained on Catholic "suggested reading" lists for decades. The *Columbian Reading Union*, for example, listed eighteen of Dorsey's books, including *Adrift*, among their recommendations for Catholic "reading circles," and strategized ways to place more copies in public libraries to reach non-Catholic readers.[12] Non-Catholic journals also noted the publication of *Adrift*. Most did not review Catholic books, but an article in *Independent* included *Adrift* along with six of Dorsey's other novels in a list of beneficial "story-books" for American girls. Since the other suggestions were concerned with female decorum and piety, Dorsey's books were presumably recommended because of their characterization of womanhood. However, the article's writer noted Dorsey's Catholicism, praising her "earnest Christian spirit" and her "devout loyalty to the Roman Catholic faith," and forestalling his readers' anti-Catholic prejudice by establishing her patriotism ("Mrs. Dorsey always proves a stanch [*sic*] upholder of the institutions and freedom of the United States") and her generous attitude toward Protestants ("the Protestant reviewer finds in these volumes less of bitterness toward Protestants than he has found of bitterness toward Roman Catholics in many stories designed for Protestant Sunday-school readers").[13] The inclusion of Dorsey's works in this list shows that at least one self-proclaimed "Protestant reviewer" perceived the prescriptive gender content of her novels as overriding their Catholic apologetics. Or perhaps he found her vision of womanhood important enough to recommend to girls despite the obvious presence of Catholic apologetics. In either case, he endorsed Dorsey's vision of womanhood—with both its traditional and its more radical elements—or he failed to perceive the more radical implications of her arguments amid the sentimentalization.

The novel traced the life of Amy Wyeth, who exhibited Marian characteristics both before and after her conversion to Roman Catholicism and who consciously modeled her life on Mary's. The first third of the novel detailed Amy's childhood, including the death of her parents and her abuse by caretakers; the second third traced her struggles to survive after being sold to a farmer as a laborer and subsequently escaping; and the final third dealt with her conversion to Catholicism, her spiritual formation, and her triumphant and gracious return to her hometown. Throughout, Amy's Marian devotion provided her emotional sustenance and led her to the Catholic fold, where she found both physical and spiritual sanctuary. Dorsey consistently described Amy in Marian terms; she had a demeanor "as modest as became a 'Child of Mary'" and a face "that the people used to say must be like Mary's when she abode in the Temple."[14] In one passage, Dorsey wrote of Amy: "She looks very lovely in her simple attire of soft gray *de laine*, a knot of pale blue ribbon fastening her linen collar, and a cluster of white and blue violets in her golden hair . . . her white Rosary-veil on her head . . . Her dress, perfectly adapted to her slender yet rounded figure, falls in soft, graceful folds around her, . . . while over her countenance is spread an indescrib-able expression—touching, yet not sad, full of pathos, yet also peace, as if her late trial and after illness had anointed her with chrisms of consecra-tion."[15] This passage could easily have been describing a painting or statue of Mary. By identifying Amy so clearly with Marian imagery, Dorsey left no doubt that she should be read as a type of Mary, a heroine whose virtues and piety would "like leaven put into a measure of meal" induce those around her to "inquire into and embrace the truth."[16]

The figure of Mary functioned in several ways in the novel. She was a marker of Catholic identity. Her presence sacralized homes, churches, and natural spaces, and devotion to her differentiated Catholics from Protes-tants. Mary was also a conduit to God. Prospective converts related to her sex and maternity, and Mary intervened in characters' lives to lead them to the Church. In particular, she heard prayers from girls and women and brought *female* concerns to God's attention. Finally, Mary modeled woman-hood, transmitting feminine ideals that were embodied by both Catholic and non-Catholic characters. Some of these characters consciously emu-lated Mary, while others inadvertently conformed to the Marian female ideal because of their own natural femininity.

Throughout the text, Dorsey characterized the Protestants who Amy en-countered in Connecticut, Philadelphia, and New York as either "Puritans" or "Presbyterians." She used "Puritan," an anachronistic term for her setting, to epitomize the harsh Calvinist theology of the Protestants in her story. (This is unexpected given the non-Calvinist orientation of the Episcopalian and Methodist communities Dorsey herself experienced, but perhaps she in-tended to give Protestant readers a way to sympathize with Catholic char-acters by differentiating between them and the "Puritan" villains.) She described Amy's religious landscape as the "land of the Puritans, . . . hedged about with the terrors of the law and kept holy to utter weariness" and re-peatedly criticized the "cold, dishumanizing tenets of Puritanism."[17] Protes-tant characters in the text, however, did not universally manifest this Puritan spirit. Several were portrayed as potential Catholics—Catholics in spirit, if not in fact. These characters did not attend Protestant churches regularly, or if they did, found themselves uncomfortable there. Rejecting theological wrangling and harsh discipline, they manifested forgiving, kindly, and ma-ternal natures. Some remembered bits of childhood prayers to Mary, the saints, and guardian angels taught by deceased Catholic parents, friendly neighbors, or passing acquaintances. These "good" Protestants later convert, or die peacefully in moving scenes accompanied by optimistic narrative commentary about their hopes for salvation.

Amy's mother, for example, grew up in this Puritan landscape, but she rejected "abstract theology," was baffled by "regeneration," and lived a "good and pure life." She died "far outside the *visible* fold of Christ," that is, the Catholic Church, but with "good will, and a confiding trust in the revealed Word as far as she knew."[18] Dorsey directly asked the reader: "Was she not of a verity one of those of whom the Good Shepherd said: 'I have other sheep that are not of this fold'; invisible members in whom His merits fill up the unevenness of spiritual knowledge?"[19] In posing this question, Dorsey did several things: she broke down hard-and-fast lines around religious identity; she emphasized the mercy of the Catholic Church as compared to a rigid Protestantism; she highlighted the natural goodness of women who embody the feminine ideal; and she differentiated Protestant people, for whom she often showed great empathy, from Protestant religion and culture, which she critiqued. Despite her interest in portraying Protestantism as false and inadequate, she allowed both Catholics and Protestants to make mistakes and manifest shortsightedness, and held out the possibility of redemption to all characters. However, only non-Catholic characters were depicted as truly violent, immoral, or cruel. "Good" Protestants were often distinguished by allusions to Mary. For example, bereaved and confused by her parents' deaths and the cruelty of her new guardians, Amy formed an attachment to a loving servant and caretaker named Ellen. Although Ellen was Protestant, she taught Amy Catholic prayers and stories of Mary—prayers and stories that Ellen's long-lost Catholic mother had once taught her. Ellen, the narrator explained, was "a Presbyterian in all things," except that she "never could, and never did, forget some little prayers that her mother had taught her to say . . . to the Blessed Mother of Jesus." Dorsey marked Ellen as implicitly Catholic by this secret devotion to Mary.

Later in the narrative, after a visitor discovered Amy's physical abuse (bruises, hunger, inadequate shelter) and threatened to divulge it, her abusive uncle sold her to a stranger, telling neighbors that he had sent her to boarding school. Amy then became a servant on a farm in western Pennsylvania, where she encountered another implicitly Catholic character, an orphaned youth named Rob. In the course of their friendship, they discussed the secret hope they have in Mary. Rob remembered that his parents had been Catholic, while Amy confirmed that Ellen had told her "such beautiful things about the Mother of Jesus."[20] They both then admitted to each other that they secretly prayed to Mary. After this exchange, in a long aside to the reader, Dorsey emphasized that Mary responded to such innocent invocations of her. She asked the reader: "Does it not seem that this simple and tender remembrance of the Mother of Jesus . . . led those two helpless souls, by God's grace and assistance, as by an invisible thread . . . into the fullness of truth and the knowledge thereof?"[21] Lines like this nudged Catholic readers to recognize the importance of early catechism and family devotions in transmitting faith, while also emphasizing that Mary is the province of Catholics, not Protestants.

Mary's importance to Amy's religious journey was revealed in an early scene when, as a young child living still with her abusive uncle, she experienced a protoconversion. In this spiritual conversion, Amy became a Catholic without knowing anything of the faith she joined. Dorsey described this moment of reflection and private prayer: "Ellie told me," Amy whispered to herself, "that the beautiful Mother Mary would love me, and hear me too, whenever I asked her for what I wanted. I'll ask Her now. Oh, Mother in Heaven, I have no friends in the world to love me! Please let me be your child." Addressing her prayer directly to Mary, she placed herself under her protection. In an aside to readers, Dorsey described Amy's prayer as "the cry of the innocent to the holy, of the human to Her who had known unspeakable human sorrows; of the soul stretching out its feeble tendrils to reach, through Her in whose being the Divine and human were united, the supernatural graces its helplessness needed."[22] Anticipating the concerns of Protestant readers, Dorsey explained and justified the Marian nature of Amy's conversion. People like Amy—the victimized, the motherless, the suffering—needed a Mother. Mary was a part of "the holy" and Mary was the person in whom the divine and human were united.

After her prayer to Mary, despite her continuing emotional and physical abuse, Amy found peace in "the sweet thought that she had a mother in heaven who would protect and love her and a bright angel friend who would help her and lead her." Immediately following the Marian prayer, Amy uttered an "Our Father," a prayer shared by Catholics and Protestants and directed to the masculine Father God. Dorsey commented to the reader that this prayer alone was inadequate to provide comfort to Amy: "Then she whispered 'Our Father': she had always said that, but as yet, 'Our Father' was so far from her conceptions, hidden, beyond the highest heavens, a Being of awful majesty and dread power, that had as yet no meaning to her, except that he was inaccessible." In a later scene, Dorsey restated the insufficiency of the "Our Father" prayer, writing: "Amy knelt down to say her prayers, but after the 'Our Father' her mind turned once more in hope to the compassionate Mother of Jesus, and the Angel whom she loved to believe walked with and guarded her, and she prayed them to pity and lead her back home."[23] The "Our Father" prayer in isolation stood for Protestantism, which offered only the starkness of a distant male God; whereas Catholicism also offered the intervention of Mary, whose vulnerability and pain were embodied in a female form and who could serve as a surrogate mother to the motherless. While Dorsey did not portray Mary as divine, she repeatedly referred to her as a part of "the Holy," capitalized pronouns referring to her, and envisioned her as an important bridge between women and the male Godhead. For Amy, and for other characters who were either female or vulnerable (including male youth), Mary's compassion and empathy mediated God's mercy and connected Him more intimately to their suffering.

In periods of abuse, Amy turned to the natural world for respite, where she also found Mary and the implicit Catholic faith Ellen had transmitted to her: "Here [where] only the birds, the squirrels and herself flitted about, her heart used to go up to God with simple childlike love; tender thoughts would come to her about the sweet Mother of His Son, and the [guardian] Angel who—all unseen—she believed ever walked with her, until some beautiful hymn burst from her lips."[24] The theme of the natural world echoing and confirming religious truth was a common Catholic literary motif, and Mary was traditionally associated with flowers (especially roses, lilies, marigolds, and bluebells) and with new life. Mary's implicit presence in nature validated the universality of Catholic truth claims.

At the farmer's house, Amy visited a clearing in the woods with the orphan, Rob. There, Amy again felt Mary's presence and fantasized aloud about one day returning to build a shrine, making Mary's presence tangible to others: "I'd build a stone grotto over this place, just in the shape it is, and I'd plant ivy so that it would run up and cover it all over except where I'd leave it open here—where this tree lies. Then I'd buy a marble image of the Blessed Virgin, as tall as Mrs. Dahl, with the Infant Jesus in her arms, and I'd stand it right over there in the corner in front of us; then, just here as if he was going in, I'd have the Angel Gabriel, because it was he who said to her, 'Hail Mary, full of grace!' O Rob! I—I will—that is, when I get rich, I'll do it!"[25] At this point in the narrative, Amy had never met a practicing Catholic, had never seen a Marian statue or painting, and was not aware of the existence of Marian shrines in grottos. Her fantasy in the clearing was unaccountable within the story, but it clearly evoked the shrines built after the famous Marian apparitions in Europe and the innocence of the children who experienced them. Youths were the main witnesses of the Marian apparitions at LaSalette in 1846, Lourdes in 1858, Pontmain in 1871, and Marpingen in 1876. Mary's presence in the scene, projected by Amy's imagination in the form of a life-size statue, transformed a wooded clearing on a farm owned by Protestants into a Catholic sacred space.

Despite Amy's fantasy of erecting the statue of Mary in the grotto, she was confused when she finally encountered such a statue in the scene described at the start of this chapter. "Do they stay there all the time, sir?" Amy naively asked the caretaker of the church. "What them statues of our Blessed Lady . . . and St. Joseph? Yes, in coorse [sic] they do."[26] Dorsey attributed Amy's inability to recognize Marian statuary as art to Protestant iconoclasm: "In [Amy's] utter ignorance of even the rudest styles of art, and still under the influence of the teachings she had imbibed against 'graven images,' she thought [the statue] was real." Amy lacked not just a religious education about Mary and the saints, but also a cultural education that valued art. Despite her initial confusion, the physicality of the statue was key to Amy's conversion; it gave material substance to the threads of faith that had long held Amy. Mary was present "at last!" and Amy rejoiced in finally having "found Mary the Mother of Jesus." The altar statue gave Mary literal feet at which Amy could lie down. Dorsey thus showed that Amy's vision at the wooded glade was a natural, naïve faith that could be made fully real only inside a Catholic church, where mature faith within the institutional Church could develop.[27]

In Amy's childhood protoconversion scene, Dorsey emphasized Mary's function as the female component of an otherwise masculine spiritual realm that was conceptually distant from the experience of women and children. Later, in Amy's full conversion, she met with the parish priest who sent her to live with a Catholic widow in a beautiful and tasteful Catholic home setting. There, she studied the Catholic catechism and learned Marian devotionalism while abiding in the female sphere of domestic life under the tutelage of a devout Catholic woman. She enjoyed the widow's patient, motherly catechism along with twice weekly instruction from the priest. This full conversion was gradual, encompassing a growing familiarity with doctrines, devotions, Catholic home life, churchgoing, and other experiences hitherto foreign to her. But Dorsey reminded the reader that this gradual growth flowed from the emotional intensity of her encounter with the statue of Mary: "Months had passed since that wonderful night in the Church of the Annunciation, and a new life and a new light has risen upon her: 'the sparrow had found for herself a home.' "[28] The night spent in the church spurred a conversion that was realized in the discovery and exploration of Catholic *home* life. In Amy's childhood conversion, she placed herself under Mary's protection; in her mature conversion, she expressed this association by joining the Church and living out her faith in domestic and community life.

In these scenes, Dorsey contrasted lavish Catholic homes and church interiors, which prominently featured Marian artwork, with stark, cold, unadorned "Puritan" interiors. She implied that warm, beautiful churches and homes were welcoming to women; while Protestant homes and churches, devoid of beauty and representations of sacred female figures, were inherently masculine spaces. Dorsey made it clear that, in a religious milieu with no female actors or devotion to female saints, the feminine was devalued. By extension, religion that affirmed women and motherhood also affirmed children. When, after her conversion, Amy observed Catholic Church life for the first time, she admiringly watched a group of children receive their first Holy Communion. All of the children wore Marian medals, "rosettes of white ribbon, in the centre of which were silver medals of the Blessed Virgin." In an aside to the reader, Dorsey reflected: "It was such a pretty scene, such as one never sees outside the Catholic Church, this blending of innocent joy and sweet friendly thoughts with holy rites, this manifestation of the sacred ties between the pastor and the flock; this leading with a strong, gentle hand the young lambs of the flock up towards the eternal hills, by such gradations that from their birth it grows with them, into a second but higher nature."[29] Mary's presence in this scene, indicated by the medals, underscored her relevance to children's inclusion in Catholic ritual. Dorsey implicitly critiqued the Puritan emphasis on adult conversion, which made children, in some sense, outsiders. In contrast, the Catholic Church included children from birth onward, in set "gradations." The Church's Marianism, she suggested, oriented it toward the maternal care of its children.

However, for Dorsey, Mary was not just a symbol of welcome and affirmation to women and children or a model of female excellence, but a powerful spiritual actor. Of the myriad names and descriptors for Mary, Dorsey most frequently called her "Protectress." She depicted Mary's protection of Amy innumerable times in the novel. While Amy's story was very grim, Dorsey insinuated that other evils—presumably sexual assault or ruin—might have occurred without Mary's protection: "Desolate indeed would she have felt . . . had not the sure solace of Mary's protection given her courage and sustained the strong simple faith that SHE who was the best safeguard of innocence, would guide and defend her."[30] And again, remarking on Amy's "heart ever, ever full of her Heavenly Protectress," Dorsey asked the reader: "Had not Mary been indeed the guiding Star of her eventful life, her shield and defence when the evil days had come upon her?"[31] Mary's sex and purity connected her to the orphaned girl whose innocence was constantly threatened. When Amy shared her trials with a priest, she reflected: " 'Father, I did not of which I need fear or be ashamed to speak; although I was placed under circumstances oftener than once, when, but for the protection of the Blessed Virgin I should probably have lost my innocence,'—a vivid glow suffusing her face and throat."[32] Dorsey acknowledged that the story of an orphaned female child in an abusive uncle's care, sold to a stranger, and then lost in a large city with no means of support, had darker implications than were realized in the narrative. Repeatedly, she emphasized that the compassionate response of the Catholic Church to female victimization and poverty stemmed directly from Mary's intervention.

Dorsey's emphases on the Catholic Church as a protective and liberatory force for women and on Mary as key to the Church's ability to value womanhood were not unique. While most Catholics found the New Woman's autonomy and sexual freedom to be both anti-American and anti-Catholic, they were eager to defend Catholicism against the charge that it oppressed women. Catholics vocally promoted the achievements of Catholic women and the Church's past accomplishments in elevating woman's status, supporting women's vocations outside of marriage, and educating girls.[33] Dorsey, however, went further than many Catholic apologists by vociferously reversing such charges. She accused Protestant churches and Protestant culture of being oppressive to women, and she developed a surprisingly nuanced analysis of patriarchal structures, especially in her later novels. This was evident in *Adrift* in her detailed and psychologically insightful portrait of domestic abuse and the ways that Protestant churches, by turning a blind eye to such abuse, perpetuated it.

Dorsey described Amy's experience of attending her abusive uncle Joe's Puritan church where he served as an elder: "Sitting there grimly, in view of her terrible uncle, she heard the terrors of the law and God's judgment preached until she used to wonder if the devil were more cruel than He?"[34]

Earlier in the narrative, when her parents were still alive, Amy's father stepped in to protect her Puritan but unconverted mother (she had not experienced saving grace) from overly enthusiastic members of this church. During her protracted illness, churchgoers repeatedly visited and exhorted Amy's mother. Afterward, when her father "heard how she had been tormented . . . his wrath exploded, and he swore a big oath that if they intruded again he'd pitch them neck and heels into the river. Knowing how good and pure his wife's life had always been, the man could not think with the least degree of patience of their having dared to talk to her as if she were the worst of sinners, and she so fragile and sensitive."[35] Dorsey portrayed Calvinist theology's harshness—particularly its insistence on human total depravity and inability to please God and the necessity of the subjective experience of conversion and rebirth—as inimical to the female spirit. The fear engendered by fire-and-brimstone preaching was inconsistent with what Dorsey perceived as the loving, nurturing, and fundamentally *domestic* goals of true religion. Female characters in *Adrift* participated in Protestant churches unwillingly, subordinating themselves to a masculine spirit of rationality and discipline, as well as to their husbands and male church elders. Significantly, many of the Catholic women in the novel were unmarried or widowed. None of the Protestant women in the text lived outside of controlling marriages and invasive churches led by domineering men. By situating her Catholic female characters in productive singleness, the religious life, or loving marriages, Dorsey implicitly contrasted the limited options outside of marriage for Protestant women with the validation of female singleness offered by Catholic religious life. Perhaps most significant was Amy's ironically named "Aunt Mercy," who was controlled by her cruel husband and her callous, patriarchal church. Mercy epitomized Protestant womanhood. Unrefined and calculating, lacking the Marian characteristics that other female characters in the text exemplified, Mercy herself was the victim of childhood abuse at the hands of her father. Although Dorsey made Mercy morally culpable for the abuse that Amy suffered—she participated in Amy's mistreatment and conspired to hide it—her complicity was accompanied by feelings of guilt and pity, feelings noticeably absent in her husband. She was the product of a religious worldview that did not honor womanhood, give women agency, or protect them from violence. As both a coperpetrator and a cosufferer of domestic abuse, Mercy needed aid—aid not available in a Protestant church that perceived her plight as her husband's private affair.

Because Mercy was afraid of her husband, Joe, and understood his capacity for violence, she cooperated with his abuse of Amy. Dorsey described Mercy's conflicted feelings and submerged feminine compassion in maternal terms: she had "a feeling of ruth [i.e., compassion], born of her motherly instinct."[36] Since Mercy's maternal instinct was depicted as inherent and natural, her participation in Amy's abuse was also a form of victimization. As Amy was made a servant in her own home—frightened, underfed, and physically beaten—Mercy cowered before her husband Joe: "The end of all her cogitations was that it was her duty to obey her husband; and when he said it would go hard with her if she didn't she knew that he was not one to be despised." Joe suppressed Mercy's womanly ethical orientation toward compassion and nurture. In a morally complex and sensitive portrait of domestic violence, Dorsey asked the reader to forbear judging a woman whose own agency was so circumscribed.

Significantly, Joe defended his abuse of Amy to his wife in religious terms, insisting that she submit to Puritan notions of severe discipline and to his God-ordained authority over her. His abuse of Amy began with the removal of signs of her innocence and her femininity: "He strode back to the veranda to continue his lecture to his wife on the necessity of strict, Christian discipline. After this, all of Amy's pretty playthings were either destroyed or locked up out of sight; her long beautiful curls that looked like spun-gold, were cropped off close to her head and thrown in to the fire without a thought of the pale, dead fingers [of her late mother] that had so often entwined and caressed them; then, after awhile, she was removed from her pretty sleeping-room to a small, dilapidated one over the buttery, directly under the eaves, where the squeaking and scampering of the rats up and down the walls . . . terrified her nearly out of her senses, and so affected her nerves that she had attacks of blinding headaches that left her wan and listless for days afterward."[37] Elsewhere in the text, Dorsey acknowledged that Joe's abuse went beyond the typical Protestant expectation of strict discipline and that he had twisted religious tenets to his own sinful ends. But she also proposed that a lack of compassion for women and children was endemic to Protestantism. For instance, when people "at meeting" noticed Amy's scrawniness and badly cropped hair, they made excuses: "They saw with their own eyes what a scarecrow they had made of Amy when they brought her to meeting dressed in her common dark calico . . . they saw that her beautiful hair was cropped close to her head, that she had a pitiful, scared look in her big blue eyes . . . but . . . they only thought that Miss'

Wythe, never having had a daughter of her own, didn't know how to slick her up like other young gals."[38] Joe maintained the respect of his congregation, who "pitied" him as a "misjudged saint," and Amy's abuse was written off as firm discipline. Joe's reputation for "piety, integrity, and forehandedness was so firmly established . . . [that he] stood high with the minister and the whole synod." But, she noted, if the community had looked closely, they would have seen that "this child whom he had tortured . . . shrank from him always with a quivering of her flesh."[39] When a few women in the congregation did remark on the possibility that Amy was being harmed, the meeting ignored their perception as slander and gossip, "for it had passed into unwritten law amongst the brethren that [Amy's parents] died in an unconverted state, [and] had no right to stand between their child and her best interests, so if she suffered vicariously for their sins and shortcomings, they thought it better for her even to endure martyrdom, if need be, for the sake of her soul, than like her parents, to die as the heathen do."[40]

In a reversal of anti-Catholic literature in which Protestant women took pity on benighted Catholic children living in large families marked by neglect and squalor, Dorsey created a story of an innocent child comforted by her spiritual Mother, Mary, and eventually saved through Catholic domestic and community life. Dorsey's sensationalized and sentimental critique of Protestantism was part of her apologetic attempt to establish Catholic moral superiority. However, condemning Protestantism as patriarchal was not the only, nor the expected, form this critique could take. At the end of the story, Amy returned home, revealing the duplicity of her aunt and uncle, whom she forgave. She also chose to embrace a single (celibate) life and minister to the community, foregoing male control and enacting independent, female domesticity. Dorsey depicted in detail how a community shaped by patriarchal assumptions and harsh theology could fail to perceive or intervene against domestic violence, tying her advocacy of Catholicism to an advocacy for women's safety and self-determination, and, possibly, subtly encouraging Catholic communities to view themselves in those terms.

Alexander Stewart Walsh's *Mary: The Queen of the House of David*

Alexander Stewart Walsh was minister of the 33rd Street Baptist Church in Manhattan and, before that, Gethsemane Baptist Church and Trinity Baptist Church in Brooklyn. Despite his promotion of a high Mariology in his book *Mary: The Queen of the House of David*, Walsh remained a Baptist throughout his life and showed no particular interest in Anglo- or Roman Catholicism. He was described in *Publisher's Weekly* as "a Baptist, but a liberal man," who "carefully avoids sectarianism and controversy."[41] He served as a chaplain during the Civil War, received an AM degree from Oberlin in 1869, and was husband to Harrietta Allen and father to several children. After his wife's illness caused him to resign from the ministry, he became a builder and ran an unsuccessful campaign for the state senate. Despite his failed campaign, he was well respected and successful, active in civic affairs, and well known as an adviser and colleague to other prominent ministers.

In *Mary: The Queen of the House of David*, Walsh intertwined a sweeping medieval romance with accounts of the life of the Virgin Mary. As many reviewers noted, despite the title, the book was not a biography of Mary, but rather a 626-page historical novel. The book drew on the same romantic nostalgia that catapulted Lew Wallace's *Ben Hur: A Tale of the Christ* to best seller status a few years before. It also evoked Walter Scott's *Ivanhoe: A Romance*, which also featured a medieval Jewish heroine. *Mary: The Queen of the House of David* told the story of Miriamne, a pious girl whose Jewish mother, after being abandoned by her Christian crusader husband, raised her to mistrust both men and Christianity, but who was eventually transformed by learning the story of the Virgin Mary's life and converting to Christianity. In turn, by self-consciously modeling her life on Mary's, Miriamne led others to salvation, conversion, and physical and spiritual healing. Walsh interrupted the meandering, convoluted tale of Miriamne's life with long retellings of Mary's life, drawn from biblical accounts and Catholic tradition. Walsh made frequent, specific, and obvious parallels between Miriamne and Mary throughout the text and emphasized his heroine's Marian womanhood by naming her Miriamne (a Hebrew version of the name Mary) and by titling the book about Miriamne "*Mary ... The Story of Her Life,*" merging the narratives of both women's lives.

The book shared many common themes and scenes with *Adrift*, including scenes in which their heroines travel alone in dangerous situations, invoke Mary's protection, are transformed by encounters with Marian art, narrowly avoid injury and seduction, minister to wayward men, experience Mary's presence in nature, astonish people with their spiritual wisdom, and struggle to ignore romantic love in favor of platonic love and service to all. Some of these elements were conventions of sentimental novels, but others were specific to Catholic fiction, especially the emphasis on Mary's watchful protection of an innocent, preternaturally pure Marian heroine who demonstrated courage, agency, and resourcefulness. Also distinctive were conversion scenes in which characters, intimidated by the masculinity of God or Jesus, were drawn to Christianity through Mary. However, since Walsh did not comment on Catholic fiction, the question of whether he was directly influenced by it or whether he merely drew on similar genres such as sentimental novels, historical fiction, and pilgrimage tales must be left to conjecture. In any case, the cultural influence of Catholic imagery and theology, which surrounded him in New York City, was readily apparent in the text.

Like Dorsey, Walsh granted many of the arguments made by woman's rights advocates. In particular, he endorsed women's educational opportunities and protested women's vulnerability and subordination in marriage and their economic dependence on men. In the text, he strongly suggested that women's moral failings were rarely their own fault, but stemmed from male abuse or from churches' failure to provide female models of holiness. He continually emphasized the moral superiority of women, which he used positively to denounce restrictions on women's agency and freedom, and, more problematically, to reinforce purity as a constitutive aspect of womanhood. Like Dorsey, he exposed the injustices of an economic and social system that oppressed women, and suggested Marian spirituality as a locus for change alongside, or in lieu of, political redress.

As in *Adrift*, there was little distance between the author and the third-person omniscient narrator. Walsh's narrator did not address the reader directly, as Dorsey's did, but his characters gave sermons and long didactic monologues that were clearly intended to instruct the reader. Despite its late medieval historical setting, Walsh clearly intended the novel to be a treatise on modern womanhood. Walsh dedicated the book "to Womankind throughout the world this story of a life most beautiful, beneficent, and inspiring." Many of the statements made by characters in the book address questions about the role, independence, and agency of women that were anachronistic in the narrative context of the story. One reviewer noted that Walsh "treat[ed] the story of Mary, the mother of Jesus, as a golden thread on which to string the pearls of his thoughts about woman and her place and mission in the world."[42] Through the examples of Mary and Miriamne, Walsh presented models of Christian womanhood that would be transformative for women, and that, in turn, would inspire men to properly understand and respect women.

Talmage's introduction to the book explicitly positioned the novel as an entry to the public debate on the role of women. He wrote: "As perhaps no other book that was ever written, this one will show us woman as standing at the head of the world. It demonstrates in the life of Mary what woman was and what woman may be. Woman's position in the world is higher than man's; and although she has often been denied the right of suffrage, she always does vote and always will vote—by her influence; and her chief desire ought to be that she should have grace rightly to rule in the dominion which she has already won."[43] Talmage apparently viewed the novel he was introducing as antisuffrage and in opposition to at least some of the goals of the woman's movement. But Walsh's treatment of both Mary and womanhood was more complex: he acknowledged and validated concerns about women's economic vulnerability and desire for meaningful work beyond marriage and motherhood, supported their vocations to preach and teach, and presented a vision of women's contributions and leadership transforming Christianity and society. His answer to the Woman Question, like Dorsey's, was a compromise: he acknowledged the injustice of current social realities, but did not advocate for political remedies. Drawing on Mary as a model of Christian womanhood, he instead suggested reforming traditional ideas about gender rather than dismantling them and building a more just society through religious rather than political channels.

Walsh's female characters were sympathetic, independent, courageous, and complex. Miriamne's mother, Rizpah, hardened by her struggle to support her three children on her own, articulated many critiques about women's economic vulnerability and mistreatment by men. Miriamne, shaped by her mother's attitudes, resisted marriage, traveled across continents, and pursued active work in the world. While Marian-drawn characters in nineteenth-century fiction often renounced marriage for chastity's sake, Miriamne instead cited concerns about physical, emotional, and economic vulnerability; childbearing; drudge work; the restriction of her agency; and her freedom to fulfill her vocation to proclaim the Gospel.

Marian spirituality pervaded Walsh's text and was the impetus for Miriamne's conversion—the book's dramatic pinnacle and turning point. Her conversion followed her intensive study of Mary's life and an encounter with a statue of Mary: "Little by little the truth dawned upon her, and she thought, 'this represents the beautiful Mary. . . .' The moonlight within the maiden's soul began to change into dawn. She gazed and gazed, and as she was so engaged, her thoughts took wing for heaven and her soul cried within itself as a babe for its mother. She knew not her way, but she knew she needed and yearned for a guide as pure as heaven and as serious as God."[44] Walsh suggested that Mary, functioning as "mother" and "guide," made it possible for Miriamne's female soul to reconcile with God. The "heaven-like" purity and "God-like" seriousness attributed to Mary indicated a quasi-divine presence. As a Baptist, Walsh would have been wary of imputing any divine qualities to Mary; however, he came very close to doing so in these lines and others. At one point in the text, a male sailor was asked whether Mary had a particular concern for sailors, and he responded: "It is enough for me to know that the Father through Mary exemplified His motherli-ness."[45] Without portraying Mary herself as divine, Walsh insisted that Mary in some ineffable way expressed the female side of the divine; and that Miriamne needed a female figure close enough to God to bridge her female human experiences and the heavenly realm.

Miriamne was unequivocal about her need for a feminine spirituality during her conversion and—like Dorsey's Amy, for whom the "Our Father" was insufficient—demanded reassurance that the female figure of Mary stood with Christ in heaven. After her encounter with the statue of Mary, Miri-amne met the priest, Father Adolphus, who talked her through her conver-sion in the following dialogue:

> "Come all ye heavy laden," measuredly replied the priest.
> "Oh, if there were someone to bear me onward; blind and weak as I am!"
> "He carries the lambs in His bosom!"
> "Alas, I feel myself cowering away from His Holiness, when I attempt to
>   approach Him alone!"
> "All to Him must go alone, in prayer as in death. He meets with a
>   plenteous mercy the confiding ones who come by sorrows' thorny
>   path . . ."
> "Is the lovely woman there, your Mary?"
> "Yes, child."
> "And she was the mother of this Saviour?"
> "Yes."
> "And was He like her?"
> "He is eternal; the 'I Am'—no was nor shall be—always."
> "Oh, yes; but is He like the woman?"
> "In my soul I so believe, to my joy; for she was godly, therefore, God-like."
> "Then I can love Him, trust Him, and I'm sure He'll pity me, at least."[46]

Like Amy, Miriamne expressed estrangement from the male figure of Christ and reluctance to approach him. In this scene, Walsh made Marian spirituality integral to the process of Miriamne's conversion, and by extension, suggested that she was important for other women who have difficulty relating to a male God and Savior. Miriamne's soul cried "like a babe for a mother," and she feared Christ until reassured that he was *like* his mother. Miriamne's prayer of conversion was not addressed to Jesus, but to Mary: "Mother of my Saviour, I need a mother! Thou and I, two women, loved of the same Lord, shall we not evermore be friends?"[47] Mary was also the impetus for the conversion and spiritual development of almost every character in the book, male and female. Unlike Dorsey, who made Mary primarily a catalyst for the weak and vulnerable, Walsh made submission to the genius of femininity, personified in Mary, necessary for *all* male characters including Miriamne's father and her (eventual) husband. For example, before his faith could be revitalized, Miriamne's apostate father had to overcome misogynistic attitudes and come to an appreciation—through a study of Mary's example—of the necessity of honoring women's unique gifts and submitting to their moral authority. Before his reconversion, in a pathetic and near-mad state, he repeatedly called the Virgin Mother "submissive" and proclaimed that in religion, like in all other things, "he the man" must be "master." After his daughter Miriamne corrected these mistaken beliefs and catechized him on Mary's life and on woman's dignity, he learned to honor Mary and reaffirmed his Christian faith, whereupon his sanity was restored. He then proclaimed: "I have praised myself as her [Mary's] champion, and, son, and devotee. Heavens! I'm abashed by the splendid revelation! I never have even dreamed of her glorious worth!"[48]

Walsh expected, and deflected, Protestant criticism of the Marian veneration in the text by having various characters voice common critiques and rebut them. These passages were anachronistic: characters vocalized nineteenth-century Protestant critiques in a pre-Protestant, late medieval setting in which Marian veneration was at its height and would not have been challenged. However, by including these critiques, Walsh anticipated his readers' discomfort with Catholic Mariology and devotionalism. At the same time, he took the opportunity to defend and explain his Marianism as intrinsic and crucial to a full understanding of Christianity.

At various points in the novel, characters defended the elevation of Mary by citing biblical passages and by emphasizing Mary's queenship. For example, a priest deflected the (unspoken) charge of Marian idolatry by emphasizing her queenship, saying: "I would that all hearts here were moved by justice to enthrone the Queen whose praise your frank youths have been sincerely singing. I am here today to proclaim her rights, and in doing so I shall appeal to that sure word which survives when all else fails. She was of David's royal line; the noblest one of all the earth. To the proof? The Christian Scriptures, from the hands of Matthew and Luke, present her ancestral descent."[49] By citing biblical texts as his only source of authority, Walsh appealed to his Protestant audience. He emphasized Mary's queenship to convey his central premise: women must be honored and elevated to a position of influence and leadership. Significantly, Walsh used terms including "justice" and "rights" to defend Marian veneration; these terms evoked nineteenth-century woman's movement rhetoric and were not generally used in Catholic apologia for Marian veneration. These echoes of woman's movement rhetoric were especially evocative in a novel written explicitly to address the Woman Question.

The priest continued: "The son and the mother here stand or fall together. If Mary was not of David's line, then the Son she bore was not, and He is left without proof of being of the seed of David. . . . The lives of mother and son are eternally intertwined. If we honor one, we just needs honor the other; abating the fame of one we degrade the other. Jesus' claims to being the Messiah depended upon the fact that His mother was of the tribe and family royal."[50] In passages like this, Walsh made a case for reinserting Mary into (Protestant) Christian spirituality by emphasizing her motherhood and queenship. Like Catholic apologists, he argued that honoring Mary honors Christ, and that neglecting to honor Mary degrades Christ.

While Walsh could not directly address changes in American social and economic life in his medieval historical novel, his commentary on gender and society was thoroughly modern. In particular, he emphasized society's need for women's ethical viewpoint. Despite Talmage's suggestion in the introduction that Walsh was antisuffrage, nothing in the book either encouraged or discouraged enfranchising women. However, Walsh did contend that men should stop blocking women's contributions and allow them a fuller scope of action. For example, in a sermon on queenship, the Hospitaller of the Knights of Mary proclaimed: "I know full well that some sneer and carp on woman's weakness, having recourse to Eden for argument. To these I reply: The enemy assailed not the weaker but the stronger first, and exhibited masterly generalship in seeking to overcome the citadel that would insure the greatest loss, the most complete victory. And note how long and arduous his siege of Eve; then remember how quickly Adam fell. Crush the woman's heart, ruin her faith, degrade her body, and then, with this work completed, we are ready to bring down the curtain over the end of the tragedy of a wrecked world."[51] Here, Walsh made a theological argument that countered misogynistic readings of Genesis; but he went further, stating his vision for society as a whole. He proposed that women had a stronger moral constitution and that society's survival depended on its willingness to protect the emotional, spiritual, and physical safety of women and encourage their contributions.

While domesticity remained a component of Walsh's understanding of womanhood, his overall approach to womanhood was not primarily domestic. Instead, he proposed that, in order for woman's ethical leadership to shape the larger society, women must be supported in following vocations beyond that of wife and mother. Likewise, he argued that women have an inviolable selfhood that transcends their domestic role: without authority to make choices for their lives and freedom to follow their vocations, women became bitter and twisted. "When men hold women to their hearts, their manhood is enlarged and their queens become their angels. . . . But when a man turns his strength against a woman . . . [h]e has brawn, and she, not having that, puts on that cunning which is the natural arm of the weaker. . . . Let men go mad over their queens become witches. Shall our queens be uncrowned, disrobed, degraded? No, no, Satan alone could say 'yea.'" While this language evokes a sentimental, essentialist understanding of female difference (that was shared by both traditionalists and some woman's rights advocates), the narrative supports a more liberatory reading of the passage. Walsh repeatedly acknowledged that men can and do harm women physically, emotionally, and economically, and the narrative directly challenged churches to acknowledge their failure to act in protecting women and to affirm women's freedom to reject marriage. He also poignantly portrayed the human cost of women's unused talents and frustrated ambitions. Granting women social influence was, in Walsh's view, the hallmark of a Christian society.

Walsh's recommendations included reinstating Marian veneration (a call implicitly directed to Protestant churches), allowing women to have some form of social power (unspecified), and, finally, reforming marriage to promote women's equality. While characters in the novel sometimes waxed on about the glories of womanhood or Christian marriage, they just as frequently pronounced pragmatic and even cynical observations on the real condition of women. In these passages, Walsh addressed nineteenth-century marriage without any attempt to accurately portray medieval marriage or account for cultural differences. A striking example was Miriamne's marriage proposal. When her lover, Cornelius, proposed to her, Miriamne invoked the virginity of Mary in her refusal: "That cannot be I fear. . . . Can't I be your ideal as Mary?" Cornelius answered: "Yes, be my Mary, and let me take the place as your Joseph. Mary was a wife and mother. The greatest of God's works in the old dispensation was to translate men; in the new dispensation, seeking to surpass the old, He presented a perfect woman, in her highest estate, as the queen of a home!"[52] Instead of allowing this sentimental vision to stand, Miriamne responded by rejecting the romantic domestic ideal and stating frankly: "At betrothal and when their wives are dead they say men are very affectionate. . . . Do not love me to death at first, vex me to death later, then go mad for love's sake after I'm gone!"[53] In an exposition on marriage she gave later in the text, she transposed the Marian ideal, with Joseph held up to men as an ideal husband: "No woman should leave all for any man," she declared, "unless she is certain of finding in him father, mother, brother, sister, companion, as Mary found in Joseph."[54] In this passage, marriage was not an unmitigated good, and potential husbands were asked to demonstrate the ability to provide friendship and emotional support for their wives. This differed markedly from domestic writings in which women are exhorted to provide emotional comfort to husbands coming home from a harsh world to the shelter of home. Significantly, husbands were here asked to be "mother" as well as "father," "sister" as well as "brother," in marriage. Walsh's language transcended restrictive gender roles in order to affirm an ideal of love in marriage that was more egalitarian.

When Miriamne eventually married Cornelius, for economic and practical reasons, her reservations about marriage came to the fore: "He entreated for a speedy wedding, and she, seeing then no alternative, consented thereto; but as she assumed love's yoke, she believed that the ambition of her life was frustrated. She was not disconsolate, neither was she tearless."[55] Walsh complicated the romantic ideal by making the sacrifice of female ambition to be a real factor in his heroine's story and grief part of her response to marrying a man she loved. After a period of time during which Miriamne supported her husband and his work, she told him that she "longed to echo nobler music," and that she believed if she continued in her current limited role, she would die young.[56] Despite having a kind and loving husband, Walsh's heroine did not find happiness in domesticity. Panicked for her well-being, Cornelius agreed to follow her vocation rather than his own, stating: "I'll work for you, with you, for God."[57] Cornelius redefined service to God as service to his wife and he willingly assumed a subordinate role. Walsh thus made the virtues of self-sacrifice and submission applicable to both sexes. Miriamne went on to found and lead a devotional community of women in which she lived and taught; she preached to mixed-sex groups that included her former priest and her husband, who were amazed and transformed by her spiritual insights. Thus, in Miriamne and Cornelius's marriage, which remained childless, Walsh demonstrated the possibility of gender equality and the necessity of a wider sphere where women could transcend domestic boundaries and bring their gifts and talents to the Church and the world. As Miriamne was directly drawn as a type of Mary, this narrative may also have reflected his understanding of Mary's role in the early Christian community, Joseph's relationship to Mary, and possibly their lack of subsequent children.

In a long exposition on marriage in the text, a priest directly acknowledged the limits of domestic happiness and the precariousness of marriage for women. "Me thinks that marriage brings the graver, heavier loads to women," the priest asserted. "The man rises by self-assertion, and wedlock does not hinder him. With the woman wedlock means self-denial; her name changes, her career is merged into that of her consort; her body is given, literally, to the new beings she bears. To woman marriage has no parallel, except death."[58] Here, Walsh echoed and affirmed some of the concerns raised by marriage reform advocates such as Ernestine Rose, Paulina Wright Davis, and Elizabeth Cady Stanton.[59] Walsh's career as a minister in New York spanned the years in which marriage reforms were passed in that state, including the 1848 Married Woman's Property Act and the 1860 Married Woman's Earning Act, as well as the 1862 repeal of sections of the later act. In various writings and addresses on marriage, Stanton observed that, once married, a woman became "civilly dead."[60] Walsh's use of the metaphor of marriage as death for women shows a serious consideration of the arguments of marriage reform advocates.

For Walsh, Marian womanhood was not merely a didactic tool, but an agent of reform: men as well as women must embrace Marian understandings of womanhood to restore women.to an elevated, influential, and just place in society. Miriamne's parents' marriage functioned in the narrative as a stand-in for the healing and transformation of larger society. In their first marriage, like in traditional society, Miriamne's father, Sir Charleroy, attempted to rule and control his wife. This resulted in an unhappy marriage culminating in his abandonment of his wife and daughter, who thereafter struggled to survive. By means of devotion to Mary and to his daughter's lectures on womanhood, Sir Charleroy reconverted to Christianity and acknowledged the genius of womanhood. When he later reconciled with his wife decades after their separation, Sir Charleroy had learned to trust her wisdom, meet her needs, allow her full control of the domestic sphere, and share decision making. After Sir Charleroy's submission to her and their subsequent reconciliation, Miriamne's mother finally converted from Judaism to Christianity. Her conversion, like the conversions of others in the story, resulted directly from her meditation on the life of Mary.

A range of fiction emerged in the later nineteenth century that supported and disseminated marriage reform goals.[61] Susan B. Anthony acknowledged the crucial role this literature played in promoting the movement. In particular, Anthony commended Elizabeth Oakes Smith's book *Bertha and Lily; or, The Parsonage at Beech Glen* and writings by Elizabeth Barrett Browning and Charlotte Bronte. Walsh's novel likewise grappled with shifting attitudes toward marriage and similarly encouraged readers to imagine more egalitarian marriages. However, unlike Smith, who was a woman's rights advocate, Walsh balanced his call for more just and egalitarian conjugal relations and an expanded sphere for women with a persistent romanticization of women's domestic role, seen most clearly in Miriamne's mother's blissful domesticity after the reconciliation of her marriage.

AMAZINGLY, NONE OF WALSH'S reviewers were alarmed by his Marian spirituality. They unanimously read the book as an entry into a public conversation on the status of women. Some reviewers sought to reassure readers that Walsh's treatment of Mary was acceptable for non-Catholics. "He does not approach it as a mariolater nor as an iconoclast, but with a discriminating caution becoming a Protestant,"[62] wrote one reviewer. Another praised Walsh's "strong" and "well-conceived" plot, noted the "sweet influence of Mary's life upon the troubled life of others," and suggested that, despite their different religious affiliations (Jewish and pre-Reformation Catholic), by novel's end, the characters "at last have their lives attuned to the principles of Christianity."[63] The *Christian Union* wrote: "The book has been highly commended by many excellent critics of many denominations. It is free from superstition, and its religious tendencies are strong and genuine."[64] The book's publisher, Hurst & Company, reassured potential buyers of the book's theological soundness, while trumpeting its aesthetic qualities. They advertised a 1901 second edition as "a charming book for presentational purposes" with "sixty full-page illustrations of the most celebrated paintings," all of which were Marian, and emphasized that the book had been "endorsed by the press and pulpit and a host of competent critics."[65] By including Marian art reproductions, this edition tied Protestant consumption of such images directly to the book's goal of promoting a Marian vision of woman's role in society. Another advertisement also noted the impressive Marian illustrations "from famous paintings of Raphael, Becker, Holman, Hunt, and others," while another emphasized Reverend Dr. Talmage's introduction to reassure readers of the book's Protestant theological credentials.[66] In marketing the book, Hurst & Company appealed to purchasers of gift books, art books, and tasteful books meant for display, as well as novel readers.

While reassurances about the theological orthodoxy of Christian-themed fiction were not uncommon in reviews, *Mary: The Queen of the House of David* received a lot of them. Perhaps this suggests that publishers and fellow clergy wanted to preempt any theological concern, and this was thus a tacit admission that some Protestant readers might have needed reassurance. Still, there was an almost willful blindness in reviewers' refusal to consider whether the theology of the extraordinarily Mary-centered book bordered on Catholic Mariology. Was Walsh's solution to the problem of woman's role so convincing that reviewers not only failed to critique him but also defended his theological orthodoxy and ignored Marian elements that they might easily have construed as "papist"? Or was this, like with the Marian art discussed in previous chapters, a matter of context priming reception: nearly Catholic positions could be held as long as they were being held by a Baptist. In part, the book's historical setting helped mitigate its Marian spirituality; scenes that might have been jarring in a modern American setting may have seemed more ambiguous in a medieval context. However, the Marian passages in the text, complete with apologia in modern theological terms, were blatantly anachronistic and overrode ambiguity. The novel's pleading for Marian spirituality and defense of autonomous womanhood were clearly based on a high reading of Mary's role in Christianity. And yet critics gave it a theological free pass, warming, perhaps, to the congeniality of Walsh's approach and his success in resolving cultural tensions around gender without radically reframing gender roles.

Catholic reviews of the book were positive, though circumspect. A *Catholic World* reviewer embraced the novel as a positive step toward ecumenism and eventual reunion, writing: "When Catholics and Protestants can sit down together and extol the virtues of Mary in concord, when they can feel their hearts thrill with equal pride in her exalted office and in her most extraordinary holiness, they have advanced one good step towards fairly reaching agreement—a step all the firmer because springing from the gentler force of the affections as well as the imperative demands of the understanding."[67] The reviewer cautioned readers that "this Protestant minister" cannot know the truth about Mary, but pleaded for readers' (and Mary's) support for Walsh because of his obvious intention of honoring her.

In surprising ways, Walsh's novel raised many of the same issues that Dorsey's did. Both authors defended Marian spirituality. Dorsey used dialogues between Catholics and Protestants about Mary to arm her Catholic readership with apologetic answers to their real-world Protestant opponents. In a necessarily more complex approach, Walsh did not include any Protestant characters in his medieval tale; and he described an intrafaith rather than an interfaith dialogue about the status of Mary. But by setting his novel in the pre-Reformation past, Walsh explored Marian veneration without signifying post-Tridentine Catholicism and drew on romanticized medieval chivalry to develop a queenly ideal of womanhood. Like Dorsey, he addressed Protestant iconoclasts and those who saw Marian veneration as a form of idolatry, but he did so implicitly and he primarily sought to persuade his readers to rethink the place of Mary in Christianity. Also like Dorsey, Walsh contended that Protestantism lacked a feminine element, and he proposed Marian spirituality as a solution. Just as Dorsey asserted that Protestantism was unable to protect women and recognize their gifts, Walsh asserted that women were unnecessarily vulnerable in churches and in a society shaped by patriarchal norms. He suggested that including Marian spirituality in Protestant Christianity would enable women to gain leadership opportunities and cultural influence, would establish more egalitarian marriages, and would ameliorate cultural stresses caused by constraints on women's agency.

The emphasis that both authors placed on the social value of women's ethical perspectives reflected Progressive Era social currents. However, while arguing for reform, they both also attempted to retain—to varying degrees—the domestic ideal of womanhood, an ideal that they feared was being lost in the rise of the New Woman. Their common approaches reveal that Mary was a uniquely attractive symbol for navigating changing gender norms while retaining certain desirable traditional functions for womanhood. Like Catharine Beecher, who identified the domestic sphere as an area of influence from which women's moral authority could flow, Dorsey and Walsh worked in a paradigm that would later develop into "maternalism," a political movement that based its calls for the expansion of women's civil rights on their moral authority and "mother-work."[68] In Mary, a traditional but empowering symbol of womanhood—maternal, pure, and domestic, as well as independent, powerful, and authoritative—they each sought an alternative to the New Woman's rejection of domesticity, call for suffrage, and demand for political agency. Walsh's approach typified this use of Marian imagery but was not unique. From literary authors like Stowe and Hawthorne, to settlement workers, to practical advice writers, Americans drew on Marian imagery to theorize womanhood, especially as gender norms were in flux.

At the end of *Mary: The Queen of the House of David*, Walsh connected Mary's queenship to the queenship of all women. At Miriamne's funeral, the presiding priest declares: "The histories of women, mostly written by men, are marred by the conceits of their writers, and are at best but obscure pictures. . . . The generality of those who discourse concerning women do it in a patronizing way. . . . The queenship of Mary is constantly disputed, and so her lot is more closely linked with that of her sex."[69] Walsh reflected (in a historical novel) on the patriarchal nature of writing history, explaining that a lack of female authorship leads to condescending and limiting visions of womanhood. For Walsh, the "queenship" of all women was disputed (as much in the late nineteenth century as in the medieval past) and required buttressing. He suggested that by honoring Mary, women would also be honored. In a novel that was intended—and reviewed—as a treatise on womanhood, Walsh's heroine and his version of Mary transcended mere domesticity and provided a model of female queenship. Walsh envisioned a world transformed by the power of women to mold society and lead people to Christ. However, in the novel, a fictional vehicle, it was unclear whether Walsh intended this transformation to be achieved through sensitivity and religious renewal alone or through legal and political action. Certainly, Talmage, in his introduction, framed the book as a call for change that stopped far short of increased legal rights for women.

Both Dorsey and Walsh used the metaphor of "queenship" to promote a strong, transformative yet traditional Marian ideal. In the last decades of the nineteenth century, this motif became ubiquitous as a descriptor of both female domesticity and female strength. As a traditional Marian-derived alternative to the New Woman, the domestic queen was an open site for discourse about female power.

CHAPTER FIVE

Queen of Heaven and Queen of the Home
Mary and Models of Domestic Queenship, 1880s–1900

The Virgin Mother, thus seated in her majesty, apart from all human beings, and in communion only with the infant Godhead on her knee, . . . and the living worshippers who come to lay down their cares and sorrows at the foot of her throne and breathe a devout, "Salve Regina!"—is, through its very simplicity and concentrated interest, a sublime conception.

—Anna Jameson, *Legends of the Madonna*

The power to heal, to redeem, to guide, and to guard . . . Will you not covet such power as this, and seek such throne as this, and be no more housewives, but queens?

—John Ruskin, "Of Queen's Gardens," in *Sesames and Lilies*

In *Mary: The Queen of the House of David*, Reverend Alexander Stewart Walsh described female characters, including his heroine Miriamne, the Virgin Mary, and other women, as "queens" or "queenly" more than seventy-five times. He used the word "royal" thirty times, "noble" forty-four times, and "reign" ten. Walsh emphasized Mary's centrality to the Christian narrative and the importance of honoring her as a queen, writing: "Jesus' claims to being the Messiah depended upon the fact that His mother was of the tribe and family royal."[1] While Walsh accentuated Mary's exceptionalism and the need to honor her as a religious figure, he also extended Mary's queenship to all women, arguing throughout the text that all women should be honored because of their "queenly" natures.

The nature of ordinary women's queenship, however, is less clear. In the novel, Father Adolphus exhorts all women to consider themselves queens: "To be a woman is to have within thee a wealth of power. To be queenly is to do in queenly spirit the work falling to thy lot. Behold the queenly women of the patriarchs! Rebecca watered the flocks. Rachel was a shepherdess. The daughter of Jethro, King of Midian, also kept the flocks. Tamar baked bread. The word of God records these things, methinks, to show in what a queenly way a queenly woman may perform a seemingly unimportant work. . . . Think of our Mary, Mother of Jesus, after her call, serving humbly as a good housewife to a carpenter."[2] While speaking of "power," Father Adolphus articulates a thoroughly domestic understanding of female queenship. Domestic tasks are ennobled and become religiously significant when they are dutifully performed by holy women. Matriarchs, princesses, and Mary herself were content with such service, as should be, by extension, all women. In the text, Walsh posited that women and society could be transformed by embracing the ideal of female queenship, but he left unclear what power domestic queens actually had. If the "wealth of power" possessed by domestic queens amounted only to the distinguished performance of "unimportant work," what good was their queenship?

IN THE FINAL DECADES of the nineteenth century, "queens" began to populate the American and British cultural landscapes. Queenship, both as a theme and as a descriptor of idealized womanhood, became pervasive.[3] In these years, the Virgin Mary was increasingly invoked under her title Queen of Heaven (*Regina Coeli*) in both devotional and popular contexts. Most Protestants, including most Low Church and many High Church Episcopalians, rejected the Catholic theological premises of Mary's Assumption and subsequent Coronation, but "Queen of Heaven" was nevertheless an increasingly popular term for the Virgin Mary in American popular culture. The domestic sphere also was increasingly romanticized as the site of a "queen's rule." From John Ruskin's "Of Queen's Gardens" in *Sesames and Lilies* (1865) to Coventry Patmore's "Regina Coeli" in the *Unknown Eros* (1890), womanhood and domesticity were described and prescribed in royal terms. Often, queenship was presented as a sort of consolation prize: rather than seek actual power and participation in public life, domestic queens were asked to be content with the "rule" of the "dominion . . . already won."[4]

Beginning in the 1880s, as woman suffrage campaigns were gaining momentum and the woman question dominated public discourse, the so-called New Woman became a cultural presence and, to a lesser degree, a social reality. One scholar found that the "New Woman" was featured "between 1883 and 1900 [in] over a hundred novels."[5] Proponents and opponents defined her in various ways, but they agreed that she was modern and autonomous. Reacting against the confining domestic ideologies of the preceding decades, the New Woman sought self-realization and freedom from domesticity. In contrast, the domestic "queen" generally exemplified and ennobled woman's traditional roles, embracing the home as a sufficient arena of authority and identity. The compensatory quality of this crowning is obvious: in contrast to the New Woman's quest for freedom, the domestic queen ruled a very limited kingdom.

In some ways, then, queenship rhetoric was just another manifestation of the midcentury Angel in the House and other idealized formulations of domestic womanhood. However, queenship rhetoric also contained the radical potential for *rule*. Queenship rhetoric was drawn—to a greater degree than is often understood—from Marian motifs and images; it implicitly and often explicitly evoked the Virgin Mary as Queen of Heaven. Mary's queenship was not merely a Catholic theological premise; it was a familiar and pervasive cultural trope that was transmitted through language and images. Like her Immaculate Conception, Mary's queenship was a site where cultural meanings and content converged at the same time theological premises diverged. The ubiquitous, late-century "domestic queen" thus transmitted a range of meanings derived from the Queen of Heaven, including typical Marian motifs such as purity and maternity, but also moral and religious *authority*. Because Mary's queenship was a traditional image of female transcendence, it provided a way to invoke female power without undermining, or appearing to undermine, social norms. Mary, as Queen of Heaven, contained enough symbolic power to be a useful site for the societal renegotiation of women's power without triggering fears of disorder and moral laxity like the New Woman.

Furthermore, queenship rhetoric both reinforced women's maternal and domestic roles and capitalized on them to broaden women's sphere of authority. In this sense, it functioned in tandem with the larger political movement that historians call "maternalism." Maternalism exalted mothering and saw it as a norm for all women. It also identified women's capacity for ethical reasoning and action as flowing from their shared experience of, or potential for, motherhood.[6] In maternalistic arguments, the moral virtues all women were assumed to possess as *mothers* justified their entry into the political realm, which Americans perceived as desperately lacking in such virtues. Domestic queenship, like other maternalistic themes, did not overturn a rhetoric of female domesticity but expanded it, imagining that women brought their moral authority and propriety with them as they stepped out into public spaces.[7]

Maternalism was broad enough to shift social norms precisely because it pulled together a diverse coalition of people who interpreted motherhood as a basis for ethical reasoning in different ways. Maternalists were both suffragists and antisuffragists, and they encompassed diverse religious and political perspectives. By focusing on the social needs of women and children, women were able to justify their increasing political activity, including organizing societies and even lobbying. A Janus-faced ideology, maternalism legitimated women's changing social roles while compensating for the gradual loss of separate-spheres ideology through a nostalgic affirmation of it. The compensatory, conservative function of maternalism hobbled its ability to transform women's reach in America, but it also legitimated and masked the first steps, enabling a broad range of Americans to accept an expansion of women's sphere. This was important for women as well as for men who feared losing their gender identity and were concerned with the implications of social change. While the conservative element of maternalism, with its essentialist gender rhetoric and sentimentality, enabled this broad coalition of activity, it also restricted its ultimate ability to achieve full rights and suffrage. But its impact in terms of legitimating women's action should not be underestimated.

In the 1890s, the "General Federation of Women's Clubs" united the various local "women's clubs" in an organization that prominently employed maternalist discourse.[8] Women's voluntary work in these clubs contributed to the development of government social policy and provided both a template for the final pushes of the suffrage movement and a group of experienced women for the early twentieth-century expansion of women into social work, teaching, and other professions. In other countries, parallel movements arose with different effects. For example, in France (where Mary was viewed as a promonarchy, antirepublican symbol), Catholic laywomen and sisters organized charity and reform societies, but these activities did not lead to calls for suffrage or woman's rights.[9] However, in America, maternalism was a precursor and important link in the chain that led to twentieth-century feminism, even though it was practiced by a coalition that included antisuffrage and traditionalist women. The development of maternalism was indebted to the ideology of domestic womanhood that developed in the mid-nineteenth century and, while easily overlooked, elements of its ideological content and visual iconography drew from the Marian imagery embraced by both American Protestants and Catholics.

On the surface, the late-century ascendance of queenly language and images in America was surprising because of its association with monarchy and Catholicism. But queenship played important cultural functions in imagining and expanding idealized womanhood. Because queenship was a royal, nondemocratic (even antidemocratic) metaphor, it did not suggest literal political power in the American context. This facilitated its use because it was clearly an abstraction, a nonthreatening, symbolic image of power. If American women were "queens," they were not congresswomen or presidents. Still, queens were real, contemporary political figures, so the word did evoke political (and not just fairy-tale) power. The success of the queenship metaphor lay in its ability to blend abstracted political authority and religious iconography. This blend of associations contributed a host of unacknowledged meanings that both propagated and mitigated the metaphor's subversive potential.

Queenship rhetoric and especially its underlying Marian associations helped to resolve the cultural anxieties generated by the emergence of the New Woman. Like maternalism, queenship rhetoric was a discourse of compromise, by turns restrictive and empowering. For traditionalists, the power implicit in the queenship metaphor could be used to espouse support for women's agency while reinforcing the boundaries of the domestic sphere. But for protofeminists, the queen's "rule" could be used to reconceive womanhood and justify the breach of traditional boundaries, especially female leadership and political agency. The power and autonomy inherent in the Queen of Heaven symbol provided a way to couch demands for social change in a reassuringly traditional religious and cultural metaphor. Thus, while queenship imagery was used in contradictory ways, some Americans used it to propose expanded roles and increased authority for women.

Queen Victoria and "American Aristocracy"

Popular American interest in Queen Victoria, and particularly in her domestic life, was an important factor in the rise of queenship rhetoric in America. British authors such as Coventry Patmore, John Ruskin, John Henry Newman, and Lewis Carroll were among the first to use queenship rhetoric to describe and comment on the status of women. As I explore later in this chapter, Queen Victoria's reign and her roles as wife, mother, and widow formed the context in which they began to utilize and employ these themes. Other factors popularizing queenship imagery included the rise of "romantic medievalism" as an aesthetic trend and the continued growth and cultural presence of Catholic Marian devotionalism.

Queen Victoria was the first British monarch to enjoy high levels of approval in America. Her commitment to British neutrality during the American Civil War and her respect of the Union blockade of the South made her popular among Northerners. The American press also romanticized Victoria's successful neutralization of the potentially explosive 1861 *Trent* affair, during which she kept Great Britain steadfastly neutral despite provocation caused by the boarding of a British ship, the *Trent*, by American captain Charles Wilkes and by the removal of two Confederate diplomats. Besides winning American approval for her politics, she established a reputation as a model woman through her fecundity and devotion to her husband, Prince Albert.

Prior to the Civil War, Americans mistrusted Victoria for both political and ideological reasons. The ideology of "Republican motherhood" imagined American women to be incubators of the next generation of male citizens and the transmitters of republican values. The European aristocracy was generally viewed as amoral, self-indulgent, and parasitical. In these years, queenship would have been both a foreign and a threatening metaphor. However, Victoria's stance during the war and her conduct during the course of her married life and widowhood won over many Americans. In particular, Victoria's consistent conformity to bourgeois gender norms mitigated her status as a member of the aristocracy and eased American mistrust of her queenship. By embracing and transmitting middle-class values, Victoria helped to reconceive queenship from an indulged and oppressive category (as it had previously appeared to Americans) to an exemplary model of femininity.[10]

As early as the 1860s, American magazines were praising Victoria's character and femininity. For example, one 1860 magazine article said of Victoria: "As the sovereign of a powerful Empire, as a Queen revered and beloved by her subjects, as a woman and a mother, she is regarded as a model of excellence." It continued, "there are few who are more meritorious in character than Queen Victoria," who, due to her domesticity, has won for "the royal family of England the respect of the civilized world."[11] In England, Victoria's domestic persona triggered ambivalence and anxieties. This was especially true in the decade after Prince Albert's death, when she abdicated many of her public responsibilities. In doing so, she brought to light the inherent incompatibility of literal political power and the domestic female role. While the domestic queen was a construction of literature, poetry, and visual arts, a real "domestic queen" was a problem.[12] However, Victoria's domesticity won her the admiration of most Americans, who approved of her exemplification of the female role and had no stake in her political leadership. On the contrary, by simultaneously embodying domestic womanhood and the office of queen, Victoria made the monarchy more acceptable to Americans and undermined the potentially radical social implications for women inherent in her visible political power.

As monarch, Victoria was a living example of "a public sphere for woman." Through her decisions—to rule over or submit to her husband, to portray herself as a political leader or a domestic figure—she explored on a grand stage the relative importance of political versus social expectations. By refusing to exempt herself from most gender norms, and by denying her support to most advocates of legal reforms for women, she effectively weakened the position of those who would espouse the "cause of woman" in her name.[13] Because of these factors, woman's rights advocates were ambivalent toward her. They objected to her dismissal of their cause—she notoriously called for an end to "this mad, wicked folly of 'Women's Rights' with all its attendant horrors"—but they often claimed her as an example of female potential. Emily Faithfull's protofeminist journal, *Victoria Magazine*, was named for the queen because her rule was symbolically significant for British women.[14]

Americans generally perceived Victoria as moderate and fair-minded on woman's rights. For example, *Scribner's Monthly* noted in 1871 that while Victoria opposed the admission of women to medical lectures at the University of Edinburgh, this was "contrary to general report and belief" about her views on "the woman-question," and added that despite her position on this issue, "an effort is being made to induce the Queen to hold up her royal hand, which has generally been shown on the side of all reasonable demands of her sex." The article also noted that Victoria's daughters' support for the "alleviation of women's ills" was evidence that "she has at least brought up her daughters to be very active in all that regards woman's welfare."[15]

A few years later, *Scribner's Monthly* ran another article on Victoria, "My Look at the Queen," by the Philadelphia Episcopal clergyman, Reverend Treadwell Walden. He reported that on a visit to England during which he worshipped at a small costal parish alongside the queen, he was able to get a "look" at her. He reflected that he would not have been interested in her at the start of her reign, but since then, "she has set the seal of personal character upon the great system of government, and justified its wisdom and beauty before the world" and also that she is revered by his fellow Americans "not only as a monarch . . . but also as the prudent good woman, the head of a model English home." Employing language very similar to contemporary descriptions of the Virgin Mary, he called Queen Victoria "a woman, sharing with the humblest of her subjects a woman's heart and a woman's sphere; but as a Queen, lifted up an immeasurable distance above her sons and daughters."[16] That Walden could consider the monarch of England a woman who resided in "a woman's sphere" was telling. Through her publicly enacted domesticity, she embodied the maternalist view that a woman's sphere accompanied her when she entered public worlds and roles. American popular interest in Victoria neutralized some of the negative connotations that royalty bore, allowing queenship to become a comfortable metaphor, and eventually *the* late-century metaphor, for idealized womanhood.

The second factor that popularized queenship rhetoric in America was the rise of romantic medievalism, a cultural affinity for medieval and aristocratic forms in art, architecture, literature, music, and liturgy. Class anxiety and the increased accessibility of European travel, among other factors, led to a late-century cultural fascination with medieval religion and art. Although there was an associated increase in conversions to High Church Episcopalianism and Catholicism, and several of these conversions involved notable individuals and were highly publicized, romantic medievalism did not trigger a significant reevaluation of contemporary Catholicism. Instead, aristocratic and religious forms were blurred as the ceremonies, objects, clothes, stories, and images of both medieval Catholicism and medieval nobility were popularized. This was triggered, in part, by rapid economic change; as one scholar put it: "Looking carefully . . . we can see a nervous ruling class discovering premodern emblems of unity, exclusivity, and cultural authority."[17] But it was also a response to changing gender norms. A highly stratified society, sanctioned by church and state, bolstered class boundaries but also maintained structured gender relations, which were romanticized as benign and protective male chivalry. In this model, medieval devotion to Mary's queenship was sentimentalized as the inspiration for chivalry. Thus, in addition to other connotations, invocations of Mary as Queen evoked images of knights and crusaders nobly protecting Christian womanhood as they marched beneath her banner.[18]

Men were less able than women to embrace and embody romantic medievalism because many upper- and middle-class men were enmeshed in modern business culture and democratic political life. Women, removed from these worlds, could live out this imaged aristocratic heritage through their refined manners and tasteful consumption of goods. Drawing on Marian characteristics such as female piety, purity, and spiritual refinement, American aspirations to cultural refinement could be demonstrated by the "queenship" of middle-class women. Meanwhile, while queenship evoked nobility and aristocracy—desired but problematic qualities for Americans— the spiritual connotations of queenship that flowed from its embedment in Marian imagery counterbalanced its connotations of wealth and privilege.

One evocative example of this pervasive rhetoric was the 1886 essay "An American Queen," in which abolitionist and woman's rights advocate Gail Hamilton (Mary Abigail Dodge) framed the life and career of female education pioneer Zilpah Grant Banister as the story of a queen. She began the piece by setting up her royal metaphor, writing: "I present herein a specimen of American aristocracy, and if the princesses and duchesses and countesses of the world would like to know whether they are of the true blood royal, they are cordially invited to examine these pages and ascertain for themselves by a careful comparison with the best standards."[19] Hamilton proceeded to describe Banister's religious upbringing, moral superiority, refinement, and, significantly, positions of leadership and authority. These factors, she claimed, transformed Banister from a woman of humble (though always "noble") origins into a virtual peer of the titled aristocracy.

Wealth was not a necessary component of Hamilton's conception of the "American aristocracy." In fact, in her view, wealth could impede its development. Banister was a "queen" who rejected wealth and, instead, valued piety. "Wealth did not attract the ambition or even the attention of these royal families," she wrote, but rather, as a child of hardworking, religiously zealous "puritans," Banister "could hardly fail to rise and rule."[20] By establishing religious piety as her standard of "noble blood," Hamilton asserted that the achievement of queenship was possible for any American woman. However, in addition to being pious and good, Banister actively used her "queenship" to "rule."

By locating America's aristocracy in its myriad "queens," writers like Hamilton transformed women's service to American democracy. No longer merely required to raise good citizens as republican mothers, women were asked, rather ironically, to ameliorate class anxieties by embodying an alternate version of aristocracy. For Hamilton, such "aristocracy" was not antithetical to democracy. "Wherever humanity gathers into society," she asserted, "an aristocracy rises to the surface as surely as cream on milk." Not only is such ordering of persons natural, according to Hamilton, but it exemplifies healthy democracy: "The character of the aristocracy is at once determined by and determinative of the character of the democracy out of which it springs." Hamilton's use of "aristocracy" as an indicator of a healthy *democracy* rather than old wealth or oppressive social hierarchy indicates how blunted the term had become in late-century America—aristocracy could be constitutive of, rather than antithetical to, a democratic state. As fears of social unrest, which had always accompanied American republicanism, increased alongside burgeoning immigration, industrialization, and urbanization, so did the identification of women with queens. Such fears were soothed by locating hope for American civilization and cultural refinement in its women at all levels of society.[21]

While the popularity of Queen Victoria and romantic medievalism both contributed to the cultural appeal of queenship, the rhetoric's power to signify idealized womanhood was derived from its association with Mary. Although Protestant Americans rejected Catholic veneration of Mary as *Regina Coeli* (Queen of Heaven) and the theological underpinnings of the descriptor, Mary's queenship was commonplace in American, both as a title and a visual image. Unlike titles that remained objectionable to Protestants, such as Mother of God and Mediatrix, or obscure ones such as Star of the Sea, by the end of the century, the title Queen of Heaven had become a common stand-in for Madonna or Blessed Mother in popular discussions of her figure. Queenly images of Mary (which included images of her Coronation as Queen of Heaven as well as other crowned or regal images such as Assumptions) abounded, as did Mary-inspired imagery of the regal female ideal. Just as idealized depictions of a woman cradling a child evoked famous Madonna and Child paintings to nineteenth-century viewers, idealized images of beautiful crowned women evoked famous paintings of the Crowned Virgin.

Regina Coeli: The Catholic Queen of Heaven

Mary's Coronation as Queen of Heaven was closely linked to the doctrines of Mary's Assumption and her Immaculate Conception. Because Mary was immaculately conceived and never subject to original sin, she was understood to have been directly assumed into heaven at the end of her life, where she was joyously received by God, Christ, and the angels, and crowned

Queen of Heaven. While the Assumption of Mary was not declared dogma until 1950 because of its dependency on Immaculate Conception theology, there was a groundswell of interest in its promulgation after the Immaculate Conception was defined in 1854.[22]

Assumption iconography was very similar to Immaculate Conception iconography. Neither depicted historical events, but rather theological doctrines, and so relied on symbolism to indicate content. Both took the Woman of the Apocalypse (described in the New Testament book of Revelation 11:19–12:18) as their model. In both, Mary was depicted in midair, surrounded by angels, usually without the infant Christ, and crowned either with a ring of stars, an imperial crown, or both. Francisco Pacheco provided the classic definition of Immaculate Conception iconography in 1649, advising that "in this loveliest of mysteries, Our Lady should be painted as a beautiful young girl, twelve or thirteen years old, in the flower of her youth . . . surrounded by the sun . . . which sweetly blends into the sky. Rays of light emanate from her head, around which is a ring of twelve stars. An imperial crown adorns her head. . . . Under her feet is the moon."[23] The crown of stars and the imperial crown tied the devotional subjects to Mary's crowning as Queen of Heaven.

In 1837 Gregory XVI provided new impetus to the veneration of Marian imagery through coronation. He held a ceremony at the Roman Marian chapel of Santa Maria Maggiore in which he adorned the famous ancient icon of Mary said to have been painted by St. Luke with two crowns, for Mary and for the infant Christ.[24] Afterward, he released the brief *Caelestis Regina*, standardizing the coronation rite, which subsequently came into widespread use. Later, at the 1854 Immaculate Conception proclamation ceremony, Pius IX reinforced coronation as a key element of Marian veneration with the crowning of the statue of Mary, reinforcing the connection between the Immaculate Conception dogma and Mary's queenship. *Ineffabilis Deus*, the Apostolic Constitution defining the Immaculate Conception, also emphasized Mary's queenship, explaining that Mary "has been appointed by God to be the Queen of heaven and earth, and is exalted above all the choirs of angels and saints, and even stands at the right hand of her only-begotten Son, Jesus Christ our Lord."[25] After the proclamation, Mary's queenship became increasingly important to American Catholics, who commemorated her Coronation during the ceremony, supported a definition of Mary's Assumption, and closely followed the ongoing Marian apparitions and connected devotions (among others, the Marian apparitions at

LaSalette, 1846; Pontmain, 1871; and Knock, 1879, were described by witnesses as crowned). Many of her devout believed that the apparitions signaled Mary was more actively asserting her agency on earth.

Pope Leo XIII strongly encouraged Marian devotionalism, especially the rosary. Beginning in 1883, Leo XIII issued eleven encyclicals specifically promoting the rosary, as well as others encouraging devotion to Mary. The fourth and fifth glorious mysteries of the rosary are Mary's Assumption and her Coronation as Queen of Heaven. Pope Leo XIII also raised the Feast of the Holy Rosary to a double of the second class (a higher ranking in the liturgical calendar) and added the title Queen of the Most Holy Rosary to the Litany of Loreto, a sixteenth-century devotional recitation of Marian titles and petitions. The rosary, a traditional, popular, widespread Marian devotion was powerful in connecting disparate groups of Catholics and drawing attention to Mary as Queen of Heaven.

Also under Leo's papacy, 1878–1903, American Catholic devotion to Mary was increasingly tied to domestic ideology. His encyclicals linked devotionalism and domesticity, tied "the safety of the family to the safety of the world," and specifically encouraged families to pray the rosary together.[26] Earlier, religious devotion was assumed to be personal and private, but with papal encouragement, Catholics increasingly conducted rosary and other Marian devotions together as families. Leo XIII's emphasis on the family as a site of devotionalism brought Mary increasingly into the center of family life and underscored her centrality to Catholic understandings of domesticity. Along with private devotionalism, church-sponsored events brought the lay community together in sodalities, at missions, and through novenas with Marian themes. The vernacular hymns that were sung in lay devotional meetings at the end of the century primarily contained motherly and queenly images of Mary.[27]

While domestic and regal images of Mary seem to be at odds, they were reconciled in the widely embraced metaphor of domestic queenship.[28] Regal images of Mary in devotional, visual, and literary forms increased alongside domestic portraits of her. If some Catholics hoped to temper the powerful model of female authority conveyed by Mary's queenship by emphasizing her domestic role, they were reacting against the powerful, nondomestic Marian images that proliferated at the same time.

Despite the powerful imagery of Mary ruling (or coruling) heaven and earth, Catholic women were significantly less likely to participate in suffrage and other woman's rights campaigns than Protestant women. In part, this was because many woman's rights advocates were anti-Catholic. Also, Catholic women's experiences as members of a persecuted religious minority strengthened their allegiance to their Church and coreligionists, preventing them from forming strong gender-based alliances across religious boundaries. They were also likely either to view Catholicism as inherently empowering to women, or to view changing social norms as threatening to their religious culture and identity. However, Catholic women, drawing on the powerful examples and religious importance of Mary and the female saints, "contested and renegotiated the parameters of their experience" within the Church.[29] While twentieth-century, second-wave-feminist Catholic women would thoughtfully explore and critique the Marian strand in Catholic thought, many Catholic women in the late nineteenth century felt empowered by the dignity and independence of Mary's model of female queenship.

Protestant Perspectives on the Queenship of Mary

As early as the 1860s, many Protestant Americans referred to Mary as "Queen of Heaven" uncritically, interchanging the term with other names for Mary. However, "Queen of Heaven" was also used to refer to the Catholic Mary in contradistinction to the "real" Protestant, or "biblical," Mary. A common refrain in Protestant articles was that Mary should be honored but not worshipped, esteemed but not enthroned as queen. One typical example from a Baptist publication analyzed the history of the term *Theotokos* (Mother of God), concluding: "She was rightly esteemed as 'blessed,' highly favored, and exalted by God among women, but it did not occur to those who first used the title [*Theotokos*] to seat her on a throne to be worshiped by angels and men as the Queen of Heaven."[30] This commentator equated her queenship with her worship while her Motherhood of God did not imply worship. This analysis points to discomfort with the term "Queen of Heaven," but was uncharacteristic; most Protestant commentators regarded Queen of Heaven as a much more acceptable term for Mary than Mother of God, especially for common, informal use. However, this article contextualized the title Mother of God in terms of its historic role in the Christological controversies of the fifth century, and argued for Protestant acceptance or tolerance of the title on the grounds that it did not indicate worship.[31]

In another example of Queen of Heaven indicating the Catholic Mary, an article in a general interest magazine about the life of twelfth-century archbishop and Catholic and Anglican saint Thomas Becket cited Mary's Coronation as Queen of Heaven as the moment she became theologically unavailable to Protestants. The author commended Becket's childhood religious instruction, especially his mother's placing him "under the protection of the Virgin, directing him 'to cast all his trust upon her after Christ,' for Mary was not as yet 'Queen of Heaven.' "[32] The author judged that this instruction was beneficial, suggesting that Mary had an important role to play in Christian faith and practice, until, at some later point, she became "Queen of Heaven." The author may have been suggesting that Mary's status changed during Becket's lifetime or more recently, perhaps with her Coronation at the Immaculate Conception ceremony. However construed, in his estimation, Mary's queenship should dissuade parents from encouraging children to trust in her because such trust would no longer be "after Christ," but *before* him.

Henry Hart Milman, Anglican scholar and dean of St. Paul's Cathedral in London, made this case succinctly in his article on history of the Latin Church and its Mariolatry: "Mary was now the Queen of Heaven instead of Christ ... the crowning act of this idolatry [was] the promulgation of the dogma of the immaculate conception."[33] Milman saw Mary's queenship eclipsing Christ's royal rule; in her Coronation, her power trumped his. He also cited the Immaculate Conception declaration as a pivotal moment of Mary's theological coronation as queen, despite his recognition that veneration of Mary as Queen had been popular for centuries.

In articles like these, Protestants used the title "Queen of Heaven" to indicate Catholic overelevation of Mary, her eclipse of Christ. However, Protestants used Queen of Heaven language in many ways. The parallel Protestant strands of response to Marian imagery in general—theological denunciation, on the one hand, and appropriation of her embodiment of the female ideal on the other—were both apparent in their usage of and reaction to the title. N. G. Batt, in an 1870 magazine article, used Mary's queenship to denounce Catholic overattention to Mary, but also to comment on Protestantism's troubling lack of female religious figures. While the author criticized Catholic Marian devotionalism—"The cultus of the Blessed Virgin Mary is every year rapidly on the increase, and threatens ere long to be the one religious idea of a large part of Christendom"—he nevertheless emphasized the human longing for a spiritual queen.[34] Positing that early Christianity had a distinctively masculine flavor compared to paganism, Batt wrote: "A King of Heaven had been revealed" with the dawn of Christianity, "but where was the Queen? Her throne stood empty." He conjectured that early Christianity was spiritually bereft because it lacked the queenly ideal that later developed in Marian theology. This queenly ideal was "inured by the habits of ages to the contemplation of womanly grace, purity, loveliness, tenderness, and, above all, maternity." "What a void," he demanded, "must have been felt on the promulgation of Christianity!" He concluded by cautioning readers not to return to paganism by improperly worshiping Mary, as Catholics did. However, he affirmed the value of Mary in her roles as Virgin, Mother, and Queen: "By a curious felicity every traditional feeling, every passionate longing . . . found what it needed in some aspect of St. Mary. As Virgin . . . As Mother (Theotokos) . . . As Queen of Heaven."[35] "Queen," along with "Mother" and "Virgin," were essential aspects of the Marian ideal that explained its resonance with human spiritual needs and its continuing appeal. The function of queenship here is significant. Batt's inclusion of queenship as a female archetype alongside motherhood and virginhood made female power and autonomy fundamental aspects of idealized womanhood.

Other Protestants who objected to the term "Queen of Heaven" resisted this aspect, specifically questioning the appropriateness of female power and a female regnant. For instance, English poet and novelist Jean Ingelow, in her serialized novel *Off the Skelligs* (simultaneously published in British and U.S. magazines) tied Mary's queenship to disordered Catholic gender norms. In the story, the female English narrator, traveling in France, repeatedly linked the elevation of Mary to the demasculinization of men. On approaching Chartres Cathedral, she first observed that carvings of "bishops, saints, apostles, and kings" on the doors showed a "want of muscle, and force, and manliness."[36] Once inside, she described the veneration of the famous black Madonna as idolatry. Her companion whispered to her: " 'Did you see the Virgin over the great door?' 'I only saw two figures,' " she replied. " 'That was our Saviour crowning Mary Queen of Heaven, and declaring her equal with Himself.' "[37] Here, the narrator's companion described Mary's Coronation as placing her on equal footing with Christ. After further objecting to various aspects of Mary's queenship, including the dedication of the cathedral to "Our Lady of Chartes . . . mighty Queen"; the priest's announcement that "behold my brothers, we are now at the feet of Mary"; and the similarity of the proceedings at Chartres to "Regent Street on the Queen's birthday," the narrator analyzed her experiences, directly equating Mary's elevation to disordered gender norms. Watching a procession, the narrator notes men in fine gowns and boys singing to Mary, and observed:

"There was the old archbishop in his golden mitre, and womanly gear reaching down to his shoes, and all stiff with gems and orfevrerie and lace . . . then in a moment [the music] flew back to its first theme, and burst upon us like musical thunder, 'God save the Queen.' It was the Queen of Heaven, who is emphatically queen at Chartres."[38] Ingelow suggested in her fictional account of Catholicism in France that as Mary was elevated to a position of ruling authority, male priests were emasculated. As in earlier Protestant responses to the Immaculate Conception, Ingelow objected to overelevation of a human figure, but focused primarily on her sex.

Poet Thomas Edward Brown grappled with the Queen of Heaven title in one of his poems in "Fo'c's'le Yarns." Like Ingelow, Mary's queenship was a problem. But for Brown, her sex explained and, perhaps, excused her overelevation. In the poem, a seaman reflects on his experience of viewing paintings of the Madonna in Italy:

Whoever thought that a woman could look
Like that—he knew the Holy Book;
He knew the mind of God; he knew
What a woman could be, and he drew and drew . . .
He was paintin' the queen—they calls her the Queen
Of Heaven, but of coorse she couldn ha' been—
But that's the sort—a woman lifted.[39]

Brown's unsophisticated sailor extols Marian painting as an accurate reflection of the mind of God (and the Bible) regarding the nature of womanhood, and, while he dismisses the theological belief in Mary as the literal Queen of Heaven, he embraces her as a "queen" and "a woman lifted."

While Protestants continued to use "Queen of Heaven" to object to Catholic "worship" of Mary, many employed the title to convey her elevation and her typification of the female ideal. The dialectic between Mary's queenship and the female queenship ideal was mutually reinforcing—models of womanhood were drawn from the Marian ideal, with its underlying Catholic theological claims; but the growing popularity of the metaphor for women normalized claims about Mary's queenship and disconnected them from theological claims. Protestants who objected to the term "Queen of Heaven" argued that Mary's elevation was excessive and saw her Coronation, with its startling image of a woman crowned in heaven, as exemplifying that problem. Like responses to the Immaculate Conception, objections to Mary's queenship often focused on her sex. At the same time, other Protestants called Mary "Queen of Heaven," citing her queenship as a personification of womanhood. In these uses, Mary's crowning was a celebration of the triumph of an abstracted ideal of womanhood, not a literal theological statement about a religious figure. This was especially apparent in the adoption of Marian queenship iconography in depictions of idealized womanhood in popular visual culture.

Queens and the Queen of Heaven in Visual Culture

Queenly visual imagery grew especially popular in the late nineteenth century. Just as painters and photographers copied Madonna and Child imagery, they also staged and re-created regal Marian art. In photographs and illustrations, noble, solitary women propagated the queenly ideal conveyed in traditional Marian compositions. These queenly images evoked the New Woman's autonomous selfhood, but since Marian imagery was associated with piety and purity, they did so in a less threatening way. These images were tied to the domestic queenship motif and were used to communicate class status and womanly ideals, not religious affiliation or theology. Queenly images of Mary were recommended by tastemakers to be displayed alongside reproductions of actual historical queens, European architecture, and other idealized representations of femininity. Other Marian subjects were also chosen and recommended for their ability to portray "elevated" womanhood.

In 1888, *Chautauquan* magazine declared *Madonnas by Old Masters* a book of the year, writing: "No art book of the year can lay claim to more permanent value and interest than *Madonnas by Old Masters*." The article continued: "Of this subject, so popular with artists for the expression of their own ideals of womanly perfection, ten of the most celebrated examples have been selected for reproduction."[40] In this and many other articles, Marian visual imagery was popularized as expressions of the female ideal rather than devotional or theological aides. The reviewer encouraged his primarily Protestant readership to purchase a book of Marian art, not for its aesthetic merit nor for its religious value, but for its inspirational gender content. In fact, he failed to consider religious faith as a factor in the historical popularity of Marian subject matter, postulating instead that the long-deceased artists had been primarily concerned with conveying idealized womanhood. Furthermore, he claimed that the female ideals achieved in these portraits of the Blessed Mother were relevant and of permanent value for his contemporary readership.

When the fair treatment, "dignity," or "elevation" of women was discussed in this period, it was understood, at minimum, as protection from excessive physical labor, sexual exploitation and abuse, physical assault and battery, and abandonment. As the woman's movement drew attention to structural inequalities in "Christian" societies, including restrictions on women's participation in public life; legal rights to children, property, and income; and sexual abuse, more essays and articles defended Christianity's history as liberatory for women—especially because of Mary's model. Commentators cited Christian societies' moral opposition to prostitution, polygamy, adultery, and "sex slavery" (sometimes including spousal rape), as well as women's rights to manage their households and "influence" choices that affected them. The intention of many of these articles was to protect the status quo by denying women's need for further emancipation; others, however, strove to demonstrate that woman's movement reforms were legitimate extensions of Christian principles. As discussed in chapter 4, some Catholics and Protestants drew on Marian imagery to directly engage changing gender norms and create more liberatory models. These Marian models of womanhood could include self-determination, meaningful work, the right to eschew marriage, partnership in child rearing, public speaking, and other forms of an enlarged sphere of influence and agency.

The historical prevalence of Marian art was often cited as a key factor in the elevation of women. Many commentators attributed Europeans' comparatively fair treatment of women to these visual reminders of Mary's embodiment of idealized womanhood and importance to God. Princeton University professor and Presbyterian minister Henry Van Dyke advanced a version of this common argument in an article on the Annunciation in art that he wrote for *Harper's*.[41] Van Dyke boastfully (and xenophobically) praised the Christian model of gender relations as more equitable than that of other world cultures, which he attributed to the prevalence of Marian art in the West. Van Dyke called the model of womanhood personified in Marian art "dignified" and "uplifted," and contrasted it to the "ignorant and degraded" status of women in other ancient cultures and of the "Arab woman of to-day." Situating the well-being of women as a core concern of God, he attributed the favored status of Jews and Christians to the gender relations they cultivated. God rewarded the Hebrews, he claimed, because they

Lorenzo Ghiberti, *The Annunciation*. From the Baptistery (North Door), Florence (Scala/Art Resource, New York).

honored and protected women; God chose them "for no other reason" than that they "cherished the purity and dignity of womanhood more perfectly than any other race of the ancient world."

The article was accompanied by eight reproductions of Annunciation paintings and reliefs, a few sketches of other Marian artworks, and several Marian poems. In his analyses of these works, Van Dyke emphasized that Marian images were typifications of womanhood rather than representations of a unique religious figure. For example, in analyzing the gilded bronze relief *The Annunciation* by Lorenzo Ghiberti, he described Mary's "slender girlish figure" and her expression of "timidity and joy," concluding that the scene "might be anywhere; it is womanhood, visited by God." In Van Dyke's reading, Ghiberti's Mary represented all women in her encounter with the divine. In another example, he discussed the painting *Ecce Ancilla Domini* by his contemporary, the pre-Raphaelite painter Dante Gabriel Rossetti. Van Dyke described the painting as "noble" in its conception of a fair and delicate Mary, half-rising from sleep, exuding "spiritual loveliness." He concluded the article with Rossetti's own Annunciation sonnet "Mary's Girlhood," which idealized the "pre-elect" Mary, a girl who was faithful, patient, wise, devout, and simple, an "angel-watered lily, that near God grows and is quiet."[42] Van Dyke approvingly echoed Rossetti, idealizing womanhood in salvific terms and representing the female ideal through Mary. It is unclear from Van Dyke's analysis whether he believed that such well-behaved women earned the "elevated" status that inspired their protection, or whether a society that protected and elevated women allowed them to achieve such rarified femininity. In either case, he propounded a Marian model of womanhood and linked it to women's safety and dignity.

Similarly, in the article "Some Types of the Virgin," frequent *Harper's* contributor Theodore Child discussed famous Marian paintings from a range of historical periods and the role they played in structuring the social order. He wrote: "The pictures reproduced [here] remain as landmarks in the history of human culture; and the very inadequate comments of the accompanying text are offered with all humility in the hope that they may be found suggestive of culture to sympathetic souls."[43] Like Van Dyke, Child argued for the superiority of Western gender relations over those of other cultures and for the role of Marian art in successfully conveying an elevated model of womanhood. In Child's opinion, Christians' embrace of Marian imagery represented the triumph of Jewish attitudes toward women over Greek (pagan) attitudes toward women. Compared to women in other

Dante Gabriel Rossetti, *Ecce Ancilla Domini* (The Annunciation). From the Tate Gallery, London (Tate, London/Art Resource, New York).

ancient cultures, he asserted, ancient Jewish women enjoyed equitable treatment. Because Mary was a Hebrew woman, the gender norms transmitted through her figure represented her culture's enlightened ideas. "If the Greek idea of the inferiority of women had prevailed," he wrote, "the history of Christianity and society in Europe would have been other than it is." Marian art disseminated beliefs about the female sex that transformed woman's place in society.

For Child, Mary's maternity was essential to her role in establishing equitable gender roles. He repeatedly used the term "Mother of God" for Mary, emphasizing her maternity and elevated spiritual status. Describing the importance of Mary's role as mother, he wrote: "By the absence of that exquisite element of sympathy and consolation, the human maternity of the Virgin, civilization would have been deprived of one of its mightiest levers, and sentiment one of its most delicate chords." Mary's motherhood was sentimentally appealing, but it was also, in Child's estimation, a great "leveler." Like some Catholic theologians, Child argued that Mary's volitional and physical participation in the incarnation allowed a woman to play a significant role in the gospel narrative, making evident women's equality before God. Child did not advocate Marian veneration or an increased religious role for Mary in Protestantism, but in this argument, he approximated Catholic arguments that theologically underpinned devotion to the Madonna (like Mary as Mediatrix). Despite this theological engagement with Mary as a religious actor, Child concluded that Marian painting continued to "fascinate and console us still" because of its renderings of "unsurpassed ideals of feminine beauty and expression" that expressed "intellectual qualities . . . elements of soul . . . [and] mirrored image of the yearnings and aspirations of noble humanity."[44]

In these and other treatments of Marian art in the 1880s and 1890s, Protestant commentators used Marian imagery to construct a female ideal that evoked traditional models of womanhood, but was more attuned to women's social equality, fair treatment, and autonomy than that of previous decades. Toward the end of the century, advice columns educating readers how to view and value art became more numerous and insistent, often quoting and promoting Anna Jameson's commentary as authoritative. Displaying Marian art became a way to evoke an aristocratic past and also to indicate general religious sensitivity. Despite the fact that it was often explicitly Catholic in its origins and underlying theology, religious art conveyed an appearance of generic spiritual refinement as well as aesthetic taste.

IN THIS NUMBER—ROMANTIC FIGURES AGAINST WAR'S GRIM BACKGROUND;
THE VIRGIN MARY ("WOMEN OF THE BIBLE SERIES"), *By Cardinal Gibbons*

HARPER'S BAZAR

Copyright, 1900, by HARPER & BROTHERS
[The Post Trust Company, Trustee]

PUBLISHED WEEKLY
VOL. XXXIII.—NUMBER 11

NEW YORK, SATURDAY, MARCH 17, 1900

TEN CENTS A COPY
FOUR DOLLARS A YEAR

"WOMEN OF THE BIBLE"—THE VIRGIN MARY.
[ILLUSTRATION BY FRANK V DU MOND.—[SEE PAGE 728]

Cover of *Harper's Bazar* 33, no. 11 (March 17, 1900). This cover illustrates another article
on Mary in a popular magazine. Unlike past issues, which contained Marian articles
written by Protestants, this feature story was contributed by Catholic Cardinal James
Gibbons. From the Mann Library, Cornell University.

Often, the Catholicity of classic religious art and its theological under-pinnings were ignored completely. For instance, the author of a series on "Christianity in Art" in the *Chautauquan* emphasized the spiritually trans-formative power of religious art as well as its ability to cultivate culture and refinement. He advised: "It is necessary that the individual shall adopt some habit of careful analysis of artworks, to be kept up at intervals for his lifetime . . . for art, like religion, is a spiritual energy of the soul. . . . The one who is un-regenerate in his tastes is contented with shapes and appearances in the world that are ugly . . . and that lack spirituality. . . . With the development of a taste for art there is a development of a love of the manifestation of the divine in sensuous forms."[45] The author emphasized the power of art to de-velop the soul and, by extension, to demonstrate to others that one's soul has been developed. The artwork he recommended, which could develop the (implicitly Protestant) soul, was primarily Marian. Like most writers of the period, he recommended the *Sistine Madonna* as the obvious place to begin, noting "the universal verdict of critics that this picture is in a rank by itself apart." The value of the painting, as he saw it, lay in its presentation of Mary as a model of transcendence—"she has the look of a woman elevated above the rank of all others"—because the image of an elevated woman would have a refining effect on the souls of viewers. Noting that the painting was synchronic with Luther's posting of his ninety-five theses, he mused: "Do the Madonna and Child perhaps see the great schism which will rend the Christian Church of Western and Central Europe in twain?" He also noted the painting's move from a holy to a secular site: "If some faint pre-monition of these things were in the mind of Raphael and received expres-sion in the supernatural earnestness of the chief personages in the *Sistine Madonna*, it was a strange fate that should carry away this Madonna out of Italy and the home of the Catholic Church into the northern home of Prot-estantism, where the Madonna received no such ceremonial homage as in Catholic countries." If moving the *Sistine Madonna* from Catholic to Protes-tant territory was a "strange fate," then, in essence, he was replicating that fate by recommending the painting to a primarily Protestant audience for its spiritual and cultural improvement.

What is more, he urged his readers to treat Marian imagery as religiously meaningful rather than merely aesthetically beautiful or sentimental. "In the Catholic religion," he explained, "the Virgin symbolically presents to the devout worshiper the tenderness and love of God, which is as that of a mother toward her infant—a love that swoops down to humanity in its utmost feebleness and helplessness, and cares for it just as much as if it were the highest and completest realization of saintliness and rationality." This was an abstracted version of Catholic Mariology; instead of actually venerating Mary as the Mother of God, he suggested that readers should spiritually engage her as a representation of God's love expressed through the metaphor of motherhood.

Yet, it was not merely her maternity that Protestants must grasp, in his view. In order to be spiritually transformed by Marian art, readers must also acknowledge her *queenship*, which he tied to her ability to represent the "Eternal-Feminine." "Goethe," he noted, "closes the second part of his 'Faust' with a 'chorus mysticus,' that celebrates the Virgin with the words: 'The Eternal-Feminine leadeth us on.'" Encouraging his readers to likewise affirm the "eternal-feminine" through Mary, he elaborated on Mary's role as Queen of Heaven in Catholicism: "By magnifying the influence of the Virgin (*Regina Coeli*) in heaven, the grace of God toward imperfect creatures" was being depicted through its only adequate symbol, "that of the mother-love." He used the title "*Regina Coeli*" (Queen of Heaven) to signify Mary's glorification, the eternal feminine, and her powerful invocation of God's love in her divine maternity.

This analysis put forward the figure of Mary, as Mother and Queen, as a metaphor for God's love and the female ideal itself as religiously meaningful and transformative. Despite its dramatic claims and poetic language, it was consistent with the ways in which tastemakers, drawing on Jameson's example, were encouraging Protestant Americans to value maternal and queenly Marian art. Currier & Ives catalogs provide evidence of the increasing popularity of queenly images of Mary and queen imagery more broadly. In the last decades of the century, Currier & Ives produced more than thirty Marian images, including "The Queen of Angels," which depicted Mary being crowned by angels while stepping on a serpent, and "The Ascension of the Virgin," which showed Mary with a dramatic crown.[46] These were sold alongside popular images of historical queens, including several depictions of Mary Queen of Scots, who was "endlessly popular as a tragic heroine ... despite or because of her intractable allegiance to popery," and Queen Victoria.[47] One particularly queenly print of Victoria represented her encircled by all her various crowns.

Images of historical queens were produced in quantity, sold well, and remain easy to find today. However, the most prolific queenly prints produced by Currier & Ives were generic depictions of beautiful, solitary, idealized

QUEEN OF LOVE AND BEAUTY.

PUBLISHED BY CURRIER & IVES 152 NASSAU ST NEW YORK.

Currier & Ives, *Queen of Love and Beauty*, ca. 1870. One of many images of beautiful, regal women titled "Queen of . . ." in the Currier & Ives catalog. From the Library of Congress, Washington, D.C. (Gale Research, Detroit, Mich.).

women, titled "queens." There were dozens of these images entitled, variously: "The Queen of Flowers," "The Queen of the South," "The Queen of the West," "Queen of Love and Beauty," "Queen of Brunettes," "Queen of the Blondes," "Queen of Hearts," "Queen of the Woods," and so on. Some of these queens were crowned, as in the "Queen of Love and Beauty," which depicted a heavily crowned and bejeweled woman looking stern and regal.[48] Others had jewels, pearls, or flowers in their hair in place of a crown. All of the images idealized womanhood as a type of queenship. Of particular interest is "Queen of the House," the only one of the "queen" images portraying a small child.[49] The girl was depicted in a bed or cradle, acting out a domestic scene with her dolls, already aspiring to domestic queenship.

Some portion of the Marian imagery produced in these decades by Currier & Ives, the Louis Prang Company, and other inexpensive printers was intended for the Roman Catholic market.[50] For example, Currier & Ives produced images such as "The Most Holy Catholic Faith," which depicted the Church as an oversized woman (possibly Mary), holding out the Eucharist to a mother and three praying women. Other images, such as "Our Lady of Knock" and "Pilgrims at the Shrine of Our Lady of Lourdes," were also obviously directed to Roman Catholic devout. It is harder to determine the audience for other Marian images. Many images, such as illustrations or reproductions of the Immaculate Conception, the Assumption, and Holy Family groups, by Raphael, Murillo, or Correggio were popular among Protestants as well as Catholics. Marian prints were also distributed by settlement workers, indicating that some portion of Marian art was intended for a broad, nonspecialized market. The workers at Hull House, for example, kept a library of art reproductions, including religious and Marian art, for distribution to their beneficiaries. While the content of art reproductions was perhaps secondary to art's status as a transmitter of high culture, many charitable workers ascribed spiritual or moral efficacy to these images, particularly those depicting Mary or angels.[51]

One account of Marian imagery in settlement work was given by Elizabeth McCracken, who wrote about her experiences in her article "Pictures for the Tenements" in *Atlantic Monthly*.[52] She described giving a print of Raphael's *Madonna of the Chair* (*Madonna della Seggiola*) to a poor woman who subsequently lost her infant. The woman placed the image over her mantel, saying of the Madonna: "It seems as if she'd even, bein' here, 'ave let me hold her baby a little while, mine bein' gone."[53] The woman does not appear to have been devoted to Mary, nor was she familiar with the painting.

She claimed to prefer it to another image donated to her, Leonardo DaVinci's *Mona Lisa*, because while both paintings were said to be "good," Raphael's Madonna offered comfort. In this account, Marian art was intended to provide cultural uplift, but the recipient found emotional or spiritual solace in the painting because of Mary's maternity.

Marian art reproductions were not only seen as culturally beneficial to the poor, but were frequently recommended for middle-class women decorating homes on a budget. In his 1887 book *The House Beautiful*, Clarence Cook wrote: "We are happy in knowing that in these days there can always be procured, at trifling expense, some copy of a noble picture—the 'Sistine Madonna' of Raphael, the 'Madonna of the Meyer Family,' by Holbein, or some one of the lesser, yet still glorious, gifts of Heaven to man."[54] The "noble" paintings he recommended included the *Madonna of the Meyer Family*, which depicts Mary as the Queen of Heaven, indicated by a crown resembling the German imperial crown, and the "lesser, yet still glorious" choices that he mentioned were likewise Marian art, or, as he calls them, "gifts of Heaven." These were all high Mariological subjects, not Madonna and Child groupings. These images, he reflected, "shall be worth living with."[55]

Protestant art critic Estelle Hurll was another important domestic tastemaker. She contributed notes to later (posthumous) editions of Jameson's *Sacred and Legendary Art* series and wrote several notable art books, including *The Madonna in Art* and *The Home Book of Great Paintings*.[56] She was particularly interested in using Mary as an archetype of femininity and motherhood. For example, in her book *The Madonna in Art*, she wrote of a Luigi Vivarini *Madonna and Child*: "Before such pictures as this, gleaming in the dim light of quiet chapels, many a heart, before unbelieving, may learn a new reverence for the mysterious sanctity of motherhood."[57] In Hurll's conception, "unbelievers" were agnostic toward motherhood as a transcendent ideal, not toward Marian dogma such as the virgin birth. This shift reflected her assumption and preference that Marian imagery be read as typological representations of motherhood rather than visual expressions of biblical narratives or theological doctrines.

In an 1894 issue of *Arthur's Home Magazine*, Hurll advised women on how to select pictures for their homes. In almost every room, she specifically recommended that Marian imagery be placed alongside other images of queens to inspire family members with an ideal of womanhood that was both pious and aristocratic. Her first suggestion was to place a reproduction of the *Sistine Madonna*, which she called "the finest work of art the world has ever seen," in the parlor. Her reasoning was that the picture would have an "elevating influence [which would] make itself felt upon all, the sweet strong spirituality of this ideal of womanhood, hastening down the centuries to present Christ to the world."[58] The primary appeal of the *Sistine Madonna* was its ability to represent both religious sentiment and the ideal of womanhood. Hurll's following recommendations were a series of historical and mythological queens. In particular she recommended paintings of Queen Louise of Prussia: "a gracious, womanly presence to have in the parlor ... the great grandmother of the present young German emperor, a noble and beautiful woman." In addition to the most well-known depiction of Queen Louise, a "full-length figure" by Gustav Richter, she also suggested an artotype of a painting by Nicolai, in which the queen is depicted holding her infant son in her lap, Madonna-like. By recommending that images of the *Sistine Madonna* and Queen Louise with her son be displayed together, Hurll constructed a female ideal that emphasized maternity, religious perfection, and nobility. In *Madonna in Art*, she elaborated on her partiality toward regal images of Mary, explaining: "In every true home the mother is queen, enthroned in the hearts of her loving children. There is, therefore, a beautiful double significance, which we should always have in mind, in looking at the Madonna enthroned. According to the theological conception of the period in which it was first produced, the picture stands for the Virgin Mother as Queen of Heaven. Understood typically, it represents the exaltation of motherhood."[59]

Hurll's recommendations for other rooms of the house recapitulated these themes. They included Holy Family groups by Murillo and *Cornelia and Her Children* by Sir Joshua Reynolds, of which she writes: "A noble Roman matron proudly displays her children as the most precious jewels of her possession." Hurll emphasized these paintings' moral function: they were "pictures from which you wish your children to gain their first lessons of character." In this set of images, idealized womanhood was directly connected to the ability to embody and transmit religious and aristocratic ideals. However, despite being idealized through unique figures—historical queens, the Virgin Mary—the shared maternity of all these women was on display, tying their lived experiences to the mother of the household and their attainment of womanly perfection to hers.

The one exception to her consistent recommendations of paintings of Mary and aristocratic women was the dining room, where formality dictated more spare decoration. There, Hurll suggested architectural imagery:

"I have recently seen some very fine large artotypes of celebrated old world castles, which would be particularly elegant for the dining-room. Of this class, 'Heidelberg,' 'Windsor,' and 'Warwick' are notable examples; and 'Melrose' and 'Tintern Abbeys' belong to the same group." European churches and castles complete the set of imagery Hurll selected for the tasteful American home. These choices, notably medieval and European, reinforced the aristocratic ideal that Hurll propounded. She recommended no naturalistic or American scenes, and no nonaristocratic or male figures (other than children). Female figures, represented by aristocratic matrons, queens, and the Madonna communicated refined taste and elevated cultural status. These visual images represented the work that American women were doing through their enacted femininity: ameliorating class anxieties and communicating refinement by becoming "queens."

As Marian and Marian-derived images populated print media and domestic sphere, the ongoing conversation about women's relationship to domesticity and their rights in the public sphere continued. While the Angel in the House was a salvific, self-sacrificing figure, the domestic queen had more potential for rule. The figure of Mary symbolized this queenly ideal primarily because it could transmit female authority while also seeming safely pious and traditional. The autonomy and authority that queenship rhetoric communicated were, in essence, a negotiation between the traditional domestic ideal and the rising pressure of the New Woman.

Ruskin's "Of Queen's Gardens"

The motif of domestic queenship originated in the writings of John Ruskin, whose use of queenship as a metaphor for womanhood predated its popularity in America. Ruskin's 1865 "Of Queen's Gardens," half of his book *Sesame and Lilies*, was, and remains, one of the best-known nineteenth-century elegies of domesticity. Drawing on the Western literary tradition, from medieval courtly romances, to Dante, to Shakespeare, he constructed an argument that woman should inspire and command male action because of her purer and more elevated moral sense. He challenged the "common idea of the marriage relation," that is, that the husband "rules" while the wife obeys without "think[ing] for herself," calling this arrangement "wholly undesirable." Instead, he argued that women have a right and duty to command men on moral questions, home life, and charity and that, if they exercised that right, men would be elevated and wars and poverty would cease. Ruskin used the metaphor of queenship to suggest a bounded, domestic version of authority, but authority nonetheless.

According to Ruskin, men should yield to women in matters big and small, reasonable and arbitrary, from courtship through marriage. "In all Christian ages which have been remarkable for their purity or progress," he wrote, "there has been absolute yielding of obedient devotion, by the lover, to his mistress. I say *obedient;*—not merely enthusiastic and worshiping in imagination, but entirely subject receiving from the beloved woman, however young, not only the encouragement, the praise, and the reward of all toil, but so far as any choice is open, or any question difficult of decision, the *direction* of all toil."[60] Ruskin emphasized that obedience should not be understood as a romanticized notion; the male lover is not merely "enthusiastic" but "subject." He works not merely for his beloved's approval but for her well-being, consulting her on any open choice or difficult decision.

After ruminating along these lines for several pages, asserting the necessity for men to defer to women and be subject to them, Ruskin reasserted masculine authority: "But how, you will ask, is the idea of this guiding function of the woman reconcilable with a true wifely subjection? Simply in that it is a *guiding*, not a determining, function."[61] By this he meant that the husband owes loyalty and obedience to his wife, but never gives up his free will and final authority. He ought to follow her wishes, but he does not have to: she is not in charge. Thus, according to Ruskin, the queen's rule is a form of power, but one that is voluntarily given and easily revoked.

The specific power that woman holds, in Ruskin's view, is the "power to heal, to redeem, to guide, and to guard." He asked his female readers: "Will you not covet such power as this, and seek such throne as this, and be no more housewives, but queens?"[62] To "be no more housewives, but queens" was, in Ruskin's view, to be spiritually and morally pure, to be worthy of inspiration, worthy of being the object (the direction) of male actions. In this essay, Ruskin strongly asserted woman's authority and then pulled back from these assertions, finally equating woman's "rule" with her ability to earn man's attention and sympathy and thus to get her way.

Kate Millet and other feminist writers have thoroughly critiqued Ruskin's vision of womanhood as patronizing and regressive. Millet admitted that Ruskin acknowledged the negative implications of patriarchy for women's lives, but disparaged his solutions as "bland disingenuousness." Writing in 1970, she called his arguments in *Sesame and Lilies* unintellectual and based only on "sentiment, a vague nostalgia about the heroic middle ages, and saccharine assertions about "the Home."[63] Comparing Ruskin's attitude toward women to "paternal racis[m] of the more genial variety," she charged him with writing in order to "ennoble a system of subordination through hopeful rhetoric."[64] Millet's conclusion that Ruskin's assertions of female "queenship" were merely compensatory language justifying a separate-spheres ideology by "reserving the entire scope of human endeavor for the one [man], and a little hothouse for the other [woman]" have influenced most subsequent readings of Ruskin.

Some scholars, however, have challenged aspects of Millet's analysis. Literary scholar Nina Auerbach, for example, perceives ambiguity in Ruskin's descriptions of queenship and recommends reevaluation of his work and its impact. In particular, she argues that Ruskin's depiction of woman-as-queen in "Of Queen's Gardens" contains within it an "awed acknowledgment of special power."[65] She contrasts this portrayal to the anxiety and "impotence" of the "kings" (men) in his parallel text "Of King's Treasuries." Placed side by side, "Of King's Treasuries" reads as a frustrated response to the everyday business of life, while "Of Queen's Gardens" is poetic and grand. Men in "Of King's Treasuries" are indeed in a separate sphere from women; however, they are neither powerful nor active. While Ruskin's vision of womanhood is romanticized and poetic, the masculine role is bounded by meaningless duty and man's agency subsumed by institutions. Ruskin, Auerbach argues, "may want to hymn domesticity, but his language evokes omnipotence, with his queen supplanting God as the sole source of light in a darkness she inhabits."

Other scholars have also interpreted "Of Queens' Gardens" as navigating between a restrictive and an empowering position. For example, Barbara Weltman writes: "Ruskin creates a notion of queenship that offers women under the reign of Queen Victoria a powerful political and mythological model for the broadening of their scope of action, thereby redefining the traditionally domestic arena to include a broad range of philanthropy and social activism. While vigorously supporting Victorian culture's strict separation of spheres for the sexes, Ruskin nevertheless encourages women to do things that other suffocating 'woman worshippers' with whom he is normally conflated, such as Coventry Patmore, oppose."[66] As I have shown previously, queenship rhetoric was often linked with maternalist arguments for increased agency for women. Ruskin, in his hymn to women as queens, suggested that women should be educated and that they should take the lead in helping the unfortunate, positions that supported larger spheres of female action. His rhetoric was different from and potentially more empowering than the Angel in the House rhetoric of Patmore and others precisely because he used the metaphor of queenship. His use of this metaphor at a time when queenship was a political reality in England gave it a weight that is missing from our current vantage point.

Lewis Carroll's *Through the Looking Glass* parodied Victoria's queenship and the growing prevalence of paeans to domesticity as queenship, taking particular aim at Ruskin's "Of Queen's Gardens." Carroll challenged the use of a symbol of power and autocracy to elegize everyday domestic life. In *Through the Looking Glass*, Alice desires to become a queen, and not just a queen, but one among several. Through the ensuing absurdity, Carroll pilloried Ruskin's attempt to persuade all women to be queens. Moreover, he attacked the very premise of domestic queenship. Rather than elevate domesticity, Carroll showed that the domestic queen "inevitably issues commands closer to those of a governess or nurse than to those of a monarch."[67] In doing so, he critiqued both Ruskin's and others' calls for domestic queenship and the reign of Victoria.

Despite Carroll's pointed (though somewhat veiled) critique, by the end of the century, domestic queenship was widely represented in British and American popular culture. While Ruskin was clearly ambivalent about woman's rights, his motif resonated with late-century cultural needs. He made "rule" central to his conception of womanhood, but vacillated between granting women power and withholding it. In his most succinct and provocative phrase, "the woman's power is for rule, not for battle," he called for agency without activity. However, he also acknowledged that women's desires for power and authority were not improper and that women must have areas of control and self-determination. He also pushed the metaphor of a queen's "rule" further, explicitly grappling with how much of men's *obedience* such power could command. Thus, Ruskin developed a metaphor for womanhood that, by explicitly addressing questions of power and agency, was particularly useful for navigating changing gender expectations and balancing traditional and more liberatory expectations for women.

"Shall Womanhood Be Abolished?"
Restrictive and Radical Domestic Queenship

In America, queenship language was employed by traditionalists who prescribed a domestic vision of womanhood, protofeminists who sought an enlarged sphere for women, and moderates who saw the domestic queen as a stronger, more modern, but still domestic figure. "The husband is the leader and representative of his family before the world; the wife shines, and charms, and reigns, queen of the consecrated home" declared the author of an 1877 *New Englander* article entitled "Shall Womanhood Be Abolished?"[68] A traditionalist, he used domestic queenship language to demarcate the home as the boundary of woman's rule. He linked the wife's queenship directly to her rule over the "consecrated home," indicating the sacredness of the domestic sphere and the moral basis for the wife's authority there. By setting up a parallel between the wife and the husband, with her sacred domain explicitly contrasted to his secular domain (i.e., the "world"), he directly countered women's advocates who were calling for a larger sphere of action and increased legal protections and rights for women. By referring to the wife as a "queen" and her domestic role as her "reign," the author asserted not just a separate sphere but also a parallel authority since "queen" implies power and control in an arena. The romanticization of domesticity characteristic of Angel in the House rhetoric is evident in this article, as are its purity, spirituality, and salvific quality. But where Angel rhetoric was wholly sacrificial, the language of queenship was compensatory, implicitly conceding that women need some site of authority.

Traditionalists refuted demands for an enlarged sphere for women by portraying domestic queens who step outside their "kingdom" as abdicating power rather than acquiring it. Most American Catholics who used queenship language to conceptualize womanhood used it in this compensatory and restrictive way. Well-known Catholic novelist Eleanor Donnelly, for example, used this strategy in a *Catholic World* article entitled "Is There a Public Sphere for Woman?" "Woman's true sphere is the domestic one," she wrote. "God made her to be the queen of home. When she is driven out of it by a resultant of forces, she is in a state of violence, her life is out of joint."[69] For Donnelly, women's confinement to the domestic sphere was a God-ordained, natural state of being. In contrast to the New Woman's transgressions into the public, the "queen of the home" enjoyed a spiritualized and dignified domesticity. Donnelly claimed that by bounding their lives within the limits of the domestic sphere, women protected themselves from a "state of violence" and self-destruction. Donnelly also argued that no contribution to society would compensate for the loss of women's work in the home and in child rearing: "What work accomplished by gifted women in art, literature, science, or statecraft can compare with the moulding of a single childish character?" Expanding the queenship metaphor, she wrote:

"Be she as rich or as largely retinued as Sheba's queen, she cannot, she dare not, shift her responsibilities to the shoulders of others. Even when her little ones are in the daily care of good religious, she is bound to look to their instruction, to the formation of their characters." In other words, even if the queenship metaphor was taken literally—indicating financial resources and actual power—it would still not justify any role for women beyond home-making and mothering.

In his 1878 book *The Mirror of True Womanhood: A Guide for Women in the World*, New York Catholic priest, Bernard O'Reilly also used queenship to indicate women's right of command within the domestic sphere: "The mother is queen there; her will, in all that pertains to the proprieties and the charities of life, no one, not even her husband, should be permitted to question."[70] O'Reilly granted a very limited authority to women, but nonetheless, he used queenship language to suggest an area where they had actual authority: the sphere in which a woman's "will" should not be questioned is the sphere in which she is "queen." But even as O'Reilly used queenship language to signify women's power, he also sought to define its limits.

Like Donnelly, O'Reilly based a woman's right to "rule" on her moral authority. "Why will you not be a queen in your own little kingdom, O wife, O mother, O sister, and make all subject to you by this ascendancy of your goodness and devotion?"[71] O'Reilly did not grant women inherent authority, but rather suggested that they earn authority—that they *become* queens—when they enact a moral and spiritual domestic role that inspires the voluntary submission of family members. Without such "goodness and devotion" a woman is not a queen, and therefore not able to command others. Thus, for O'Reilly, queenship establishes and bounds female authority: queenly authority is bounded by location, the home; by topic, the proprieties and charities of life; and by proper rule, she must prove moral authority.

While both Catholic and Protestant writers used the theme of queenship to grapple with changing gender norms and pivotal issues such as woman's suffrage, and nearly all tied queenship to domesticity, casting it as a private and largely symbolic form of female authority, queenship rhetoric was multivalent. Ultimately, the notion of a queen's *rule*, implicit in this rhetoric, could be used to justify the transgression of the public-private boundary. Advocates for woman's rights used the moral authority and underlying agency of the queenship metaphor to bridge the divide between the Angel in the House and the New Woman. According to them, women could act publicly as "queens," while retaining their connection to the home and bringing their moral authority into their public lives.

For example, in Hamilton's article on Zilpah Grant Banister discussed earlier, she used queenship rhetoric to legitimate and consecrate Banister's career. Because queenship was already widely used to represent idealized womanhood and because it implied female authority, Hamilton employed the metaphor to argue that the public life of Banister was not transgressive. "Queen Zilpah," Hamilton wrote, "entered upon the full duties of her kingdom" when, after "teaching awhile," she became "the head of her own schools." Unlike Ruskin's and O'Reilly's version of queenship, in which queenship is attained through morality, Hamilton asserted that Banister did not attain the full status of a queen until she took a position of public authority as the head of her own school—that is, until she actually had power.

Hamilton further distanced Banister from radicalism by emphasizing her Puritan spirituality and traditional values. In doing so, she also made Banister's unique accomplishments normative: when Banister became an education reformer, she was not acting as an agitator for woman's rights, but as a normal Christian woman, a queen. "She did not talk of her mission," Hamilton explained admiringly, "but she taught as one having authority. She did not talk of her rights; she exercised them." Banister's authority extended not just over her students but also over the all-male school board. Hamilton recounted that when the male directors of the Adams Academy, where Banister was head of school, disputed the theological instruction that Banister mandated, she overruled them. "Doubtless they were upright, gentle, pious men, but they were . . . at their wit's end before this female sovereign." Hamilton directly tied Banister's queenship to her ability to command men.

Hamilton also used the metaphor of queenship to explain Banister's marital harmony. After marrying late in life, Banister accepted "subordinacy" to her husband, as Hamilton wrote, "like a queen." She "seems to have insinuated her own way upon Mr. Banister in all things, under the prevailing impression, both in himself and herself, that it was his way—as it certainly became." Hamilton's language was tongue in cheek: Banister accepted subordinacy like a queen in that she upheld domestic queenship standards; however, she also accepted subordinacy like a queen in that she resisted it, ruling rather than being ruled. There are echoes of Ruskin in this description. Banister made herself a queen by inspiring devotion and taking authority without challenging the appearance of her husband's leadership. Hamilton characterized Mr. Banister's obedience to his wife as voluntary (Ruskin's distinction between guiding and determining), but also involuntary to a degree that was imperceptible to him.

Hamilton's queenship rhetoric actually had much in common with New Woman rhetoric. Despite the New Woman's radicalism, she was the product of an essentialist feminism that was less antithetical to domesticity than is often presumed.[72] Sarah Grand (Frances Elizabeth Bellenden Clarke), the originator of the term "New Woman" and an influential contributor to the genre of New Woman essays and books, cautioned women to resist marriage because of fears of class pollution rather than desires for autonomy. She was primarily concerned with empowering women in order to create strong, healthy, and racially pure citizens. Grand wrote: "Emancipated women consider motherhood the most important function of their lives. . . . For this reason . . . they have begun to demand a much higher standard of morals and physique than usual to satisfy them in their husbands, and to demand every advantage in every way of education and civil rights for themselves."[73] For Grand and others who contributed to the construction of the New Woman at the end of the century, female authority was linked to eugenic concerns; financially independent women would be empowered to choose not to mate if appropriate men were unavailable. In 1896, Grand called for the marriage of "certain men" to be made illegal. Aspects of this construction of the New Woman can be seen in Hamilton's use of "queenship," in which the notion of a "blood royal" echoed society's interest in the transformational power of female holiness and the responsibility of women to uphold class and status markers through their purity, moral authority, and control over less-pious men.

By the twentieth century, domestic queenship was an utterly commonplace motif, but its underlying connection to the Virgin Mary was not lost. New Woman writer and suffragist Mary Ives Todd (author of *The Heterodox Marriage of a New Woman* among other novels) used Marian womanhood as the central motif of her 1908 book *An American Madonna: A Story of Love*, which was a passionate endorsement of nontraditional (legally and religiously unsanctioned) marriage. It was dedicated to her sisters, "Jennie and Vina, Loyal wives; devoted mothers; staunch friends; Queens of Home!"[74] The novel was serialized in the periodical, *Wheel of Life*, which described it as "a beautiful presentation of the essentially modern problem of the Woman in Business." The heroine, trained in business and about to inherit a company and its significant financial assets, faced the choice between her desire for success and her "old primal instinct that drives all women toward wifehood and motherhood."[75] Todd used Marian imagery throughout the book to theorize "modern" womanhood, navigating between perceived extremes and offering a religious sanction of her heroine's radical choices by construing her as an "American Madonna." Like Dorsey and Walsh, Todd objected to the economic, legal, and emotional repression of women in traditional marriages. However, while Dorsey and Walsh answered the marriage problem by reaffirming traditional marriage with the caveat that society (or the Church) monitor against violence, abuse, and economic dependency, Todd advocated for civil contractual marriage and nontraditional "free unions." Marian imagery, present on nearly every page of the story, coupled with the author's sisters, reigning as Queens of Home on the dedication page, clothed the frankly radical subject matter in traditionalist religious and moral trappings.

The book's heroine, Harriet, is a young woman "with smiling grace and madonna tenderness," whose Italian lover affectionately styles her "Raphael's American Madonna" and enjoys watching her "ply her Madonna gifts." Todd contrasts the Madonna woman with the New Woman: "America breeds clever women, handsome women, intellectual women, brave, independent women; but madonna women! *Dio mio*, never!" However, this dichotomy is complicated in the narrative, as Harriet, described continually as the "American Madonna," also fully embodies the New Woman's freedoms. She is the levelheaded executive of a corporation, she eschews marriage (in favor of a "free union" with her lover), and she locks the door on her "husband's" conjugal desires when she chooses, yet these choices establish rather than undermine her status as a "Madonna woman."

The Marian motif not only enables the merger of new womanhood and traditional womanhood, it also functions as a catalyst that allows the autonomous heroine to retain her freedom while embracing her maternal and passionate desires. In two remarkable scenes, Harriet makes the decision to "give herself to her lover" and become open to childbearing; and later, pondering her choices in her "Madonna room" (which she had created as a child, spending all her allowance on reproductions of the great Madonnas by Raphael and "other great masters"), decides to do so without the sanction of a legal or religious marriage. Out of deference to her dying father, Harriet had initially chosen to become a "woman of business," rejecting her lover and foregoing marriage. However, on entering her Madonna room, Harriet sees Raphael's *The Sposalizio* with fresh eyes and is transfixed by its overpowering evocation of motherhood and Italy (the romanticized Old World land where she met her lover). Envisioning herself as Mary and her lover, Ivo, as Joseph, she has a catharsis that shifts the narrative arc: her tears "gushed forth from some hitherto sealed fountain . . . She was saved!" In response, she "dropped to her knees . . . underneath the picture," prostrating herself beneath the Marian painting and resolving to allow herself to become a complete woman—businesswoman as well as "wife" and mother.[76] Like Walsh's and Dorsey's Marian heroines, Harriet's Marian art–facilitated conversion opens her up to a fully realized, Mary-like womanhood. However, unlike them, Todd's heroine is not saved religiously but in her ability to reconcile autonomous and domestic womanhood.

In another scene, Harriet invites her family and friends to the Madonna room, where she questions her uncle about her late father's intent for her to stay single. She is told that her father's concern was that her lover, as a European, would be profligate, have loose morals, and bring her to a land of "decadence" and "decaying castles," where her children would be "reared aristocrats instead of solid, sturdy, common-sense Americans." When Harriet objects that she would prevent that fate, her uncle replies that she would be unable to do so as a married woman: "When a woman is married, she is no longer her own boss. She is a minor. Poor woman! First a beast of burden, then a domestic animal, then a slave, then a servant, then a minor. Your father did not like you playing the part of minor after training you to boss big business interests and complications." Like Walsh and Dorsey, Todd critiques traditional marriage's restriction of women's rights and autonomy while affirming the "primal desire" of women for domestic life. Harriet suggests that she take her lover "on a free union basis." While some of her family and friends object that such a marriage is equivalent to "free love" or "free lust," others affirm her rejection of traditional marriage and her solution. Blaming Catholic priests, "who refuse to marry at all," for creating the "indissoluble marriage system," one character opines: "Once they [priests] get a man and woman unequally yoked together, no matter how unequally, no matter if both find the yoke crushing the life prematurely out of them, just the same, they must put up with it, until, by George, the life too often *is* crushed out of 'em." Harriet responds that free unions affirm American values: "It is a crime against human nature, and particularly American human nature, supposed to have infused into it more love of liberty than any other kind—to insist that every couple pledge away all domestic liberty when they get married."[77] She suggests that a dual system be established, with religious marriage offered to those who prefer divorce to be allowed only through "anguish and alimony," and civil marriage offered to those who "hold common-sense views of matrimony" and who desire "to go to a civil servant and be married by him with the right to have their marriage contract dissolved in the usual way by another civil servant . . . and be at liberty to make a new marriage if desired." Harriet herself chooses neither, uniting with her lover in a completely unsanctioned way. While Todd's use of Marian imagery may have been radical or even shocking, it is not dissimilar to the creative uses of Marian imagery that Dorsey and Walsh employed to theorize answers to the Woman Question.

Like other models of Marian womanhood that emphasized female domesticity and moral superiority as antidotes to increasing industrialization, Todd's vision was also a response to the prominence of industrialization and business culture. Ivo, Harriet's lover, declares at one point: "To what end this demoralizing, devitalizing, enslaving worship of the new god these Americans have set up—which they call Business, and for which they prostitute life, love and liberty? Race suicide of *bona fide* Americans? . . . Ah, but it is a pity to see sweet women and even children infected with this lust for business and money, and thousands of homes broken up in consequence!"[78] Todd gave full reign to the fears of those who believed that industry undermined childhood and social stability; but rather than recommend a return to traditional domesticity, she argues instead that Marian womanhood is completely liberating. A free woman, living out the purity of her Madonna-like wifehood and motherhood, could be trusted to exist outside of the bounds of state or church, where, unfettered, she could rehabilitate society and, Todd dares to add, even business culture itself. Like Dorsey and Walsh, Todd is able to successfully employ the symbol of Marian womanhood to her argument because of its inherent strength, autonomy, and queenship along with its reassuring, self-giving maternity. Into the first decade of the twentieth century, Marian imagery remained useful in proposing new ideas about women's place in society in a traditional idiom.

QUEENSHIP RHETORIC, as a late nineteenth-century ideological construction, was deeply indebted to and engaged with the maternalist and Marian strains in American gender ideology. It transcended its apparent compensatory function, becoming a language of disputation that was used variously to rein in, promote, and reimagine female authority. As women were repeatedly cast as queens, the limits and possibilities for their action in larger public worlds was explored. Queenship, evocative of both European nobility and Marian spirituality, became one of the primary modes of describing and re-framing woman's role in America because it resonated with the romantic medievalism, class anxieties, and increased interest in Mary that character-ized these decades.

Like the domestic "Angel," queenship tied woman to the domestic sphere (the primary arena of "rule") and evoked spiritual transcendence—in this case, by evoking the queenship of Mary. However, queenship implied a stronger, more authoritative role for women. While the rhetoric was used both to resist and to promote legal and cultural reforms, queenship imagery established a less sacrificial model of womanhood: an angel ministers, but a queen rules. The authority and autonomous selfhood evoked by queenship rhetoric marked a significant change from previous idealized womanhood metaphors. While still emphasizing the connection between women and the domestic sphere and the essential female role of motherhood, queen-ship rhetoric was more responsive to changing gender norms. Mary's ability to suggest and contain multiple, conflicted meanings facilitated a shift in pub-lic consciousness of the boundaries of a woman's authority and the meaning of her life and work.

Epilogue

The Immaculate Conception Proclamation Semicentennial, 1904

On December 8, 1904, the headline of the *Boston Daily Globe* declared: "Celebration of the Immaculate Conception: World-Wide Observance of the Semicentennial of the Solemn Definition of the Dogma."[1] The full-page account of the observance was accompanied by an illustration of Murillo's *Immaculate Conception* and Pius IX's portrait, an exposition of the Immaculate Conception doctrine by Jesuit Father Thomas Gasson, Pius IX's original apostolic letter promulgating the doctrine, and a reprint of the paper's coverage of the declaration fifty years prior. Pope Pius X marked the semicentennial of the proclamation by declaring a jubilee year: Catholics received a plenary indulgence for visiting specific churches in Rome or their home cities, praying specific prayers, fasting, going to confession, and receiving the sacrament. This jubilee indulgence was universal rather than local; that is, it was available in all parts of the world, not only at a specific site. It was plenary rather than partial; that is, it granted full remission of the temporal punishment (in purgatory) of sin, rather than some portion of it.

According to the *Globe*, New England Catholics enthusiastically participated in the indulgence:

> No event in the church's history has, in New England, met with such general observance as that of this jubilee. In Boston alone more than 200,000 persons have conformed to the requirements for gaining the indulgence awarded to those taking part in the exercises. For three months the cathedral of the Holy Cross has been open from early in the morning until late at night, and thousands have visited its solemn precincts. Very numerous have been the pilgrimages from the parishes within the city limits, the people following their pastor or curate marching in a body to the cathedral. Today, the feast of the Immaculate Conception, the jubilee exercises will end with solemn services in Catholic churches throughout the world.[2]

In addition to Boston Catholics' observance, the *Globe* reported on worldwide festivities. In a section titled "Scenes in the Cathedral of the

World to Be Even More Elaborate than 50 Years Ago," the paper detailed the events planned at the Vatican. The writer emphasized the luxury of the proposed ceremony, particularly the crown fabricated for the planned ceremonial coronation of the statue of the Virgin, made of "solid gold, studded with precious jewels . . . having been contributed by Catholics all over the world," as well as the richness of the pope's "magnificent white and gold" vestments.

The semicentennial of the Immaculate Conception declaration is a fruitful moment to reexamine the contested place of Mary in American culture. By comparing the coverage of the original declaration to its fifty-year commemoration, the changes in Catholics' and Protestants' views of Mary, and of each other, are apparent. In response to the 1854 declaration, Protestant critics attempted to engage with Catholic theology through persuasive or combative rhetoric; however, during the semicentennial, most simply reported on the event, detailed the history of the doctrine, or noted the proclamation's anticipation of papal infallibility. A few commentators rehashed the critiques raised in the 1850s or expressed concerns about Mary's sex and her eclipse of Christ, but the tone of the coverage had changed. It focused less on the doctrine itself and on the figure of Mary, and more on the occasion and what its extravagance said about the Roman Catholic Church. Critics mainly applauded the reduction of the pope's political power over the previous fifty years and critiqued the lavish spending for the occasion. Compared to Protestant critics' emotional reactions to the 1854 declaration, the neutral tone of the semicentennial coverage and its lack of interest in Mary suggest that American Protestants had already begun ceding Mary to Roman Catholicism. She no longer seemed crucial enough for Protestants to debate her theology or claim for themselves.

Outside of Boston, which had an unusually large celebration of the semicentennial, coverage of the event was both shorter and more cynical. Coverage by the *New York Times*, for instance, was concise and fairly neutral. The paper briefly noted several minor events leading up to the occasion, including Pope Pius X's intention to announce a jubilee year, the diocese of New Orleans' gift of jeweled, golden sandals for the pope to wear during the celebratory mass, the American delegates' trip to Rome, and the blessing of Mary's crown before the ceremony (specifying—in the headline—the crown's $30,000 value).[3] The *Times* informed readers of the times and locations of New York City masses for the occasion, and the events in Rome received brief notice in a short, factual column. There were only minor hints of editorial bias, like the brief remark that the procession to St. Peter's was "imposing in the extreme."[4] Other large American newspapers similarly provided brief, factual coverage.[5]

The coverage in Protestant religious publications was more critical, though still moderate. The Methodist *Zion's Herald* ran a story written by contributor Josephine Fisk, who was present in Rome for the celebration.[6] She dwelled extensively on the richness and splendor of the occasion, describing the Swiss Guard's "gay, picturesque uniforms," other Vatican guards' "handsome black velvet knee breeches with gold buckles, and high white neck ruffles," and Pope Pius X's "beautiful shimmering robe, sparkling with jewels, and . . . gold mitre studded with diamonds." She amusingly commented that while the cardinals and bishops wore extremely costly vestments, the guards' outfits were "less rich and expensive . . . but they fitted better, and I certainly admired them much more."[7] Fisk closely chronicled the day's events, noting expensive items such as the "chalice of solid gold set with diamonds" and Mary's crown, "composed of twelve stars in diamonds, costing $30,000." Her tongue-in-cheek account conveyed amused condescension—she admired the pageantry, but remained cynical about the cost. While the article's title, "Is it Christianity or Paganism," was derogatory, Fisk attacked the Catholic Church through brief satirical digs rather than focused argument. For example, after praising the "glorious" singing at the ceremony, she remarked: "The words I could not understand, but I suppose they were something like, 'All hail the power of Mary's name!'" Or again, after describing the "gorgeous pageant" processing out of St. Peter's, she concluded: "Again the blast of silver trumpets, and again the devout ones knelt as the Pope was borne back to his prison in the Vatican, and the great crowd dispersed" (referring to the pope's dissatisfaction with his political relationship to the Italian state). With hindsight, most critics easily drew a connection between Pius IX's augmentation of spiritual power in pronouncing the Immaculate Conception dogma on his own authority and his loss of temporal power. After the events of 1870, when the Vatican Council decided the doctrine of papal infallibility mere months before Pope Pius IX's final loss of Rome and the occupation of the Vatican and the Leonine City by Italian forces, the link became clear even to those who failed to notice it in 1854. By calling attention to Catholic claims that the pope was imprisoned in the Vatican, Fisk reinforced how limited papal power had become on the world stage. But while there were a few snide remarks about Catholic veneration of Mary, the article mocked papal weakness and Catholic extravagance, not Marian theology.

Coverage of the semicentennial by the *Watchman*, a Baptist paper, raised similar themes. After the celebration, the *Watchman* ran a story on the history of the Immaculate Conception doctrine, which concluded by pronouncing Catholicism to be essentially Marian. In a mild version of an argument that, by this point, was well trodden, the author reflected: "We may almost call the Roman Catholic Church the Church of the Virgin Mary—not the real Virgin of the Gospels, but of the apocryphal Virgin of the imagination, whose worship overshadows even the worship of Christ."[8] A few months later, the *Watchman* ran the report of contributor Nathan Bishop Wood, who was at the Vatican for the celebratory mass.[9] He decried the profligate spending on the event, its "gaudiness," and the absurdity of "solemnly plac[ing] a diamond crown ... upon the head of an image of the Virgin." Wood briefly raised some of the critiques that had emerged a half century before: he noted that Marian art in Rome—especially the Francesco Podesti frescos in the Vatican's *Sala Immaculata*—seemed to put Mary before Christ, divinizing her; that the Immaculate Conception declaration was an outdated, regressive superstition; and that the declaration proved that the Catholic Church does change over time. Despite such critiques, the *Watchman*'s coverage was mild in comparison to similar coverage fifty years earlier. Wood's article, like Fisk's, focused more on the Church's wasteful expenditures than on the figure of Mary.

DESPITE A FEW PROMINENT exceptions, in the early decades of the twentieth century, American Protestants grew less interested in using Mary as an emblem of womanhood and motherhood and were more likely to see her only as an emblem of Catholic identity. Although U.S. Catholicism was thriving, the Church's loss of temporal power made the "Catholic threat" seem less menacing. Articles like the *Independent*'s on the semicentennial predicted the Church's imminent demise and reassured readers that there was no remaining menace: "The Papacy has shrunk more and more into its narrow shell. Its nunciatures are disappearing. France is a foe to the Church. The Temporal Power ended in the breach of Porta Pia, never to be restored in all likelihood; Italy is a kingdom in spite of Pope and Jesuit; the '*non-expedit*' against the Italians' voting has proven a boomerang; a free Church in a free State holds the ground ... [and] the Catholic revival in England has faded out among the children of Rome, and has its only vitality in the Anglican Church."[10] The author contextualized the commemoration of the declaration as meaningless in light of the Catholic Church's failed ambitions on the world stage. Not only was the declaration no longer relevant due to the Church's weakness, but it proved that spiritual power could not make up for temporal power: if it could, Mary presumably would have aided the papacy. "Pius IX," the *Independent* asserted, "dreamed that his new dogma would insure Mary's protection," and yet the Church's eschatological hopes had proven false: "Before her Immaculate Conception the powers of darkness would be vanquished. What are the facts?" While the author's intention was to embarrass the Catholic Church, his commentary revealed one reason that many American Protestant critics were uninterested in engaging and denouncing the doctrine: Catholicism was no longer as threatening. While anti-Catholic sentiment and fear of papal influence in American politics would continue for decades to come, the papacy's loss of temporal power lessened Protestant anxieties. At the same time, Catholic success in America, along with other cultural changes, heightened the association of Mary with Catholic identity and diminished the availability, power, and usefulness of Mary as a shared cultural symbol.

On the occasion of the semicentennial, American Catholics took both a celebratory (though perhaps less hopefully jubilant) and apologetic stance. One of the primary apologies for the doctrine, Bishop Ullathorne's *The Immaculate Conception of the Mother of God*, was reprinted for the occasion in a new edition revised by Reverend Canon Iles. The *American Catholic Review* praised the timeliness of the reissue, hoping that it would be beneficial "at a time when attention of the whole Christian world is drawn to the blessed subject."[11]

Pope Pius X outlined the procedures for the jubilee indulgence in his encyclical, *Ad Diem Illum*, which had an oddly conciliatory tone.[12] Like his predecessors Leo XIII and Pius IX, he expressed his deep devotion to Mary, high Mariology, and eschatological hopes; however, he explicitly acknowledged the failure of the 1854 proclamation to bring about the radical changes that Catholics had hoped it would. He also indirectly addressed Protestant theological critique through a series of rhetorical questions and answers. In the first paragraphs of the encyclical, Pius X raised the topic of failed eschatological hopes: "Why should we not hope to-day after the lapse of half a century when we renew the memory of the Immaculate Virgin, that an echo of that holy joy will be awakened in our minds, and that the magnificent scenes of that distant day, of faith and of love towards the august Mother of God, will be repeated?" He continued, "Many, it is true, lament the fact that until now these hopes have been unfulfilled, and are prone to repeat the words of Jeremias: 'We looked for peace and no good came; for a time of healing and behold fear' (Jeremias viii.15). But all such will be certainly rebuked as 'men of little faith.'"[13] This was a jarringly defensive sentiment with which to begin an encyclical celebrating the promulgation of the Immaculate Conception, but it reflected the beleaguered tone of other Church communications that encouraged Catholics worldwide to continue to support the reinstatement of papal political power and holdings. Mitigating this early lamentation, the letter turned to historical events that could be construed as triumphant for the Church, including the remarkable length of Leo XIII's pontificate and Mary's apparition at Lourdes.

Pius X then began to address the topic of Marian veneration through a series of rhetorical questions, including: "Can any one fail to see that there is no surer or more direct road than by Mary for uniting all men in Christ?" "Who more than his Mother could have a far reaching knowledge of the admirable mysteries of the birth and childhood of Christ?" and "For is not Mary the Mother of Christ?" He concluded this apologetic section on Catholic Mariology with the declaration: "We are thus, it will be seen, very far from declaring the Mother of God to be the author of supernatural grace which belongs to God alone." This statement responded to implicit Protestant challenges. By discussing both Catholic disappointment and Protestant criticism at the start of the encyclical, Pius X placed his commentary on the Immaculate Conception in a defensive and embattled light.

Pius X's tone was in keeping with the Catholic Church's conciliatory stance regarding Marian theology in these years. The Church conscientiously rebutted Protestant "misunderstandings," even when that meant mitigating strong claims for Mary. For example, in a minor but telling episode that was widely publicized in the United States, the Sacred Congregation at Rome denied official approval to an "Immaculate Conception crucifix" because it could lead to Protestant misunderstanding and criticism.[14] The crucifix was a depiction of Murillo's *Immaculate Conception* superimposed on the cross. The letter of nonapproval claimed that such an image could lead to "superstition or erroneous conceptions of doctrine." The author asserted that a "true Catholic" would admire the pious intent of the devotional aid while rejecting its "false combination of religious symbolism." He argued that the theological message of the crucifix is "utterly misleading" because "to place upon the Cross our Blessed Lady, who, however exalted she is among the children of men, differs from her Divine Son by the illimitable distance that exists between the Creator and the creature" would lead to confusion. In denying the Church's approval for the devotional aid, the author alluded to Protestant critiques about Catholics' supposed divinization of Mary.

The *Independent* approvingly reported the Catholic Church's rejection of the crucifix, titling their coverage of the story "A Creditable Decision."[15] The paper asked Catholic scholar Dr. James Nilan to explain the incident to its readers. Nilan stated baldly that the letter of nonapproval was chiefly motivated by Protestant censure: "I believe it was feared that the meaning which Catholics give to the crucifix might be misapprehended in some cases, especially by Protestants. . . . The Propaganda, knowing the propensity of those outside the Church to charge Catholics with holding doctrines which these abhor, may have found it proper to remove this occasion of error from our Protestant brethren." While emphasizing that he spoke unofficially, Nilan proclaimed the letter "practically a condemnation of this medal" and asserted that concern over Protestant interpretation was the Church's "motive . . . [for] non-approval."

Similarly, while American Catholic newspapers and magazines enthusiastically covered the semicentennial and the jubilee year, they also often remarked on or alluded to Protestant censure. For instance, the author of a fictional essay treating Pope Pius IX's legacy, entitled "Romance in the Land of Pius IX," called the declaration "controversial."[16] In the story, a military general remarks to Pius IX's niece: "I suppose it was [Pius IX's] great love for her [Mary] which induced him to enforce the dogma of the Immaculate Conception, but surely it was not altogether a popular movement." She responds: "No, it caused a good deal of contention; as also did the dogma of the 'Infallibility.'" Since the niece was a devout Italian contessa, and the declaration was not controversial among Italian Catholics or among the Church's hierarchy, the author may have projected the American Catholic experience of "controversy" surrounding the proclamation (due to nativism) onto her Italian characters. The Catholic press also ran stories about Protestant understandings of Mary, such as the *American Catholic Review*'s story, "Attitude of Modern Protestants towards the Virginity of Our Blessed Lady."[17] American Catholics remained wary of Protestant critiques of Catholic Mariology, and this wariness resurfaced as the semicentennial brought Catholic Marian theology back into the public conversation.

While, by the turn of the century, most Protestants talked much less about Mary, a set of conservative Protestants, some of whom would join together in a new "fundamentalist" movement, granted Mary a significant but limited role. The "Virgin Birth of Christ" was the topic of one of the articles in a series entitled *The Fundamentals*, published by the Bible Institute of Los Angeles between 1910 and 1915. In the article, Scottish Presbyterian minister James Orr argued that Christ's virgin birth underlay his miraculous and sinless nature and that the doctrines could not be separated. This became so important that it eclipsed other possible uses of her figure. Part of the reason that early fundamentalists ceased using Mary, even in sentimentalized ways, to conceptualize womanhood was because she performed a concrete and specific function that did not allow for blurred boundaries or metaphor. Other groups of Protestants, who were less concerned about shoring up theological orthodoxy in response to threats such as Darwinian evolution and higher biblical criticism, continued to use Mary as a sentimentalized symbol of motherhood. The most obvious group was the "Kindergarteners," who frequently used Marian imagery in their publications and recommended reproductions of Marian art in kindergarten and primary school classrooms.[18] However, this usage declined abruptly in the second decade of the twentieth century.

In basic frequency searches of magazines such as *Atlantic Monthly*, *Independent*, *Christian Advocate*, and *Harper's*, references to the "Madonna" and "Virgin Mary" peaked in the 1870s through the 1890s and then dropped off. The *Independent*, for example, mentioned the "Madonna" or the "Virgin Mary" in 79 articles in the 1850s (including a peak in 1854, when the Immaculate Conception was promulgated), 65 in the 1860s, 110 in the 1870s, 129 in the 1880s, and 165 in the 1890s, dropping to 91 in the 1900s and only 50 in the 1910s. *Atlantic Monthly* showed a similar arc, climbing from 50 mentions of the "Madonna" in the 1850s to 78 in the 1890s. *Harper's* references to Mary peaked in the 1870s, with more than 45 articles mentioning the "Virgin Mary," and declined sooner, dropping to 15 in the 1890s. In the collection of magazines indexed by the American Periodicals Series Online, the term "Madonna" appeared in approximately 800 articles in the 1850s, increased steadily by decade throughout the nineteenth century, and peaked in the 1890s, appearing in 2,095 articles; however, it dropped to 800 references in the 1900s, and to 370 in the 1910s.[19] By the second decade of the twentieth century, there were significantly fewer references to Mary in popular, non-Catholic newspapers and magazines. While the American Catholic community grew steadily in these decades, references to Mary in general-audience sources dropped, as Protestants stopped using Mary as a symbol of idealized womanhood.

I suspect that there were four main causes of the waning of popular Marian imagery in early twentieth-century America. The first was Catholic success: Catholics achieved large and stable communities and used Mary as a symbol of Catholic identity. As Catholics became established, this usage of Mary became dominant. The second cause was the entrenchment of the market economy. While an ideology of domesticity persisted well into the twentieth century, a strictly demarcated separate sphere for women was less essential as Americans adjusted to the capitalistic economy, reducing the need to conceptualize idealized womanhood through Marian imagery. The third cause was the success of feminist reforms. As the early goals of the woman's movement, including local and state suffrage, were achieved, and the movement became more established and broader in its goals, feminists no longer found it necessary or effective to couch their requests in traditional, religious idioms. Finally, the fourth cause was the emergence of Protestant fundamentalism. While fundamentalists drew on Mary, they envisioned a specific and limited religious function for her that precluded metaphorical use of her figure. Taken together, these changes diminished the availability of Mary as a Protestant cultural symbol, as well as the need for her figure to represent idealized womanhood. In effect, in the decades-long battle for Mary as an American cultural symbol, her function as an emblem of Catholic identity and unity began to dominate, while various Protestant uses of her imagery faded.

ULTIMATELY, ANNA JAMESON fulfilled her desire to translate Mary "into poetry"—a symbol extricated from its theological substratum and available to all—but only for a few decades. Mary's multivalence enabled her to flourish as a popular cultural symbol from the 1850s through the turn of the century. Despite American Catholics' ongoing use of Mary as a symbol of Catholic distinctiveness during these decades, Protestants continued to find meaning in Mary as an example of Christian womanhood, maternity, and female purity, and claimed the right to use and define her. Later, her ability to evoke traditional female values as well as elevated, autonomous womanhood made her a site for the renegotiation of women's agency and power. By the twentieth century, incoming Catholic ethnic groups each brought distinctive cultural content and devotional traditions (from Italian American devotion to Our Lady of Mount Carmel to Mexican veneration of Our Lady of Guadalupe and Cuban American veneration of the Virgen de la Caridad) that would thereafter define the American Madonna. Her figure continued to be a site of disputation and hope for Americans, but the conversation increasingly became intra- rather than interdenominational. Only in the final decades of the twentieth century would Protestants rediscover Mary as a site for spiritual contemplation.

In the 1970s and 1980s, scholars including Maria Warner and Rosemary Radford Ruether examined the theological possibilities inherent in Mary, offering critiques of her historical uses and possible avenues for feminist reclamation of her figure.[20] More recently, Protestant writer Kathleen Norris shared her personal spiritual engagement with Mary and examined Mary's relevance for women in her book *Meditations on Mary*.[21] And feminist spiritual writer Sue Monk Kidd, after rejecting Mary as a passive and subordinate figure, has come to see her as her "primary icon of devotion." She muses, like her nineteenth-century forbearers, about Mary's potential to transform society: "What might happen if such a feminine symbol actually began to function in the big spiritual picture—in the minds and hearts of people, in cultural and political institutions . . . if the picture widened out to include a creative, loving Mother or Sister?"[22]

Contemporary Catholic women have also offered accounts of how Marian elements fit into their feminist spiritual journeys. Literary scholar Patricia Hampl's *Virgin Time: In Search of the Contemplative Life*, for example, is an account of her pilgrimage to Lourdes and other sites to find a living faith within the Catholic tradition. And Beverley Donofrio's *Looking for Mary; or, The Blessed Mother and Me* is a conversion memoir in which Donofrio finds her path back to Catholicism facilitated by Mary, who allows her to grapple with her identity as a daughter and a mother, and reveals a strong female element within the Catholic tradition.[23] In works like these, Americans are once again using Mary to conceptualize womanhood and a feminine aspect of the divine.

Notes

Introduction

1. Duyckinck and Duyckinck, *Cyclopaedia of American Literature,* s.v. "Francis Lieber."

2. Particular claims about the transformational power of the *Sistine Madonna* were a mainstay of German romanticism. U.S. Protestants were likely influenced by romantic and even mystical claims made about the painting by Wolfgang Goethe, Friedrich Nietzsche, Richard Wagner, and, later, Thomas Mann. However, while American Protestants understood the *Sistine Madonna* to be in a class by itself, they recounted similar experiences in response to a range of Marian paintings.

3. Hopkins, "Application of the Kindergarten Theory," 104.

4. Gatta, *American Madonna,* 10–32, 49.

5. Ibid., 53–71. For Charles Beecher's interest in Mary, see also Beecher, *The Incarnation; or, Pictures of the Virgin and Her Son.*

6. Adams, *Our Lady of Victorian Feminism.*

7. Johnston, *Seeing High and Low,* 55–61.

8. See Smith, "Continuity and Discontinuity," 73; and Orr, "The Virgin Birth of Christ."

9. Aquinas, *Summa Theologiae,* 3.25.5.

10. Morgan, *Protestants and Pictures,* 220.

11. My approach has been influenced by Thomas Tweed, whose book *Retelling U.S. Religious History* I read early in my graduate studies. It prompted me to approach religious communities from a rubric of exchange and mutual influence. As he points out in the book, "When individuals and groups meet across social and political boundaries they exchange things. They give and receive beliefs and artifacts, practices and people, and (more abstractly) meaning and power," 19. My attention to religious communities' proximity and shared cultural and physical spaces has also been shaped by Tweed's theoretical approach outlined in *Crossings and Dwellings,* and the work of Peter D'Agostino and R. Laurence Moore.

12. D'Agostino, *Rome in America,* 9.

13. Dominican missions, in particular, were known for promoting the rosary, a structured prayer that includes the repetition of the angel Gabriel's salutation to Mary and meditation on events in her life and the life of Christ. Redemptorist missions were also well known for promoting Marian devotions. See Dolan, *Catholic Revivalism,* 226–27; Taves, *Household of Faith,* 24; and Chinnici, *Living Stones,* 83, on the particular significance of the Immaculate Conception devotion in the United States.

14. On the role of devotionalism in unifying immigrant Catholics, see Chinnici, *Living Stones*, 83–85.

15. See especially Cott, *Bonds of Womanhood*; and Sklar, *Catherine Beecher*.

16. McDannell, *The Christian Home*, 52.

17. For example, in *Religious Outsiders*, Moore draws attention to the replication of Protestant hegemony implicit in telling history as if Protestantism were a unified and normative entity, 48–71.

18. For a reflection on Protestant cultural power, see Marty, *Pilgrims in Their Own Land*, 337.

19. Summers, *Methodist Pamphlets*.

20. For the role of public schools in consolidating mainstream Protestant identity, see Goen, *Broken Churches, Broken Nation*, 34–35.

21. See especially Franchot, *Roads to Rome*. Note also that Andrew Stern's recent book *Southern Crucifix, Southern Cross* complicates our understanding of this history by showing regional differences, and particularly how much less significant anti-Catholicism was in the hierarchical culture of the South.

22. Freeman, "Alterity and Its Cure," 405, quoting Jonathan Z. Smith.

23. Auerbach, *Woman and the Demon*, 10.

24. *Oxford English Dictionary*, 2006.

Chapter One

1. Veuillot, "Immaculate Conception Declared."

2. "Religious Intelligence," *New York Evangelist*, 2.

3. Ibid.

4. These fears were expressed most vividly in Rebecca Reed's and Maria Monk's best-selling, pseudoautobiographical accounts of abusive and disturbing experiences as novices in convents, published in 1835 and 1836, respectively. These writings anxiously described the political power of the pope and Catholic gender expression and sexual behavior, particularly the seclusion and celibacy of nuns and priests, as nefarious and dangerous to the stability of American democracy. They charged Catholic priests and women religious with crimes ranging from sexual slavery to brutality to murder. An early version of Reed's account may have been a factor in triggering the 1834 burning of the Ursuline convent near Boston by a Protestant mob.

5. The feast of the "Conception of Mary" was established in Palestine by the seventh century; it may have occurred earlier in Syria. The feast of the "Immaculate Conception" was celebrated in Naples as early as the ninth century and migrated to England by the eleventh. Ecclesiastical feasts, also called Holy Days, commemorate a religious dogma or saint by mandating rest from labor and attendance of mass.

6. Bernard of Clairvaux, *Letters*, epistle 174. Bernard argued that Mary was purified immediately after her conception rather than during it, and that her conception itself was commonplace and should not be celebrated.

7. For examples in decades prior to the declaration, see "The Pernicious Effects of Party Zeal," *Weekly Museum*; "Letters from Spain," *Ladies' Literary Cabinet*, 81; and "Miscellaneous," *Correspondent*, 12.

8. Gaeta is located in central Italy in what was then the Kingdom of the Two Sicilies and is now the region of Lazio. After his chief minister, Pellegrino Rossi, was assassinated in 1848 and the Swiss Guard disbanded, Pius IX fled to Gaeta and lived there in exile from 1848 to 1850.

9. Chinnici, *Living Stones*, 83.

10. "Article IX: Book Notices," *The Church Review*, 456.

11. Maguire, "Article V-2. The Abbé Laborde in Rome," 102–7. See also Laborde, *The Impossibility of the Immaculate Conception*. The *Index Librorum Prohibitorum* was the List of Forbidden Books maintained by the Catholic Church in various forms from the sixteenth century until 1966.

12. Veuillot, "Immaculate Conception Declared," 6.

13. "Religious Intelligence," *New York Evangelist*, 26. The pamphlet was written by [Sir] George Bowyer, Car. OP IX.

14. Catholic Church and Pius IX, *Letters Apostolic* (also published in Bryant, *Immaculate Conception*, 289); Orsini, *Life of the Blessed Virgin Mary*, 316; Smith, "Dogma of the Immaculate Conception"; and Lambruschini, *Polemical Treatise*, 177.

15. Catholic Church and Pius IX, *Letters Apostolic*.

16. "Jansenists vs. Jesuits," *New York Daily Times*, 4 (emphasis in original).

17. Anglicans, Methodists, and Lutherans accepted the formulations of the first seven ecumenical councils as authoritative; other groups, such as Baptists, rejected the authority of the councils but generally accepted their theological formulations; while others, notably Unitarians, rejected them.

18. "Jansenists vs. Jesuits," *New York Daily Times*, 4.

19. "European Affairs," *New York Daily Times*, 2. The initial description of Rome being "intoxicated with joy" is attributed to French theologian Abbé Jean-Joseph Gaume, who reported on the proclamation from Rome.

20. "From Our French Correspondent," *Independent*, 394.

21. D'Agostino has shown that the "Roman Question" (the status of the papacy and the Vatican lands in the Kingdom of Italy) also generated significant interest among U.S. non-Catholics and received widespread coverage in the American media. See also Stern, *Southern Crucifix, Southern Cross*; and Franchot, *Roads to Rome*.

22. Maguire, "Article V-2. The Abbé Laborde in Rome," 107. M. the Abbé Laborde of Lectoure, France, attributed the belief that the definition of the Immaculate Conception would end all war to the eighteenth-century prophet Leonard of Port Maurice. He claimed that Pius IX was familiar with the prophecy and observed that, in advance of the ceremony, placards advertising the prophecy were posted throughout Rome.

23. Veuillot, "Immaculate Conception Declared," 6.

24. Alzog, *Manual of Universal Church History* estimated that in 1878 in the Dutch provinces of Utrecht and Haarlem, there were five thousand schismatic Jansenists in

twenty-five congregations. The manual also noted their protest against the Immaculate Conception declaration, 847.

25. Veuillot, "Immaculate Conception Declared," 6.

26. *Manual of the Immaculate Conception.* The *New York Times* reported on an Astor Place book trade event five years later, noting high attendance and heavy sales of Catholic books, including the sale of fifty-four copies of the *Manual of the Immaculate Conception* in one afternoon, at a range of prices reflecting varying quality bindings. Sales of Abbé Orsini's *Life of the Blessed Virgin Mary* and books by Catholic novelists were also noted. See "Book Trade Sales," *New York Times.*

27. See McGreevy, *Catholicism and American Freedom*, 29; and D'Agostino, *Rome in America*, 32. McGreevy attributes American Catholic affinity for ultramontanism to the coincidence of American Catholic institutional development and the rise of global ultramontanism, as well as to an increased likelihood that missionary priests and sisters wishing to work in the United States had ultramontane leanings. D'Agostino demonstrates that U.S. Catholics' experiences of persecution aligned with the "redemptive suffering" expressed through "Ultramontane devotionalism" and that Catholics "suffered vicariously with Pius" in exile.

28. See Hatch, *Democratization*; Prothero, *American Jesus*, 44–52; and Carroll, *American Catholics* on the role of populist rhetoric in Church growth.

29. See Prothero, *American Jesus*, 55. Prothero argued that, among other factors, a new form of preaching characterized by pulpit storytelling prioritized an affective relationship with Jesus, leading to a shared and cohesive "Jesus piety" across denominations.

30. Several religious historians have examined the ways that the political populism of the period affected religious discourse. Most notably, Hatch in *Democratization* characterized the period between 1780 and 1830 as a time of sweeping change when religious rhetoric mirrored political populism, undermining the authority and influence of "central ecclesiastical institutions and high culture." While Hatch has been criticized for not sufficiently accounting for the authoritative (and sometimes authoritarian) power of the "firebrands" who built the evangelical movement, and for using the term "democratization" instead of "populization," which may more accurately describe their use of democratic rhetoric but failure to build democratic structures, he marshals a wealth of evidence about the appeal of democratic rhetoric and the ascent of populist religious movements in the period.

31. Smith, "Dogma of the Immaculate Conception," 286. This article was reprinted with an introduction and brief omissions as "Immaculate Conception of Mary," tract no. 30 in the *Methodist Pamphlets for the People* series, and vol. 3 of the collected pamphlets.

32. Summers, *Methodist Pamphlets for the People*, no. 48, "Giant Pope," 238–40.

33. Catholic Church and Gregory, *Mirari Vos*, "On Liberalism and Religious Indifferentism," encouraged obedience and respect for the divine authority of the Church; denounced challenges to clerical celibacy and the indissolubility of marriage; and opposed "religious indifferentism." Point 14, which the tract loosely quotes, read in

part: "This shameful font of indifferentism gives rise to that absurd and erroneous proposition which claims that liberty of conscience must be maintained for everyone. It spreads ruin in sacred and civil affairs, though some repeat over and over again with the greatest impudence that some advantage accrues to religion from it. 'But the death of the soul is worse than freedom of error,' as Augustine was wont to say . . . . Thence comes transformation of minds, corruption of youths, contempt of sacred things and holy laws—in other words, a pestilence more deadly to the state than any other. Experience shows, even from earliest times, that cities renowned for wealth, dominion, and glory perished as a result of this single evil, namely immoderate freedom of opinion, license of free speech, and desire for novelty."

34. The author of "Giant Pope" misdated *Mirari Vos*, from which these lines were loosely excerpted, to August 15, 1852.

35. For more on American Protestant perceptions of Pius IX, see D'Agostino, *Rome in America*, 1–3, 19–21. Protestants initially celebrated Pius IX's ascendancy to the papal seat, believing he would institute reforms in the Catholic Church and support the Risorgimento (the campaign for the political unification of Italy), but as the situation unfolded, Protestants generally supported "Liberal Italy" against the political aspirations of the papacy in exile, viewing Pius IX as the enemy of modernity and democracy.

36. "Immaculate Conception," *National Era*, 6.

37. Neumann, "Pastoral Letter" (quoted in Bryant, *Immaculate Conception*, 232).

38. *Brownson's Quarterly Review*, unsigned review of *Jesus the Son of Mary*, 286.

39. Kenrick, "Pastoral Letter."

40. Ibid.

41. Cumming, "Dr. Cumming on the Immaculate Conception Dogma," 1.

42. Laborde, *Impossibility of the Immaculate Conception* (emphasis in original).

43. "Rome Self-Convicted of Error," *Church Review*, 435.

44. Smith, "Dogma of the Immaculate Conception," 277, 281.

45. Ibid., 284.

46. Ibid., 311; "Religious Scarecrow of the Age," *National Magazine*, 524; Cumming, "Dr. Cumming on the Immaculate Conception Dogma," 2.

47. Cumming, "Dr. Cumming on the Immaculate Conception Dogma," 2.

48. For other treatments of historical opposition to the Immaculate Conception, see the following articles published in, respectively, a Baptist and an Episcopal journal: "Catholicity of the Roman Church" and "New Article of Faith."

49. Cumming, "Dr. Cumming on the Immaculate Conception Dogma," 2. The line comes from the "Holy Scriptures" decree proclaimed at the Council of Trent (a counterreformation council) in Session 4, 1546. The council also issued a decree "On Original Sin" that specifically omitted Mary: "This same holy Synod doth nevertheless declare, that it is not its intention to include in this decree, where original sin is treated of, the blessed and immaculate Virgin Mary, the mother of God" (Council of Trent, Session 5, 1546).

50. Ibid.

51. Summers, *Methodist Pamphlets for the People*, no. 31.

52. "Jansenists vs. Jesuits," *New York Daily Times*, 4. See also Ripley and Dana, *American Cyclopaedia*, s.v. "Jansenists."

53. Ullathorne, *Immaculate Conception*, 202.

54. De Charbonnel, "Definition of the Immaculate Conception," 239.

55. "Immaculate Conception: Sermon by Archbishop Hughes," *New York Daily Times*, 1.

56. Ibid. The Socinians were a sect who followed the teachings of sixteenth-century religious leader Faustus Socinus. They were anti-Trinitarian and did not believe in the divinity of Christ. They also objected to the phrase "mother of God" in reference to Mary.

57. Bryant, *Immaculate Conception*, 121.

58. Ibid., 122.

59. Orsini, *Life of the Blessed Virgin Mary*, 24.

60. Ullathorne, *Immaculate Conception*, 196.

61. Ibid., 193.

62. "Pastoral of Francis Patrick Kenrick," *Catholic Herald*, 145.

Chapter Two

1. "Rumors of Relics," *New York Daily Times*, 8.

2. Ibid.

3. Ibid.

4. One of the statues was described as Mary standing alone and the other as Mary cradling the infant Jesus.

5. "New York City," *New York Daily Times*, 1.

6. "Notices of New Books," *New York Daily Times*, 3.

7. Ibid. (emphasis in original).

8. Ibid.

9. See Daly, *Beyond God the Father*, 87; and Carr, "Mary in the Mystery," 8.

10. See Brekus, *Strangers and Pilgrims*, introduction.

11. Langland, *Nobody's Angels*, 11.

12. Ibid., 8. For more on female sentimental culture, see also Berlant, *Female Complaint*. Berlant emphasizes women's agency in creating female sentimental culture as a way of constructing a ground of meaning as well as social belonging to lives circumscribed by unjust social conditions: "In this discursive field the emotional labor of women places them at the center of the *story* of what counts as life, regardless of what lives women actually live," 35 (emphasis in original).

13. In addition to counterbalancing the emerging capitalistic market, female domesticity also provided a foil to the masculine domain of politics. Their hospitality and neighborliness created the illusion of a unified community that mitigated the

divisive nature of local and national politics. Hence, early calls for female suffrage were in direct opposition to the cultural function that women had as sustainers of community. See Baker, "Domestication of Politics."

14. The Church fathers called Mary "Ark of the Covenant" because she bore the physical presence of the living God in the same way as the ark contained God's physical presence. The Immaculate Conception affirmed this role because the necessity of Mary's total physical purity was compared to the requirement that the setim wood of the ark be unblemished in order to bear God's presence.

15. Orsini, *Life of the Blessed Virgin Mary*, 53.

16. Donnelly, *Poems*, "Maria Immaculata," 123.

17. See chapter 5 for a description of the visual iconography of the Immaculate Conception.

18. Taves, *Household of Faith*, 45.

19. Taves observed that these devotions stressed ways in which Mary "transcended the human condition and emphasized the impossibility of any human being living up to her ideal standard," ibid., 101.

20. Bryant, *Immaculate Conception*, 321.

21. Ibid., vii.

22. Ibid., 257.

23. Rohner, *Life of the Blessed Virgin*, 49.

24. Ibid., 40.

25. Patmore, *Angel in the House*.

26. For example, Gilbert and Gubar, in *Madwoman in the Attic*, write that "clearly, behind and before the Angel in the House stands the Virgin Mary in a number of guises," 20.

27. For example, Trudgill writes in *Madonnas and Magdalens* that "Mary as a literal religious figure was one thing, however; Mary as a glorious model was another . . . once Marian virtue was embodied in the semi-secularized forms of sentimental heroines, it won widespread reverence." Lootens makes a similar argument in *Lost Saints*.

28. Adams, *Our Lady of Victorian Feminism*, 52.

29. Ibid., 97.

30. "Expressionism in Art: Painting," *Lippincott's Magazine*, 57.

31. "Objections against Chromos Considered," *Prang's Chromo*, 3.

32. Ibid.

33. See Martinez, "At Home with Mona Lisa," 169.

34. "The Arts," *Appleton's Journal*, 602.

35. Raphael's *Sistine Madonna* had a unique place in nineteenth-century culture. Diverse thinkers claimed that it was not only the finest painting ever made, but that it represented a symbolic, spiritual ideal that could transform the viewer. Turn-of-the-century thinkers Johann Wolfgang von Goethe and Rudolph Steiner made specific, strong claims for the painting's effects on viewers, as did Auguste Comte. For a

discussion of the importance of the *Sistine Madonna* to Comte and his followers see Lootens, *Lost Saints*, 51–54.

36. Morgan, *Protestants and Pictures*, 181.

37. Currier & Ives, "Infancy of the Virgin"; "Sacred Heart of Mary"; "The Infant Savior with Mary and Joseph"; "Madonna Di San Sisto."

38. Parton, "Mr. Parton on Prang's Chromos," 1.

39. Stowe, "Mrs. Stowe on Prang's Chromos," 2.

40. Nealy, "Popular Art," 551.

41. See the 1865 Julia Margaret Cameron photograph, *Blessing and Blessed*.

42. Martinez, "At Home with Mona Lisa," 171.

43. See Lindley, *"You Have Stept Out of Your Place,"* 63.

44. On the 1857–58 revival, see: Corrigan, *Business of the Heart*; and Long, *Revival of 1857–58*. Long demonstrates that women were deeply affected by the revival and converted as frequently as men. However, the leaders of the revival—especially in its urban, downtown setting—deliberately limited women's participation in order to identify the meetings with businessmen.

45. Long, *Revival of 1857–58*, 73.

46. See "Forward Movement Ends Its Campaign," *New York Times*. The Young Men's Christian Association (YMCA) was founded in London, England, in 1844; its first American branch opened in Boston in 1851. Many prominent American Protestant leaders were involved with the organization, which was considered one of the main proponents of "muscular Christianity" in the nineteenth and early twentieth centuries.

47. Seymour, *Mornings among the Jesuits at Rome*.

48. Many similar travelogues denounced Catholicism or "explained" the faith in patronizing terms. One notable example is Cummings, *Italian Legends and Sketches*.

49. Seymour, *Mornings among the Jesuits at Rome*, 45.

50. Ibid., 51.

51. Ibid., 50.

52. Ibid., 51.

53. Ibid., 58.

54. Ibid., 47.

55. Ibid.

56. Ibid., 118.

57. *Fiat* is Latin for "let it be done," and was commonly used to refer to Mary's response to the angel Gabriel's message during the Annunciation. It was drawn from Luke 1:38, where Mary replies: "Be it unto me according to thy word."

58. Seymour, *Mornings among the Jesuits at Rome*, 118.

59. Ibid., 121.

60. Ibid., 123.

61. "Seymour's *Mornings among the Jesuits*," *Littell's Living Age*, 249.

62. Ibid.

63. The Oxford controversy (variously called the Oxford movement, Anglo-Catholicism, and Tractarianism) was a movement of High Church Anglicans to reintroduce traditional elements of liturgy and tradition into the Anglican Church, closing some of the distance between Anglicanism and Roman Catholicism. It was centered at Oxford, and led by thinkers such as Edward Pusey, John Keble, and John Henry Newman.

64. "Notices of New Books: *Mornings among the Jesuits at Rome,*" *United States Democratic Review* (emphasis in original).

65. Ibid.

66. *Princeton Review,* unsigned review of *Morning among the Jesuits at Rome,* 143–59.

67. "Is the Church of Rome Idolatrous?" *Biblical Repertory & Princeton Review.*

68. *Princeton Review,* unsigned review of *Morning among the Jesuits at Rome,* 150.

69. Ibid., 149.

70. Ibid., 151.

71. Horne and Jarvis, *Mariolatry.*

72. *Princeton Review,* unsigned review of *Morning among the Jesuits at Rome,* 150.

73. "Is the Church of Rome Idolatrous?" *Biblical Repertory & Princeton Review,* 247.

74. Ibid.

75. "Dick Tinto on His Travels," *New York Daily Times,* 2.

76. Ibid.

77. Ibid.

78. Ibid.

79. Smith, "Dogma of the Immaculate Conception," 311.

80. Ibid.

81. Ibid., 304.

82. Ibid.

83. See Monk, *Awful Disclosures;* Reed, *Six Months in a Convent;* and Sherwood, *The Nun.*

84. McDannell, *Christian Home,* 14.

85. Prentice, "Bohemian Journal," 207.

86. Washington, *Echoes of Europe,* 699 (emphasis in original).

87. Ibid., 73.

88. Ibid., 641.

89. Ibid., 371 (emphasis in original).

90. Ibid., 303.

91. "Paintings and Painters in Italy," *Hours at Home,* 325–32.

92. Ibid., 328.

93. Ibid., 329 (emphasis in original).

94. Ibid., 332.

95. "A New *Stabat Mater,*" *Hours at Home,* 50.

96. "Francis Lieber," *Southern Literary Messenger,* 366.

97. "Miscellanea at Munich," *Southern Literary Messenger*, 101.

98. *Overland Monthly and Out West Magazine*, "Current Literature," 486.

99. These themes would later be famously taken up by Henry Adams in his 1900 essay, "The Dynamo and the Virgin."

100. See, for example: Benson, "The Pagan Element in France," 203–9; Batt, "Corruption of Christianity by Paganism," 202; and Child, "Resemblances between the Buddhist and the Roman Catholic Religions," 660–65. Jameson, in *Legends of the Madonna*, which I examine in detail in chapter 3, also extensively (but not derogatorily) compared the veneration of Mary to the cults of pagan goddesses, 21.

101. For an excellent treatment of the intersection between Catholic religious and gender identities, see Cummings, *New Women of the Old Faith*, 17–58.

102. Catholic Church and Pius IX, *Apostolic Constitution Ineffabilis Deus* (emphasis mine).

103. "And I will put enmity between thee and the woman, and between thy seed and her seed; it shall bruise thy head, and thou shalt bruise his heel." Gn 3:15 KJV.

104. Ullathorne, *Immaculate Conception*, 207.

105. Rohner, *Life of the Blessed Virgin*, 56.

106. Wissel, *Redemptorist*, 213. St. Alphonsus Liguori lived from 1696 to 1787 in Naples. The first American edition of *Glories of Mary*, translated from the Italian, was published in New York by Edward Dunigan and Brothers in 1852.

107. Wissel, *Redemptorist*, 213.

108. For more on the role of Mary in midcentury Great Britain, see chapter 3. See also Lootens, *Lost Saints*, 50–57.

109. Ullathorne, *Immaculate Conception*, 30.

110. See, for example, Anderson, "Mary's Difference," 183–202.

111. Ibid.

112. Ullathorne, *Immaculate Conception*, 30.

113. Ibid., 8.

114. Ibid., 187.

115. Ibid.

Chapter Three

1. "Rumors of Relics," *New York Daily Times*, 1.

2. Ibid. (emphasis in original).

3. "Religious Scarecrow of the Age," *National Magazine*, 523.

4. "Was Shakespeare a German?" *New York Times*, 4.

5. See chapter 2. An editorial comment followed the initial letter to the editor implicitly endorsing nativism through a facetious reference to the Know-Nothing Party.

6. "Mr. Aspinwall's Murillo," *New York Times*, 5; "Murillo Controversy," *New York Times*, 5; "Still Another Picture," *New York Times*, 4.

7. "Rumors of Relics," *New York Daily Times*, 8.

8. For one example, see "Murillo's Celebrated Picture," *New York Times*, 6.

9. "Mr. Aspinwall's Murillo," *New York Times*, 5.

10. Ibid.

11. Ibid.

12. As Adele Holcomb and other art historians have noted, there was a particular value placed on statuary in the nineteenth century: "Respect for sculpture as a more noble art than painting because of its abstract intellectual character seems one of the more conservative ideas to endure in nineteenth-century art criticism." Both religious art and religious statuary could evoke veneration: the portrait icon, the crowned statue. However, in the American context, religious statuary was less familiar in art galleries and museums and thus more directly evocative of Roman Catholic devotionalism than painting, which could be found in multiple contexts. Holcomb, "Anna Jameson," 173.

13. "Burning of the Compania," *Harper's Weekly*, 71.

14. Ibid. The coverage in the *New York Times* suggested that over the altar stood a statue of Mary, not a painting. "Terrific Tragedy in Chili," *New York Times*, 1.

15. "Table-Talk," *Appleton's Journal*, 106.

16. Thomas, *Love and Work Enough*, 212.

17. Holcomb cites Mariana Starke's *Letters from Italy* (1800), William Hazlitt's *Sketches of the Principal Picture—Galleries in England* (1824), and Maria Callcott's *Descriptions of the Chapel of the Annunziata dell'Arena or Grotto's Chapel, in Padua* (1835), as well as Jameson's own early book *Visits and Sketches at Home and Abroad* (1834) as travel writings that influenced the art historical genre, 171.

18. "Sacred and Legendary Art," *Crayon* 4, 176.

19. Nathaniel, "Mrs. Jameson," 463. The article was originally published in the *New Monthly Magazine* and reprinted in several American publications.

20. Jarves, "Writers on Art," 155. He called Charles Callahan Perkins dry, Alexis-François Rio bigoted and distorted, and Lord Alexander Lindsay unoriginal, but promoted Jameson's books.

21. "Notices of Books," *New Englander and Yale Review*, 252.

22. Ibid., 252–53.

23. Steegman, *Consort of Taste*, 186.

24. Holcomb, "Anna Jameson," 177–79.

25. For more on Jameson's relationship to these thinkers, see Adams, *Our Lady of Victorian Feminism*, 84.

26. "History of Our Lord in Art," *Living Age*, 435.

27. Ibid., 436.

28. Lovelace Papers, Oxford University, 56–57.

29. Needler, *Letters of Anna Jameson*, 188, letter no. 153.

30. Jameson, *Legends of the Madonna*, xvi.

31. "Our Positions and Prospects," *Rambler*, 4.

32. Ibid., 5.

33. Singleton, "Virgin Mary and Religious Conflict," 23 (quoted in Lootens, *Lost Saints*, 53).

34. Ibid. For anti-Catholicism in Britain and the role Mary played in British Catholic and Anglican identities, see Lootens, *Lost Saints*, chaps. 1 and 2.

35. Jameson, *Commonplace Book*, 141 (emphasis in original).

36. Ibid.

37. Jameson, *Legends of the Madonna*, xvi.

38. Jameson, *Commonplace Book*, 56.

39. Ibid., xix.

40. Ibid.

41. Ibid., 20.

42. Ibid.

43. Ibid., 29.

44. Lovelace Papers, Oxford University, 152–55.

45. Ibid.

46. I take the term "nostalgic medievalism" from John Gatta, who uses it in *American Madonna* to describe the tenor of the Romantic era in the United States, 6.

47. Jameson, *Legends of the Madonna*, 187.

48. Ibid., xix.

49. Ibid., 192 (quoting Wordsworth, *Excursion*) (emphasis in original).

50. Ibid., xx. Jameson elaborated on the gendering of virtue in her *Commonplace Book*: "A man who requires from his own sex manly direct truth, and laughs at the cowardly subterfuges and small arts of women as being *feminine*; a woman who requires from her own sex tenderness and purity, and thinks ruffianism and sensuality pardonable in a man as being *masculine*—these have repudiated the Christian standard of morals which Christ, in his own person, bequeathed to us—that standard which we have accepted as Christians—theoretically at least—and which makes no distinction between 'the highest, holiest manhood,' and the highest, holiest womanhood," 86 (emphasis in original).

51. Jameson, *Commonplace Book*, 85 (emphasis in original).

52. Stanton wrote in *Woman's Bible*: "We are told that the whole sex was highly honored in Mary being the mother of Jesus. . . . I think that the doctrine of the Virgin birth as something higher, sweeter, nobler than ordinary motherhood, is a slur on all the natural motherhood of the world," 465.

53. Jameson, *Legends of the Madonna*, xx (quoting Augustine, Opera Supt. 238, Sermon 63).

54. Ibid., 212.

55. Ibid., 213 (emphasis in original).

56. Ibid., 29. In this passage, Jameson called the Misericordia "beautiful and . . . acceptable to our feelings."

57. Ibid., xl.

58. Ibid., 29.

59. Ibid., 12.

60. Ibid.

61. Ibid., 43.

62. Ibid., xxviii.

63. Ibid., 84.

64. Ibid., 85, fig. 2. Virgin of San Venanzio (Mosaic, AD 642).

65. Ibid., xli.

66. Ibid.

67. Jameson, *Commonplace Book*, 91.

68. Jameson, *Legends of the Madonna*, 251.

69. Ibid., 259.

70. Jameson, "Statement on the Position of Women," in Needler, *Letters of Anna Jameson*, 233 (all emphasis in original).

71. Ibid.

72. Jameson, *Legends of the Madonna*, 166.

73. In one of many examples from these decades, the author of the 1882 *Chautauquan* series "Christianity in Art" cited Jameson's opinion on the relative merits of Marian works as authoritative: "Next to the Sistine Madonna, thinks Mrs. Jameson, is that of Holbein." "Christianity in Art VI: The Madonna and Child," *Chautauquan*, 395.

Chapter Four

1. Dorsey, *Adrift*, 513.

2. Ibid. (emphasis in original).

3. Ibid., 516.

4. Walsh, *Mary: The Queen of the House of David*, 340.

5. Callon, "Converting Catholicism," 148. Based on his research in the archives of Catholic University of America, the Archdiocese of Baltimore at St. Mary's Seminary, and Georgetown University, Callon describes Dorsey as "a woman on intimate terms with some of the most important clerical figures in nineteenth-century America, including Cardinal James Gibbons."

6. Ibid., 193.

7. See McDannell, *Christian Home*, 10–12.

8. Cummings, *New Women of the Old Faith*, 26, 86–87.

9. Kenneally, *History of American Catholic Women*, 25. Kenneally helpfully enumerates four categories of nineteenth-century Catholic novels: (1) early novels that were directed at the moneyed Catholic establishment; (2) apologetic novels, often written by converts, that sought to reach Protestant readers and rebut nativist attacks; (3) prescriptive novels directed to recent immigrants that established acceptable Catholic domestic and social norms; and (4) late-century novels that sought to buttress the Catholic community against overassimilation. Dorsey's multidecade career produced works in all categories: she had the status and contacts to speak to the Catholic

elite, the background to mount an effective apologetic defense in terms Protestants understood, the breeding to transmit domestic ideals and define gender norms for recent immigrants, and the long view and influence to buttress Catholic identity at the end of the century.

10. I owe this insight to Callon's reading of Dorsey's conversion, "Converting Catholicism," 178.

11. Mary Agnes Tincker and Kate O'Flaherty Chopin were two of the only Catholic writers widely considered protofeminist. However, other Catholic writers including Lelia Hardin Bugg and Madeline Vinton Dahlgren cautioned women against overdependence on men and marriage and endorsed women working outside the home. See Kenneally, *History of American Catholic Women*, 38.

12. "Columbian Reading Union," *Catholic World*, 304.

13. "Literature: American Story-Books for Girls," *Independent*, 16.

14. Dorsey, *Adrift*, 489, 481.

15. Ibid., 603 (emphasis in original).

16. Ibid., 638–39.

17. Ibid., 398.

18. Ibid., 61 (emphasis in original).

19. Ibid., 78.

20. Ibid., 403.

21. Ibid., 542.

22. Ibid., 175–76.

23. Ibid., 390.

24. Ibid., 398.

25. Ibid., 456.

26. Ibid., 512, 518.

27. William S. Paley's 1802 book *Natural Theology* popularized the study of God as revealed by the natural world in the nineteenth century. The book was an immediate best seller, and was required reading at Cambridge University well into the twentieth century. Catholic theologians, drawing on Thomas Aquinas's understanding of the relationship between natural and revealed truths, particularly emphasized the role of nature as witness to theological truths for those outside the institutional Church.

28. Dorsey, *Adrift*, 476.

29. Ibid., 529.

30. Ibid., 556.

31. Ibid., 647.

32. Ibid., 691.

33. Cummings, *New Women of the Old Faith*, 38, 41.

34. Dorsey, *Adrift*, 216.

35. Ibid., 54.

36. Ibid., 106.

37. Ibid., 61.

38. Ibid., 253.

39. Ibid., 270.

40. Ibid., 211.

41. "Henry P. Allen, N.Y." *Publisher's Weekly*, 621.

42. *Independent*, unsigned review of *Mary: The Queen of the House of David*, 12.

43. Talmage, introduction to *Mary: The Queen of the House of David*, vii.

44. Walsh, *Mary: The Queen of the House of David*, 340.

45. Ibid., 416.

46. Ibid., 340.

47. Ibid., 351.

48. Ibid., 434.

49. Ibid., 539.

50. Ibid., 543.

51. Ibid., 506.

52. Ibid., 536.

53. Ibid., 479.

54. Ibid., 562.

55. Ibid., 511.

56. Ibid., 516.

57. Ibid., 518.

58. Ibid., 575.

59. For an in-depth treatment of marriage resistance and rejection in the late nineteenth century, see Richardson, "Eugenization of Love," 227–55.

60. "He has made her, if married, in the eye of the law, civilly dead." Stanton, "Seneca Falls Declaration."

61. See Miller, "From One Voice a Chorus," 152–89.

62. *Independent*, unsigned review of *Mary: The Queen of the House of David*, 12.

63. "Talk about Books," *Chautauquan*, 128.

64. *Christian Union*, unsigned review of *Mary: The Queen of the House of David*, 23.

65. Walsh's book included illustrations of "Mary and the Infant Savior" by Frederick Goodall, "The Birth of Mary" by Murillo, "Rizpah Defending the Dead Bodies of Her Relations" by Becker, "The Education of Mary" by Carl Muller, "The Marriage of Mary and Joseph" by Raphael, "The Shadow of the Cross" by Morris, "Jesus at the Age of Twelve with Mary and Joseph on Their Way to Jerusalem" by Mengelburg, "The Youth Jesus Yielding to the Wishes of His Mother" by W. Holman Hunt, "The Wedding at Cana" by Paul Veronese, and "Mary and St. John" by Plockhorst. "Advertisement 48," *Independent*, x.

66. "Hurst & Co.," *Literary World*, 157; *Christian Union*, unsigned review of *Mary: The Queen of the House of David*, 23.

67. "New Publications," *Catholic World*, 572.

68. See Sklar, *Catharine Beecher*. Also see chapter 5 of this volume.

69. Walsh, *Mary: The Queen of the House of David*, 613.

Chapter Five

1. Walsh, *Mary: The Queen of the House of David,* 543.

2. Ibid., 490.

3. Auerbach notes that in Victorian-era Britain, "actual queens and queenly women proliferate in literature and art," *Woman and the Demon,* 36.

4. Talmage, introduction to *Mary: The Queen of the House of David,* vii.

5. Richardson and Willis, *New Woman in Fiction and in Fact,* 1.

6. See Koven and Michel, "Womanly Duties," 1076–108.

7. See Baker, "Domestication of Politics," 631.

8. Ibid., 640.

9. Koven and Michel, "Womanly Duties," 1088.

10. For in-depth treatments of American attitudes toward Victoria, see Weltman, " 'Be No More Housewives, but Queens' "; and Leoffelholz, "Crossing the Atlantic with Victoria."

11. "Royal Family of England," *Eclectic,* 56B1.

12. White, "Domestic Queen, Queenly Domestic," 112.

13. "Culture and Progress Abroad," *Scribner's Monthly,* 683.

14. See Weltman, " 'Be No More Housewives, but Queens,' " 118.

15. "Culture and Progress Abroad, " *Scribner's Monthly,* 683.

16. Walden, "My Look at the Queen," 217.

17. Lears, *No Place of Grace,* 184.

18. See also Franchot, who evocatively calls postbellum medievalism a "rallying cry against the manifold psychic deprivations of modernization," *Roads to Rome,* 10.

19. Hamilton, "An American Queen," 329.

20. Ibid., 330.

21. See Lears, *No Place of Grace,* 28.

22. Mary's Assumption, like her Immaculate Conception, was a doctrine, feast, and artistic subject centuries before it was defined by Pope Pius XII in 1950 in the encyclical *Munificentissimus Deus,* which also established papal infallibility, or the right of a pope to declare doctrine without a general council, as Pius IX had done when declaring Mary's Immaculate Conception in 1854. Before the official definition, the question of whether Mary had physically experienced death remained undecided. Similarly, Mary was venerated as Queen of Heaven or *Regina Coeli,* which was also a classic art subject. It was also defined by Pius XII in his 1954 encyclical *Ad Caeli Reginam,* along with an official feast in its honor, the feast of the Queenship of Mary. *Munificentissimus Deus* made the connection between the doctrines clear: "According to the general rule, God does not will to grant the just the full effect of the victory over death until the end of time has come. And so it is that the bodies of even the just are corrupted after death, and only on the last day will they be joined, each to its own glorious soul. Now God has willed that the Blessed Virgin Mary should be exempted from this general rule. She, by an entirely unique privilege, completely overcame sin

by her Immaculate Conception, and as a result she was not subject to the law of remaining in the corruption of the grave, and she did not have to wait until the end of time for the redemption of her body. Thus, when it was solemnly proclaimed that Mary, the Virgin Mother of God, was from the very beginning free from the taint of original sin, the minds of the faithful were filled with a stronger hope that the day might soon come when the dogma of the Virgin Mary's bodily Assumption into heaven would also be defined from the Church's supreme teaching authority."

23. Orsi quoting Francisco Pacheco's 1649 *Del Arte de la Pintura* (Art of Painting), "Many Names of the Mother of God," 98.

24. The ceremony occurred on August 15, 1837. The painting, *Salus Populi Romani* (Protectress of the Roman People), was also known as *Regina Caeli* (Queen of Heaven). While it does not depict crowns on the figures' heads, Mary is holding a *mappula*, a type of handkerchief indicating Church or imperial authority. It has been crowned repeatedly over the centuries, most famously by Clement VIII in response to Protestant iconoclasm at the close of the sixteenth century.

25. Catholic Church and Pius IX, *Apostolic Constitution Ineffabilis Deus.*

26. McDannell writes: "Beginning in 1878 with *Inscrutabili*, and then in 1880 (*Arcanum*), 1890 (*Sapientiae Christianae*), and 1891 (*Rerum Novarum*), he denounced the trends of divorce, family limitation, and state influence in child rearing. Under Leo XIII, for the first time, the family became the guardian of purity of both society and Christianity," *Christian Home*, 15–16. See also McDannell, "Catholic Domesticity, 1860–1960," 62.

27. See Kane, "Marian Devotion since 1940," 117.

28. McDannell wrote that in these years, Catholic writers "placed [Mary] within the domestic structure of life in Nazareth. No longer the queen of the universe, Mary became a Hebrew housewife who looked after the needs of husband and child," "Catholic Domesticity," 60. She recognizes an important shift that should not be minimized. At the same time, these seemingly conflicting roles and images also coexisted.

29. Cummings, *New Women of the Old Faith*, 5. Cummings also carefully analyzes Catholic women's participation in Progressive Era reforms and their relationship to late-century woman's rights campaigns.

30. Dobbs, "Mother of God," 331.

31. The vast majority of Protestants actually accepted the theology of *Theotokos*, or Mary as Mother of God, which claimed that Jesus was divine at his conception and did not become divine later in his life. However, many misunderstood the term to imply that Mary was also mother of the triune God, or God the Father, and thus found it idolatrous.

32. "Becket, Archbishop of Canterbury," *Living Age*, 480.

33. *Biblical Repertory and Princeton Review*, "Article II—History of Latin Christianity," 269.

34. Batt, "Corruption of Christianity by Paganism," 202.

35. Ibid.

36. Ingelow, "Off the Skelligs, Part XII," 242.

37. Ibid., 243.

38. Ibid., 245.

39. "Poems of Thomas Edward Brown," *Living Age*, 709.

40. "Talk about Books," *Chautauquan*, 187.

41. Van Dyke, "Annunciation," 3–14. The "Annunciation" refers to the New Testament pericope, Luke 1:26–38, in which the angel Gabriel appears to Mary to inform her that she will conceive Jesus without a human father. Her response, "Be it unto me according to thy word," is known as her *fiat*, from the Latin "let it be done."

42. Van Dyke, quoting Dante Gabriel Rossetti's 1848 sonnet "Mary's Girlhood," in "Annunciation," 14.

43. Child, "Some Types of the Virgin," 57.

44. Ibid., 59.

45. "Christianity in Art VI," *Chautauquan*, 395.

46. Currier & Ives, "Queen of Angels," and "Ascension of the Virgin."

47. Leoffelholz, "Crossing the Atlantic with Victoria," 39. Currier & Ives, "Mary Queen of Scots," "Mary Queen of Scots Leaving France," "Queen Victoria," "Queen Victoria's Coronation," "Queen Victoria's Court Quadrilles," and "Queen Victoria" (*with crowns*).

48. Currier & Ives, "Queen of Love and Beauty."

49. Currier& Ives, "Queen of the House."

50. Currier & Ives, "Most Holy Catholic Faith," "Our Lady of Knock," and "Pilgrims at the Shrine of Our Lady of Lourdes."

51. For examples, see Martinez, "At Home with Mona Lisa," 164.

52. Ibid., 160–76. See also McCracken, "Pictures for the Tenements," 519.

53. Ibid.

54. Cook, *House Beautiful*, 122.

55. Ibid.

56. Hurll, *Madonna in Art* and *Home Book of Great Paintings*.

57. Hurll, *Madonna in Art*, 181.

58. Hurll, "Selecting Pictures for the Home," 235.

59. Hurll, *Madonna in Art*, 37.

60. Ruskin, *Sesames and Lilies*, 66 (emphasis in original).

61. Ibid., 67 (emphasis in original).

62. Ibid., 81.

63. Millet, *Sexual Politics*, 89, 92.

64. Ibid., 98.

65. Auerbach, *Woman and the Demon*, 59.

66. Weltman, " 'Be No More Housewives, but Queens,' " 105.

67. White, "Domestic Queen, Queenly Domestic," 110.

68. Stowell, "Shall Womanhood Be Abolished?," 545.

69. "Woman Question among Catholics," *Catholic World*, 677.

70. O'Reilly, *Mirror of True Womanhood*, 160.

71. Ibid., 28.

72. I owe this insight to Richardson, "Eugenization of Love," 228.

73. Grand, "Letter to Prof. Viëtor," 94.

74. Todd, *American Madonna*.

75. Ibid., frontispiece.

76. Ibid., 110–11.

77. Ibid., 157.

78. Ibid., 254 (emphasis in original).

Epilogue

1. "Celebration of the Immaculate Conception," *Boston Daily Globe*, 9.

2. Ibid.

3. "Pope's First Official Document," *New York Times*, 6; "Jeweled Sandals for Pope," *New York Times*, 2; "American Pilgrims to Rome," *New York Times*, 7; "Pope Blesses $30,000 Crown," *New York Times*, 5.

4. "Rome Ablaze for Jubilee," *New York Times*, 6.

5. See "Immaculate Conception Day," *Washington Post*, 9; "Will Crown Statue of Virgin," *Chicago Daily Tribune*, 1; "Brilliant Consistory," *Los Angeles Times*, 5.

6. Fisk, "Is It Christianity or Paganism?" 11.

7. Ibid.

8. Cressey, "The Immaculate Conception," 10.

9. Wood, "Rome in a Festival," 10.

10. "To-Day's Golden Jubilee in Rome," *Independent*, 1335. The "breach of Porta Pia" refers to the final success of the *Risorgimento*—the campaign for the unification of Italy. On September 20, 1870, the forces of General Raffaele Cadorna met the much smaller papal forces—consisting of the Swiss Guard and assorted volunteers—in a largely symbolic battle. The Aurelian walls surrounding Rome were breached at Porta Pia, and Italian forces moved into Rome, briefly occupying the Leonine City and the Vatican. Rome was annexed to the Kingdom of Italy. The "*non-expedit*" ("it is not expedient") was a controversial papal injunction barring Italian Catholics from voting in Italian parliamentary elections.

11. "The Immaculate Conception of the Mother of God," *American Catholic Quarterly Review*, 821.

12. Catholic Church and Pope Pius X, *Ad Diem Illum*. See also "Encyclical Letter of Our Holy Father Pius X," *American Catholic Quarterly Review*, 209.

13. Catholic Church and Pope Pius X, "*Ad Diem Illum*."

14. "Cross of the Immaculate Conception," *American Ecclesiastical Review*, 504.

15. "A Creditable Decision," *Independent*, 1152.

16. Alexander, "A Romance in the Land of Pius IX," 657.

17. Maas, "Attitude of Modern Protestants towards the Virginity of Our Blessed Lady," 209.

18. See the following in *Kindergarten Magazine*: "Better than the Theater," 302; "Book Reviews and References," 492; Brown, "The Evolution of a Primary Teacher," 190; "Current Work—News–Reports," 482; Harrison, "Signs of the Coming Era," 179–84; Partridge, "How to Increase the Attractiveness and Educative Power of School Environments," 38; and Peck, "Raphael," 323.

19. Search of the American Periodicals Series Online, June 2011. Results limited to magazines that had multiyear runs in the mid- to late nineteenth century.

20. Warner, *Alone of All Her Sex*; Ruether, *Sexism and God-Talk*.

21. Norris, *Meditations on Mary*.

22. Kidd and Taylor, *Traveling with Pomegranates*, 249, 281.

23. Hampl, *Virgin Time*; Donofrio, *Looking for Mary*.

Bibliography

Primary Sources

Adams, Henry. "The Dynamo and the Virgin (1900)." In *The Education of Henry Adams*. Boston: Houghton Mifflin, 1918.

"Advertisement 48." *Independent* 53, no. 2766 (December 5, 1901): x.

Alexander, Mrs. "A Romance in the Land of Pius IX." *Catholic World* 70, no. 419 (February 1900): 657.

Alzog, Johannes Baptist, ed. *The Manual of Universal Church History*. Translated with additions by F. J. Pabisch and Rev. Thomas Byrne. Cincinnati, Ohio: R. Clarke, 1878.

"American Pilgrims to Rome: Several Delegations Arrive for Jubilee of Immaculate Conception." *New York Times*, December 3, 1904, 7.

"Art." *Atlantic Monthly* 33 (February 1874): 247.

"The Arts." *Appletons' Journal* 14, no. 346 (November 1875): 602.

Batt, N. G. "Corruption of Christianity by Paganism." *Living Age* 105, no. 1351 (April 1870): 202.

"Becket, Archbishop of Canterbury." *Living Age* 65, no. 834 (May 26, 1860): 480.

Beecher, Charles. *The Incarnation; or, Pictures of the Virgin and Her Son*. New York: Harper & Brothers, 1849.

Benson, Eugene. "The Pagan Element in France." *Galaxy* 1, no. 3 (June 1866): 203–9.

Berington, Joseph, John Kirk, James Waterworth, and Thomas John Capel, eds. *The Faith of Catholics Confirmed by Scripture, and Attested by the Fathers of the First Five Centuries of the Church*. New York: Pustet, 1885.

Bernard of Clairvaux. *The Letters of St. Bernard of Clairvaux*. Translated by Bruno Scott James. Chicago: Henry Regnery, 1953.

"Better than the Theater." *Kindergarten Magazine* 10, no. 5 (January 1898): 302–4.

Biblical Repertory and Princeton Review. "Article II—History of Latin Christianity." Unsigned review of *History of Latin Christianity: Including That of the Popes to the Pontificate of Nicholas V*, by Henry Hart Milman. Vol. 36 (April 1864): 269.

"Book Reviews and References." *Kindergarten Magazine* 10, no. 7 (March 1898): 492.

"Book Trade Sales." *New York Times*, September 20, 1870.

"Books of the Month." *Atlantic Monthly* 328 (February 1885): 283.

"Brilliant Consistory: Festivities in Honor of Jubilee of Immaculate Conception Begin at Rome—Pope on Concordat." *Los Angeles Times*, November 15, 1904, 5.

Brown, Kate L. "The Evolution of a Primary Teacher, Chapter II—A Bit of Color." *Kindergarten Magazine* 10, no. 3 (November 1897): 185–91.

Brownson's Quarterly Review. Unsigned review of *Jesus the Son of Mary*, by
John Brande Morris. Vol. 6 (July 1852): 286.

Bryant, John Delavau. *The Immaculate Conception of the Most Blessed Virgin Mary,
Mother of God: A Dogma of the Catholic Church*. Boston: Patrick Donahoe, 1855.

"Burning of the Compania at Santiago, Chili." *Harper's Weekly* 8, no. 30 (January 30,
1864): 71.

Callcott, Maria. *Description of the Chapel of the Annunziata dell'Arena or Giotto's
Chapel, in Padua*. London: the author, 1835.

Catholic Church and Gregory. *Mirari Vos*. August 15, 1832.

Catholic Church and Pius IX. *Apostolic Constitution Ineffabilis Deus*. December 8,
1854.

———. *Letters Apostolic of Our Most Holy Lord Pius IX, by Divine Providence Pope,
concerning the Dogmatic Definition of the Immaculate Conception of the Virgin
Mother of God*. 1855.

Catholic Church and Pope Pius X. *Ad Diem Illum*. February 2, 1904.

"The Catholicity of the Roman Church as Affected by the Progress of the
Nineteenth Century: Seen in the History of the Dogma of the Immaculate
Conception." *Christian Review* 89 (July 1857): 380–403.

"Celebration of the Immaculate Conception: World-Wide Observance of the
Semicentennial of the Solemn Definition of the Dogma." *Boston Daily Globe*,
December 8, 1904, 9.

Child, Lydia Maria. "Resemblances between the Buddhist and the Roman Catholic
Religions." *Atlantic Monthly* 26, no. 158 (December 1870): 660–65.

Child, Theodore. "Some Types of the Virgin." *Harper's New Monthly Magazine* 86,
no. 511 (December 1892): 57–59.

"Christian Art." *Catholic World* 30, no. 176 (November 1879): 229.

Christian Union. Unsigned review of *Mary: The Queen of the House of David*,
by Alexander Stewart Walsh. Vol. 37, no. 1 (January 5, 1888): 23.

"Christianity in Art VI: The Madonna and Child." *Chautauquan: A Weekly
Newsmagazine* 2, no. 7 (April 1882): 395.

Church Review. "Article IX: Book Notices." Unsigned review of *The Impossibility of
the Immaculate Conception as an Article of Faith*, by M. the Abbé Laborde of
Lectoure. Vol. 8, no. 3 (October 1855): 456–57.

"Columbian Reading Union." *Catholic World* 52, no. 308 (November 1890): 304.

Cook, Clarence. *The House Beautiful: Essays on Beds and Tables, Stools and
Candlesticks*. New York: Scribner, Armstrong, 1878.

"A Creditable Decision." *Independent* 53, no. 273 (May 1901): 1152.

Cressey, Frank B. "The Immaculate Conception: History of the Doctrine."
Watchman 86, no. 50 (December 1904): 10.

"Cross of the Immaculate Conception." *American Ecclesiastical Review: A Monthly
Publication for the Clergy* 24 (1901): 504.

"Culture and Progress Abroad." *Scribner's Monthly* 1, no. 6 (April 1871): 683.

Cummings, J. W. *Italian Legends and Sketches*. New York: Edward Dunigan and Brother, 1858.

Cumming, John. "Dr. Cumming on the Immaculate Conception Dogma, and Its Consequences." *New York Daily Times*, January 23, 1855, 2. Reprinted in the *Christian Observer* 34, no. 9 (March 1855): 1.

"Current Work—News–Reports." *Kindergarten Magazine* 10, no. 7 (March 1898): 482.

Currier & Ives. "Ascension of the Virgin" (print nos. C0285, G0304).

——. "Infancy of the Virgin" (print nos. C3098, G3306).

——. "The Infant Savior with Mary and Joseph" (print nos. C3109, G3315).

——. "Madonna Di San Sisto" (print nos. C3861, G4189).

——. "Mary Queen of Scots" (print nos. C4058, G4412).

——. "Mary Queen of Scots" (print no. G4413).

——. "Mary Queen of Scots Leaving France" (print nos. C4061, G4415).

——. "The Most Holy Catholic Faith" (print nos. C4222, G4589).

——. "Our Lady of Knock" (print nos. C4641, G5033).

——. "Pilgrims at the Shrine of Our Lady of Lourdes" (print no. G5182).

——. "The Queen of Angels," (print nos. C4995, G5539).

——. "Queen of the House" (print nos. C5012, G5436).

——. "Queen of Love and Beauty" (print nos. C5003, G5426).

——. "Queen Victoria" (print nos. C5023, G5451).

——. "Queen Victoria" (print nos. C5024, G5449).

——. "Queen Victoria" (*with crowns*; print nos. C5021, G5450).

——. "Queen Victoria's Coronation" (print nos. unknown).

——. "Queen Victoria's Court Quadrilles" (print nos. C5027, G5455).

——. "Sacred Heart of Mary" (print nos. C5283, G5725).

De Charbonnel, Armand-Francois-Marie. "Definition of the Immaculate Conception." *Latter-Day Saints' Millennial Star* 17 (April 14, 1855): 239.

"Dick Tinto on His Travels: Madonnas and Madonnaism." *New York Daily Times*, January 30, 1855, 2.

Dobbs, C. E. W., DD. "The Mother of God." *Baptist Review* 3, no. 11 (July 1, 1888): 331.

Donnelly, Eleanor C. *Poems*. Philadelphia, Pa.: H. L. Kilner, 1892.

Donofrio, Beverley. *Looking for Mary; or, The Blessed Mother and Me*. New York: Viking Compass, 2000.

Dorsey, Anna Hanson. *Adrift*. Baltimore, Md.: John Murphy, 1887.

——. *Old Gray Rosary: "Refuge of Sinners."* New York: P O'Shea, 1869.

Duyckinck, Evert Augustus, and George Long Duyckinck, eds. *Cyclopaedia of American Literature*. New York: Charles Scribner, 1855.

"Encyclical Letter of Our Holy Father Pius X." *American Catholic Quarterly Review* 29, no. 114 (April 1904): 209.

"European Affairs." *New York Daily Times*, January 8, 1855, 2.

"Expressionism in Art: Painting." *Lippincott's Magazine* 2 (July 1868): 57.

Fisk, Josephine S. "Is It Christianity or Paganism?" *Zion's Herald* 83, no. 1 (January 1905): 11.

"Forward Movement Ends Its Campaign." *New York Times*, April 25, 1912, 12.

"Francis Lieber." *Southern Literary Messenger* 22, no. 5 (May 1856): 366. Reprinted from Duyckinck and Duyckinck, *Cyclopaedia of American Literature*, s.v. "Francis Lieber."

"From Our French Correspondent, Franc Parleur." *Independent* 6, no. 315 (December 1854): 394.

Grand, Sarah. "Letter to Prof. Viëtor, 15 December 1896." In *The Late Victorian Marriage Question: A Collection of Key New Woman Texts*, edited by Ann Heilmann, 93–95. London: Routledge, 1998.

Hamilton, Gail. "An American Queen." *North American Review* 143, no. 359 (October 1886): 329.

Hampl, Patricia. *Virgin Time*. New York: Farrar, Straus and Giroux, 1992.

Harrison, Elizabeth. "Signs of the Coming Era: Address at Opening of the Chicago Kindergarten College, Oct. 4, 1897," *Kindergarten Magazine* 10, no. 3 (November 1897): 179–84.

Hazlitt, William. *Sketches of the Principal Picture—Galleries in England*. London: Taylor and Hessey, 1824.

"Henry P. Allen, N.Y." *Publisher's Weekly*, no. 770 (October 30, 1886): 621.

"The History of Our Lord in Art." *Living Age* 82, no. 1057 (September 1864): 435.

Hopkins, Louisa Parsons. "Application of the Kindergarten Theory to Later School Life." *Kindergarten Magazine* 8, no. 2 (October 1895): 95–104.

Horne, Thomas Hartwell, and Samuel Jarvis. *Mariolatry; or, Facts and Evidences Demonstrating the Worship of the Blessed Virgin Mary, by the Church of Rome*. Hartford: H.S. Parson, 1844.

Hurll, Estelle. *The Home Book of Great Paintings*. Boston: Houghton-Mifflin, 1899.

——. *The Madonna in Art*. Boston: L. C. Page, 1898.

——. "Selecting Pictures for the Home." *Arthur's Home Magazine* 64 (March 1894): 235.

"Hurst & Co." *Literary World* 32, no. 10 (October 1, 1901): 157.

"The Immaculate Conception." *National Era* 9, no. 419 (January 1855): 6.

"Immaculate Conception Day: Elaborate Celebration of Fiftieth Anniversary of Pope Pius IX's Decree." *Washington Post*, December 8, 1904, 9.

"The Immaculate Conception of the Mother of God." *American Catholic Quarterly Review* 29, no. 116 (October 1904): 821.

"The Immaculate Conception: Sermon by Archbishop Hughes." *New York Daily Times*, April 2, 1855, 1.

Independent. Unsigned review of *Mary: The Queen of the House of David*, by Alexander Stewart Walsh. Vol. 39 (February 17, 1887): 12.

Ingelow, Jean. "Off the Skelligs, Part XII." *St. Paul's Magazine* 10 (December 1872). Republished in *Littell's Living Age* 114, no. 1468 (July 1872): 243.

"Is the Church of Rome Idolatrous?" *Biblical Repertory & Princeton Review* 26, no. 2 (April 1854): 247.

James, Henry. *The American.* London: Macmillan, 1921.

Jameson, Anna. *A Commonplace Book of Thoughts, Memories, and Fancies, Original and Selected.* London: Longman, Brown, Green, and Longmans, 1854.

———. *Legends of the Madonna as Represented in the Fine Arts.* Boston: Ticknor and Fields, 1853.

———. *Memoirs of the Loves of the Poets.* Boston: Houghton, Mifflin, 1885.

———. *Visits and Sketches at Home and Abroad.* London: Saunders and Otley, 1834.

"Jansenists vs. Jesuits—The Doctrine of Papal Infallibility." *New York Daily Times,* May 16, 1857, 4.

Jarves, James Jackson. "Writers on Art." *Appleton's Journal* 10, no. 228 (August 1873): 155.

"Jeweled Sandals for Pope: New Orleans Church Sends Gold and Silver Pair." *New York Times,* October 15, 1904, 2.

Kenrick, Francis P. "Pastoral Letter of May 1842." Philadelphia: M. Fithian, 1842.

Kidd, Sue Monk, and Ann Kidd Taylor. *Traveling with Pomegranates: A Mother and Daughter Journey to the Sacred Places of Greece, Turkey, and France.* New York: Penguin Books, 2009.

Laborde, M. [the Abbé of Lectoure]. *The Impossibility of the Immaculate Conception as an Article of Faith: In Reply to Several Works That Have Appeared on That Subject of Late Years. To Which Is Added the Author's Letter to the Pope.* Translated by A. Cleveland Coxe. Philadelphia: Herman Hooker, 1855.

Lambruschini, Luigi. *A Polemical Treatise on the Immaculate Conception of the Blessed Virgin.* New York: Sadlier, 1855.

"Letters from Spain." *Ladies' Literary Cabinet* 4, no. 11 (July 21, 1821): 81.

Liguori, Alphonsus. *Glories of Mary.* New York: Dunigan and Brothers, 1852.

"List of Publications." *Brownson's Quarterly Review* 3, no. 4 (October 1855): 549.

"Literature: American Story-Books for Girls," *Independent* 40, no. 2057 (May 1888): 16.

"Literature and Art: Copies of Great Paintings." *Galaxy* 6, no. 3 (September 1868): 432.

Lovelace Papers. Bodleian Library, Oxford University, 56–57, 152–55. Quoted in Judith Johnston, *Anna Jameson: Victorian, Feminist, Woman of Letters.* Brookfield, Vt.: Scolar, 1997.

Maas, Anthony. "Attitude of Modern Protestants towards the Virginity of Our Blessed Lady." *American Catholic Quarterly Review* 28, no. 110 (April 1903): 209.

Maguire, Robert. "Article V—2. The Abbé Laborde in Rome: His Protest and Persecution; Being a Narrative of the Opponents of the Novel Dogma of the

Immaculate Conception. From the French." *Church of England Quarterly Review* 38, no. 4 (1855): 102–7.

The Manual of the Immaculate Conception: A Collection of Prayers for General Use, Including the Most Approved Devotions to the Blessed Mother of God. New York: P. O'Shea, 1865.

McCracken, Elizabeth. "Pictures for the Tenements." *Atlantic Monthly* 98, no. 1906: 519.

"Miscellanea at Munich." *Southern Literary Messenger* 25, no. 2 (August 1857): 101.

"Miscellaneous." *Correspondent* 3, no. 1 (January 26, 1828): 12.

Monk, Maria. *The Awful Disclosures of Maria Monk, as Exhibited in a Narrative of Her Sufferings during a Residence of Five Years as a Novice and Two Years as a Black Nun, in the Hotel Dieu Nunnery in Montreal.* New York: Maria Monk, 1836.

"Mr. Aspinwall's Murillo." *New York Times*, January 21, 1858, 5.

"Mrs. Jameson." *Living Age* 4, no. 505 (January 21, 1854): 147–52.

"The Murillo Controversy." *New York Times*, February 3, 1858, 5.

"Murillo's Celebrated Picture *The Conception*." *New York Times*, January 25, 1858, 6.

Nathaniel, Sir. "Mrs. Jameson." *New Monthly Magazine* 99 (1853): 457–66. Reprinted in *Living Age* 40, no. 505 (January 21, 1854): 147–52, and *Eclectic Magazine of Foreign Literature, Science, and Art* 31 (February 1854): 211–17.

National Education Association of the United States. *Addresses and Proceedings.* Vols. 1866–70.

Nealy, Mary E. "Popular Art." *Ladies Repository* 36, no. 12 (December 1876): 551.

Needler, G. H., ed. *Letters of Anna Jameson to Ottilie von Goethe.* New York: Oxford University Press, 1939.

Neumann, John Nepomucen. "Pastoral Letter of 4 November 1854." Philadelphia: Town Printer No. 4, 1854. Reprinted in the *Catholic Herald of Philadelphia*, November 9, 1854.

"The New Article of Faith, and the Consequent Position of the Church of Rome." *Protestant Episcopal Quarterly Review and Church Register* 2 (April 1855):161–89.

"New Publications." *Catholic World* 44, no. 262 (January 1887): 572.

"A New *Stabat Mater*." *Hours at Home* 5, no. 1 (May 1867): 50–58.

"New York City." *New York Daily Times*, July 10, 1855, 1.

"New-York City: Triduan—Inauguration of a Statue." *New York Daily Times*, August 13, 1855, 1.

Norris, Kathleen. *Meditations on Mary.* New York: Viking Studio, 1999.

"Notices of Books." *New Englander and Yale Review* 19, no. 73 (January 1861): 252.

"Notices of New Books." *New York Daily Times*, April 27, 1855, 3.

"Notices of New Books: *Mornings among the Jesuits at Rome*." *United States Democratic Review* 25, no. 136 (October 1849): 384.

"Objections against Chromos Considered." *Prang's Chromo: A Journal of Popular Art* 1, no. 1 (January 1868): 3.

O'Reilly, Bernard. *The Mirror of True Womanhood: A Book of Instruction for Women in the World.* New York: P. F. Collier, 1878.

Orr, James. "The Virgin Birth of Christ." In *The Fundamentals: A Testimony to the Truth, Vol. 1*, edited by R. A. Torrey and A. C. Dixon et al, 7–20. Los Angeles: Bible Institute of Los Angeles, 1910.

Orsini, Abbé Matthieu. *The Life of the Blessed Virgin Mary, with the History of the Devotion to Her: Completed by the Traditions of the East, the Writings of the Holy Fathers, etc.* Translated by Rev. F. C. Husenbeth, DD. New York: Virtue and Yorston, 1861.

"Our Positions and Prospects." *Rambler, a Catholic Journal of Home and Foreign Literature* 11, no. 61 (January 1853): 4.

Overland Monthly and Out West Magazine. "Current Literature." Unsigned review of *Reminiscences of European Travel*, by Andrew P. Peabody. Vol. 1, no. 5 (November 1868): 486.

Oxford English Dictionary. 2nd ed. Oxford: Oxford University Press, 2006.

"Paintings and Painters in Italy." *Hours at Home* 4, no. 4 (February 1867): 325–32.

Paley, William. *Natural Theology: Or, Evidences of the Existence and Attributes of the Deity, Collected from the Appearances of Nature.* Philadelphia: H. Maxwell, 1802.

Parton, James. "Mr. Parton on Prang's Chromos." *Prang's Chromo: A Journal of Popular Art* 1, no. 1 (December 1866): 1.

Partridge, William Ordway. "How to Increase the Attractiveness and Educative Power of School Environments." *Kindergarten Magazine* 10, no. 1 (October 1897): 38.

"Pastoral of Francis Patrick Kenrick, Archbishop of Baltimore." *Catholic Herald* (May 1842): 145.

Patmore, Coventry. *The Angel in the House.* London: Macmillan, 1863.

———. *The Unknown Eros.* 3rd ed. London: George Bell, 1890.

Peck, Lilian. "Raphael." *Kindergarten Magazine* 10, no. 5 (January 1898): 323.

"The Pernicious Effects of Party Zeal." *Weekly Museum* 10, no. 7 (August 5, 1797).

"Poems of Thomas Edward Brown." *Living Age* 218, no. 2827 (September 1898): 709.

"Pope Blesses $30,000 Crown: Great Gathering of Prelates at Beatification Ceremony in Rome." *New York Times*, December 6, 1904, 5.

"Pope's First Official Document." *New York Times*, September 9, 1903, 6.

Prentice, George. "A Bohemian Journal." *Ladies Repository* 2, no. 3 (September 1868): 207.

Princeton Review. Unsigned review of *Morning among the Jesuits at Rome*, by M. Hobart Seymour. Vol. 22, no. 1 (January 1850): 143–59.

Reed, Rebecca Theresa. *Six Months in a Convent.* Boston: Russell, Odiorne, and Metcalf, 1835.

"Religious Intelligence." *New York Evangelist*, January 11, 1855, 2.

"The Religious Scarecrow of the Age." *National Magazine* 5 (December 1854): 523–24.

Ripley, George, and Charles A. Dana, eds. *The American Cyclopaedia: A Popular Dictionary of General Knowledge.* New York: D. Appleton, 1874.

Rohner, Beatus, OSB. *Life of the Blessed Virgin*. New York: Benziger Brothers, 1897.

"Rome Ablaze for Jubilee: Celebration of the Immaculate Conception Anniversary Is Begun." *New York Times*, December 9, 1904, 6.

"Rome Self-Convicted of Error." *Church Review and Ecclesiastical Register* 3 (October 1850): 435.

"The Royal Family of England." *Eclectic* 49, no. 1 (January 1860): 56B1.

"Rumors of Relics and Miraculous Madonnas Coming." *New York Daily Times*, January 31, 1855, 8.

Ruskin, John. *Sesames and Lilies: Three Lectures Delivered in 1864 and 1868*. New York: James Millar, 1884.

"Sacred and Legendary Art." *Crayon* 4, no. 6 (June 1857): 176.

Seymour, Michael Hobart. *Mornings among the Jesuits at Rome: Being Notes of Conversations Held with Certain Jesuits on the Subject of Religion in the City of Rome*. New York: Harper & Bros., 1849.

"Seymour's *Mornings among the Jesuits*." *Littell's Living Age* 23, no. 286 (November 1849): 249.

Sherwood, Mary Martha. *The Nun*. Princeton, N.J.: Moore Baker, 1834.

Simpson, A. H. "Petrarch." *Littell's Living Age* 122, no. 1576 (August 1874): 486.

Smith, Henry Boynton. "The Dogma of the Immaculate Conception." *Methodist Quarterly Review* 7 (April 1855): 275–311.

"Special Catholic Services: Immaculate Conception Promulgation to Be Celebrated Tomorrow." *New York Times*, December 7, 1904, 9.

Stanton, Elizabeth Cady. "Seneca Falls Declaration of Sentiments and Resolutions." Rochester, N.Y.: Printed by John Dick at the North Star Office, 1848.

———. *The Woman's Bible*. New York: Arno, 1895.

Starke, Mariana. *Letters from Italy, Between the Years 1792 and 1798*. London: R. Phillips, 1800.

Steegman, John. *Consort of Taste: 1830–1870*. London: Sidgwick and Jackson, 1950.

"Still Another Picture." *New York Times*, March 6, 1858, 4.

Stowe, Harriet Beecher. "Mrs. Stowe on Prang's Chromos." *Prang's Chromo: A Journal of Popular Art* 1, no. 1 (December 1866): 2.

Stowell, A. D. "Shall Womanhood Be Abolished?" *New Englander* 36, no. 3 (July 1877): 545.

Summers, Thomas O., DD, ed. *Methodist Pamphlets for the People, Vol. 3*. Nashville, Tenn.: Southern Methodist, 1857.

"Table-Talk." *Appleton's Journal* 6, no. 121 (July 1871): 106.

"Talk about Books." *Chautauquan* 7, no. 2 (November 1886): 128.

Talmage, Rev. T. De Witt. Introduction to *Mary: The Queen of the House of David*, by Alexander Stewart Walsh. New York: Henry S. Allen, 1888.

Taylor, Bishop Jeremy. *The Great Exemplar, Vol. II*. New York: Robert Carter & Bros., 1859.

"Terriffic Excitement in a Church." *New York Daily Times*, February 14, 1855, 6.

"Terrific Tragedy in Chili: Two Thousand Five Hundred Persons Roasted to Death in a Church." *New York Times*, January 18, 1864, 1.

"To-Day's Golden Jubilee in Rome." *Independent* 57, no. 2923 (December 8, 1904): 1335.

Todd, Mary Ives. *An American Madonna: A Story of Love*. Binghamton, N.Y.: Binghamton Book, 1908.

———. *The Heterodox Marriage of a New Woman*. New York: R. L. Weed, 1898.

Ullathorne, William Bernard. *The Immaculate Conception of the Mother of God: An Exposition*. Baltimore, Md.: John Murphy, 1855.

Van Dyke, Henry J. "The Annunciation." *Harper's New Monthly Magazine* 84, no. 499 (December 1891): 14.

———. "The Nativity in Art." *Harper's New Monthly Magazine* 72, no. 427 (December 1885): 16.

Veuillot, Louis. "The Immaculate Conception Declared the Faith of the Roman Catholic Church." *New York Daily Times*, January 5, 1855, 6.

Walden, Treadwell. "My Look at the Queen." *Scribner's Monthly* 17, no. 2 (December 1878): 217.

Walsh, Alexander Stewart. *Mary: The Queen of the House of David and Mother of Jesus; The Story of Her Life*. New York: Henry S. Allen, 1888.

"Was Shakespeare a German?" *New York Times*, May 24, 1868, 4.

Washington, E. K. *Echoes of Europe; or, Word Pictures of Travel*. Philadelphia, Pa.: J. Challen & Son, 1860.

"Will Crown Statue of Virgin: Pope Pius X Supervises Preparations for Ceremony, Which Will Be Replica of One Held 1854." *Chicago Daily Tribune*, August 22, 1904, 1.

Wissel, Joseph. *The Redemptorist on the American Missions*. New York: Arno, 1875.

"The Woman Question among Catholics: A Round Table Conference—Alice Timmons Toomy, Eleanor C. Donnelly, Katherine E. Conway." *Catholic World* 57 (August 1893): 677.

Wood, Nathan Bishop. "Rome in a Festival." *Watchman* 87, no. 38 (September 1905): 10.

Wordsworth, William. *The Excursion, Being a Portion of the Recluse, a Poem*. London: Longman, Hurst, Rees, Orme, and Brown, 1814.

Selected Secondary Sources

Adams, Kimberly VanEsveld. *Our Lady of Victorian Feminism: The Madonna in the Work of Anna Jameson, Margaret Fuller, and George Elliot*. Athens: Ohio University Press, 2001.

Anderson, Janice Capel. "Mary's Difference: Gender and Patriarchy in the Birth Narratives." *Journal of Religion* 67, no. 2 (April 1987): 183–202.

Auerbach, Nina. *Woman and the Demon: The Life of a Victorian Myth*. Cambridge, Mass.: Harvard University Press, 1982.

Baker, Paula. "The Domestication of Politics: Women and American Political Society, 1780–1920." *American Historical Review* 89, no. 3 (June 1984): 631.

Berlant, Lauren. *The Female Complaint: The Unfinished Business of Sentimentality in American Culture*. Durham, N.C.: Duke University Press, 2008.

Brekus, Catherine. *Strangers and Pilgrims: Female Preaching in America, 1740–1845*. Chapel Hill: University of North Carolina Press, 1998.

Brush, Lisa D. "Love Toil, and Trouble: Motherhood and Feminist Politics." *Signs* 21, no. 2 (Winter 1996): 430.

Callon, David Jerome. "Converting Catholicism: Orestes A. Brownson, Anna H. Dorsey, and Irish America, 1840–1896." Ph.D. diss., Washington University in St. Louis, 2008.

Carr, Anne. "Mary in the Mystery of the Church." In *Mary According to Women*, edited by Carol Frances Jegen, BVM, 5–32. Kansas City, Mo.: Leaven, 1985.

Carroll, Michael P. *American Catholics in the Protestant Imagination: Rethinking the Academic Study of Religion*. Baltimore, Md.: Johns Hopkins University Press, 2007.

Chinnici, Joseph P. *Living Stones: The History and Structure of Catholic Spiritual Life in the United States*. New York: Macmillan, 1989.

Corrigan, John. *Business of the Heart: Religion and Emotion in the Nineteenth Century*. Berkeley: University of California Press, 2002.

Cott, Nancy. *The Bonds of Womanhood*. New Haven, Conn.: Yale University Press, 1977.

Cummings, Kathleen Sprows. *New Women of the Old Faith: Gender and American Catholicism in the Progressive Era*. Chapel Hill: University of North Carolina Press, 2009.

Cunneen, Sally. *In Search of Mary: The Woman and the Symbol*. New York: Ballantine Books, 1996.

D'Agostino, Peter. *Rome in America: Transnational Catholic Identity from Risorgimento to Fascism*. Chapel Hill: University of North Carolina Press, 2004.

Daly, Mary. *Beyond God the Father: Toward a Philosophy of Women's Liberation*. Boston: Beacon Press, 1985.

Dolan, Jay P. *Catholic Revivalism: The American Experience, 1830–1900*. Notre Dame, Ind.: University of Notre Dame Press, 1978.

Douglas, Ann. *The Feminization of American Culture*. New York: Macmillan, 1977.

Franchot, Jenny. *Roads to Rome: The Antebellum Protestant Encounter with Catholicism*. Berkeley: University of California Press, 1994.

Freeman, Curtis. "Alterity and Its Cure." *Cross Currents* 59, no. 4 (December 2009): 404–41.

Gatta, John. *American Madonna: Images of the Divine Woman in Literary Culture*. New York: Oxford University Press, 1997.

Gilbert, Sandra M., and Susan T. Gubar. *The Madwoman in the Attic: The Woman Writer and the Nineteenth-Century Literary Imagination*. New Haven, Conn.: Yale University Press, 1979.

Goen, C. C. *Broken Churches, Broken Nation*. Macon, Ga.: Mercer University Press, 1985.

Hatch, Nathan. *The Democratization of American Christianity*. New Haven, Conn.: Yale University Press, 1989.

Hewitt, Nancy. *Women's Activism and Social Change: Rochester, New York, 1822–1872*. Ithaca, N.Y.: Cornell University Press, 1984.

Holcomb, Adele. "Anna Jameson: The First Professional English Art Historian." *Art History* 6 (1983): 171–87.

Johnston, Judith. *Anna Jameson: Victorian, Feminist, Woman of Letters*. Brookfield, Vt.: Scolar, 1997.

Johnston, Patricia, ed. *Seeing High and Low: Representing Social Conflict in American Visual Culture*. Berkeley: University of California Press, 2006.

Kane, Paula M. "Marian Devotion since 1940: Continuity or Casualty?" In *Habits of Devotion: Catholic Religious Practice in Twentieth-Century America*, edited by James M. O'Toole, 89–130. Ithaca, N.Y.: Cornell University Press, 2004.

Kelley, Rosemary Skinner, Ann Braude, Maureen Ursenbach Beecher, and Elizabeth Fox-Genovese. "Forum: Female Experience in American Religion." *Religion and American Culture* 5, no. 1 (Winter 1995): 1–21.

Kenneally, James K. *The History of American Catholic Women*. New York: Crossroad, 1990.

Koven, Seth, and Sonya Michel. "Womanly Duties: Maternalist Politics and the Origins of Welfare States." *American Historical Review* 95, no. 4 (October 1990): 1076–1108.

Langland, Elizabeth. *Nobody's Angels: Middle-Class Women and Domestic Ideology in Victorian Culture*. Ithaca, N.Y.: Cornell University Press, 1995.

Lears, T. J. Jackson. *No Place of Grace: Antimodernism and the Transformation of American Culture, 1880–1920*. Chicago: University of Chicago Press, 1981.

Leoffelholz, Mary. "Crossing the Atlantic with Victoria: American Receptions, 1837–1901." In *Remaking Queen Victoria*, edited by Margaret Homans and Adrienne Munich, 33–56. Cambridge: Cambridge University Press, 1997.

Lindley, Susan Hill. *"You Have Stept Out of Your Place": A History of Women and Religion in America*. Louisville, Ky.: Westminster John Knox Press, 1996.

Long, Kathryn Teresa. *The Revival of 1857–58: Interpreting an American Religious Awakening*. New York: Oxford University Press, 1998.

Lootens, Tricia. *Lost Saints: Silence, Gender, and Victorian Literary Canonization*. Charlottesville: University Press of Virginia, 1996.

Marsden, George. *Fundamentalism and American Culture*. New York: Oxford University Press, 2006.

Martinez, Katharine. "At Home with Mona Lisa: Consumers and Commercial Visual Culture, 1880–1920." In *Seeing High and Low: Representing Social Conflict in American Visual Culture*, edited by Patricia Johnston, 160–76. Berkeley: University of California Press, 2006.

Marty, Martin. *Pilgrims in Their Own Land: 500 Years of Religion in America.* New York: Little, Brown, 1984.

McDannell, Colleen. "Catholic Domesticity, 1860–1960." In *American Catholic Women: A Historical Exploration*, edited by Karen Kennelly, 48–80. New York: Macmillan, 1989.

———. *The Christian Home in Victorian America, 1840–1900.* Bloomington: Indiana University Press, 1986.

McGreevy, John T. *Catholicism and American Freedom: A History.* New York: W. W. Norton, 2003.

Miller, Diane Helene. "From One Voice a Chorus: Elizabeth Cady Stanton's 1860 Address to the New York State Legislature." *Women's Studies in Communication* 22, no. 2 (Fall 1999): 152–89.

Millet, Kate. *Sexual Politics.* New York: Doubleday, 1970.

Moore, R. Laurence. *Religious Outsiders and the Making of Americans.* New York: Oxford University Press, 1986.

Morgan, David. *Protestants and Pictures: Religion, Visual Culture, and the Age of Mass Production.* New York: Oxford University Press, 1999.

Orsi, Robert. *The Madonna of 115th Street: Faith and Community in Italian Harlem.* New Haven, Conn.: Yale University Press, 1985.

———. "The Many Names of the Mother of God." In *Divine Mirrors: The Virgin Mary in the Visual Arts*, edited by Melissa R. Katz, 3–15. New York: Oxford University Press, 2001.

Pelikan, Jaroslav Jan. *Mary through the Centuries: Her Place in the History of Culture.* New Haven, Conn.: Yale University Press, 1996.

Prothero, Stephen. *American Jesus: How the Son of God Became a National Icon.* New York: Farrar, Straus and Giroux, 2003.

Richardson, Angelique. "The Eugenization of Love: Sarah Grand and the Morality of Genealogy." *Victorian Studies* 42, no. 2 (2000): 227–55.

Richardson, Angelique, and Chris Willis. *The New Woman in Fiction and in Fact: Fin-de-siècle Feminisms.* New York: Palgrave, 2001.

Ruether, Rosemary Radford. *Sexism and God-Talk.* Boston: Beacon Press, 1983.

Ryan, Mary. *The Cradle of the Middle Class: The Family in Oneida County, New York, 1780–1865.* New York: Cambridge University Press, 1981.

Singleton, John. "The Virgin Mary and Religious Conflict in Victorian Britain." *Journal of Ecclesiastical History* 43, no. 1 (January 1992): 23.

Sklar, Kathryn Kish. *Catharine Beecher: A Study in American Domesticity.* New Haven, Conn.: Yale University Press, 1973.

Smith, Daniel Scott. "Continuity and Discontinuity in Puritan Naming: Massachusetts, 1771." *William and Mary Quarterly* 51, no. 1 (January 1994): 73.

Stern, Andrew. *Southern Crucifix, Southern Cross.* Tuscaloosa: University of Alabama Press, 2012.

Taves, Ann. *Household of Faith: Roman Catholic Devotions in Mid-Nineteenth-Century America*. Notre Dame, Ind.: University of Notre Dame Press, 1986.

Thomas, Clara. *Love and Work Enough: The Life of Anna Jameson*. Toronto: University of Toronto Press, 1967.

Trudgill, Eric. *Madonnas and Magdalens: The Origins and Development of Victorian Sexual Attitudes*. New York: Holmes and Meier, 1976.

Tweed, Thomas. *Crossings and Dwellings: A Theory of Religion*. Cambridge, Mass.: Harvard University Press, 2006.

———. *Retelling U.S. Religious History*. Berkeley: University of California Press, 1997.

Warner, Maria. *Alone of All Her Sex*. New York: Knopf, 1976.

Welter, Barbara. "The Cult of True Womanhood: 1820–1860." *American Quarterly* 18, no. 2 (Summer 1966): 151–74.

———. "The Feminization of American Religion: 1800–1860." In *Dimity Convictions: The American Woman in the Nineteenth Century*. Athens: Ohio University Press, 1976.

Weltman, Sharon Aronofsky. " 'Be No More Housewives, but Queens': Queen Victoria and Ruskin's Domestic Mythology." In *Remaking Queen Victoria*, edited by Margaret Homans and Adrienne Munich, 105–22. Cambridge: Cambridge University Press, 1997.

White, Laura Mooneyham. "Domestic Queen, Queenly Domestic: Queenly Contradictions in Caroll's *Through the Looking Glass*." *Children's Literature Association* (2007): 112.

Zimdars-Swartz, Sandra. *Encountering Mary: From LaSalette to Medjugorje*. Princeton, N.J.: Princeton University Press, 1991.

Index

Adams, Henry, 2

Adams, Kimberly VanEsveld, 47

Ad Caeli Reginam (Pius XII), 212 (n. 22). *See also* Queen of Heaven (*Regina Coeli*)

Ad Diem Illum (Pius X), 191–92. *See also* Immaculate Conception of the Virgin Mary

Adrift (Dorsey): about, 121–23, 132–34; abuse in, 130–32; analysis of, 14, 117–18; on Catholic aesthetics, 115, 128; on children, 128; conversion to Catholicism in, 127–28; critical reception of, 121–22; encounter with Virgin Mary in, 114–16, 127; Marian spirituality in, 123–29, 137; natural world in, 126; on "Our Father" prayer, 125–26; patriarchal critique in, 129–31; Protestants in, 123–24, 129–32, 144; and womanhood, 144–45. *See also* Dorsey, Anna Hanson

American, The (James), 89

American Catholic fiction, 118, 119–20, 209 (n. 9), 210 (n. 11). See also *Adrift* (Dorsey); Dorsey, Anna Hanson

American Catholicism: anti-Catholic propaganda and violence, 6, 10–11, 18, 26, 66–67, 74, 191, 198 (n. 21); as constructed category, 10, 11–12; contemporary reflections of Virgin Mary in, 196; growth of, 7; identification with Virgin Mary, 80, 81, 87, 190, 191, 195; and Immaculate Conception, 20, 22, 24–25, 30, 38, 42, 74–76; "otherness" of, 12, 19, 40; power

inequality of Protestants over, 12; Protestants on, 10–11, 19, 30–31, 192–93, 198 (n. 4); and queenship rhetoric, 179–80; sale of Catholic books, 200 (n. 26); and social norms, 9, 74, 119–20; theological debates with Protestants, 28–29; and ultramontanism, 25–26, 30–31, 200 (n. 27); use of Virgin Mary by, 80–81; and Virgin Mary's queenship, 156–57; and womanhood ideal, 75–77, 80, 120. *See also* American Catholic fiction; Catholic devotionalism; Catholic women; Marian devotionalism; Roman Catholic Church

American Catholic Review, 191, 193

American domestic fiction. *See* Domestic fiction

An American Madonna (Todd), 182–85

"An American Queen" (Hamilton), 154–55, 181–82

Angel in the House motif, 46–47, 179, 203 (n. 26)

Annunciation (Ghiberti), *164*, 165

Annunciation of Mary, 33, 214 (n. 41)

Anthony, Susan B., 142

Appleton's Journal, 50, 88

Aquinas. *See* Thomas Aquinas

Architectural imagery, 174–75

Aristocracy rhetoric, 154–55. *See also* Queenship rhetoric

Art: for education, 51, 53; for home decoration, 174, 175; reproductions of, 50–51, 53, 55, 84, 170, 172; writing, 89, 207 (n. 17)